ANXIETY

IN RELATIONSHIP

2 BOOKS IN 1

STOP OVERTHINKING, OVERCOME YOUR FEAR OF
ABANDONMENT, NARCISSISTIC ABUSE, AND TOXIC
ATTACHMENT STYLE AND IMPROVE YOUR RELATIONSHIP
THROUGH LOVE LANGUAGES AND COUPLE SKILLS

PHILIP RELATION

THIS BOOK INCLUDES

BOOK 1:
ANXIETY IN RELATIONSHIP
THE MOST COMPLETE MANUAL TO OVERCOME ANXIETY AND CONFLICT IN A RELATIONSHIP
MANAGE YOUR EMOTIONS TO IMPROVE YOUR EXISTING COUPLE OR TO CULTIVATE A NEW ONE

BOOK 2:
JEALOUSY IN RELATIONSHIP
THE BEST GUIDE TO OVERCOME JEALOUSY AND USE IT TO STRENGTHEN THE RELATIONSHIP
MINDFULLY MANAGE YOUR FEELINGS TO GET OVER YOUR TRUST ISSUES

© Copyright 2021 - All rights reserved.

Table of Contents

Anxiety in Relationship

Jealousy in Relationship

ANXIETY
IN RELATIONSHIP

THE MOST COMPLETE MANUAL TO OVERCOME ANXIETY
AND CONFLICT IN A RELATIONSHIP
MANAGE YOUR EMOTIONS TO IMPROVE YOUR EXISTING
COUPLE OR TO CULTIVATE A NEW ONE

PHILIP RELATION

Introduction

A nxiety affects nearly every facet of every relationship. When someone enters into a relationship, there have relatively simple expectations that go along with it. First and foremost, you assume the other person can fulfill the role of a partner. Being a partner involves the solid ability to communicate openly, offer companionship, contribute financially, hold on to a stable job, and eventually raise a family.

Communication is particularly important when it comes to romantic relationships. Being able to discuss all issues freely, make plans, and set goals for the future are all vital for a successful relationship. Otherwise, how could two partners handle their responsibilities, challenges, and expectations?

However, what happens if one of you is suffering from anxiety? Of course, it depends on how severe the anxiety is. However, no matter its level of development, a personal connection will be in some way affected. You or your partner might encounter difficulties in reacting in a healthy way when either of you expresses an opinion or an emotion. For instance, it is common to misread someone's intent or misinterpret the meaning of individual conversations. Anxiety works in many ways as a filter, and when it clouds your vision, you might act in a way that will eventually damage your relationship. Any joke, comment, or harmless critique can lead to an overreaction that will put a strain on any couple, even more than the anxiety itself.

If you find yourself in such a situation, you should take a break and see what warranted such a negative reaction or outburst. Your partner may be suffering from a form of anxiety, and they are overwhelmed by the strain. On the other hand, if you are the one with this problem, you need to acknowledge what's wrong and express it. If not, your partner will think you're cruel or aggressive for no reason, or that they are the problem.

Anxiety has a severe emotional effect on people, and the partner is always affected in some way as a result of seeing his or her significant other suffering and going through the whole life-crippling experience. And many cases in which the one suffering from anxiety will suppress any emotion or feeling. Emotions carry a great deal of power, and some people find it too challenging to face them. Those who are afraid to express themselves emotionally have likely lived in a household where the behavior was discouraged.

The act of suppressing emotions is a sign that the person is trying to hold on to a semblance of control. If you find yourself behaving this way, it might be because you are scared at the thought of losing that control and allowing the locked-up feelings to overwhelm you. Naturally, the biggest issue here is when it comes to negative emotions as they have such a substantial impact on a person's life. You might think that if you let it all out, you will change your partner's feelings. And whatever good opinions and thoughts he or she has about you will be gone, and cause damage to the relationship. However, while you may think of this as a solution, it leads to even more problems. Acting this way will increase the amount of anxiety you experience. You will find less and less peace of mind until one day when it will all come out in a wild burst. It's difficult to suppress those feelings forever, and when they do come to the surface, the feeling will cloud all judgment.

Communication anxiety can also manifest itself without involving any emotional suppression. For instance, let's say your partner unloads only her most powerful feelings and emotions regularly. Some people cannot hold back on certain beliefs, so they lash out, and as a result, both of you end up feeling overwhelmed and confused, leading to another problem. Experiencing these outbursts often enough, you can start feeling that it's your job to find a solution to your partner's issues. It's not enough to notice the anxiety and the strain it's putting on your relationship. You get the feeling you are the sole savior of this partnership. Unfortunately, this usually makes things worse as your partner could start developing resentment towards you for their behavior.

Another communication problem is when you consider expressing yourself as a risky affair. Maybe you are wondering what will happen if you reveal what you honestly think. It is enough to trigger your anxiety as you are afraid of the uncertainty of the outcome. Frequently, this symptom stems from not having confidence in yourself and you are worried about an adverse reaction from your partner. In this case, you might be taking a great deal of time to rehearse what you will say and complicate things further by imagining all the possible scenarios.

Also, anxiety can have even worse repercussions if you or your partner will refuse to admit that you are suffering from it. Not acknowledging that there is a problem, especially one as grave as anxiety, will only lead to anger and irritable behavior that pushes the other person away. Running away from this problem often feels like it's an easier solution, especially by thinking that doing so will shelter the other person. Many people then act based on instinct and don't notice they're avoiding the problem or derailing the discussion by acting irritated. This defensive reaction is almost always caused by anxiety. They don't feel comfortable during the conversation, so they react without even thinking about their behavior, commonly leading to frustration and resentment for both parties.

With that said, now is the time for a little exercise, and you can ask yourself whether you or your partner are exhibiting signs of communication anxiety. The best approach to this little investigation is to take a journal and start making notes of any possible clues. Prepare several lists where you write down what kind of out-of-place signals you detect in a conversation. Don't just think about your partner, because you might be the problem without even realizing it. You should also take some time to reflect on how you react when you have a conversation with your partner. Think about his or her responses, as well. Finally, you can perform a mental exercise where you think about what you could've done to handle the conversation better. Make a list of situations where better communication would've prevented any feelings of resentment or anger between the two of you.

Social Situations

Being in certain social situations is difficult for many people who don't even suffer from any form of anxiety. However, those with anxiety will encounter other problems that wouldn't cross other people's minds. It's typical behavior to deny meal invitations from coworkers or friends, ignore unnecessary phone calls, and even avoid small family gatherings. While social situations are more specific and don't occur every day, there are also daily occurrences that can cause extreme amounts of anxiety. For instance, some have issues performing any task or responsibility as long as another human is being in their presence, looking over their shoulder.

Isolating yourself from any social situation usually leads to more than just personal social isolation. In some cases, this behavior can turn into a never-ending cycle of avoidance. The social aspects of life causing you anxiety, can, in turn, create even more tension in new situations. Avoidance reduces your ability to cope, and you will be dealing with even more fear during the next social gathering. This self-perpetuating cycle often leads to relationship problems, especially breakups, especially if one party is not suffering from any anxiety.

CHAPTER 1:

Understanding Anxiety in Relationships

A great relationship can be one of the most fascinating and pleasurable things throughout everyday life. It is something that the vast majority of us anticipate encountering and assembling. Nonetheless, contemplating the complexities associated with a relationship can be a prolific rearing ground for emotions and musings that lead to uneasiness. Tension in a relationship can emerge at any phase of the romance or even marriage. Numerous youngsters can get sentiments of nervousness and stress just from the contemplations of seeing someone. At the beginning of a relationship, individuals may get sentiments of weakness, prompting more nervousness. One can encounter stressing considerations, for example, "Does this individual truly like me?" "How genuine is this relationship?" "Will it work out?"

One may imagine that the sentiments of tension at the beginning of a relationship will die down once the individual understands that the relationship will last, for example, through getting hitched or realizing that the accomplice won't hurt them. Indeed, this isn't generally the situation. For certain couples, the sentiments of uneasiness get increasingly extreme as the two individuals draw nearer. Destabilizing considerations, for example, "Do I truly like this individual?" "Would I like to spend a mind-blowing remainder with him/her?" "Will he/she free enthusiasm for me?" "Am I sufficient?" come flooding in like a tempest.

Every one of these concerns can cause an individual to feel desolate in any event, when in a relationship. Truth be told, these nervousness-activating contemplations can make an individual remove him/herself from his/her accomplice. More terrible still, tension seeing someone can make us abandon love completely. It is thusly critical to get uneasiness and its triggers and the outcomes. Understanding nervousness while seeing someone can assist us in detecting the negative considerations and activities that damage the affection in our lives. How might one hold the sentiments of tension within proper limits and defeat the relationship unleashing emotions?

Truly, falling and being infatuated causes difficulties for us from numerous points of view. Some of these difficulties are unforeseen and when we face them on the first run-through, our human instinct makes us cautious. For example, if you love somebody without question, and he/she makes you extremely upset, odds are, you will abstain from being helpless. On a specific level, we as a whole dread being harmed, intentionally or unknowingly. Unexpectedly, this dread will in general increment when we are getting what we need. If a relationship is acceptable, one begins to consider dread the 'effect of a separation.' Consequently, he/she begins to take the safeguard, making separation and in the end cutting off the association. If we are given love and are treated in a bizarrely decent manner, we become tense.

That protective strain turns into a hindrance. Note that nervousness in a relationship doesn't just emerge on account of the things going between the two gatherings included. This inclination may likewise emerge on account of our observation. The things you enlighten yourself regarding a relationship, love, fascination, want, and so forth will influence our lives. The famous 'Internal voice' is extremely hazardous if it is negative. This psychological lounge chair can reveal to us things that fuel our dread of closeness. The basic internal voice can take care of our negative guidance, for example, "You are excessively monstrous for him/her" "Even the others have left you previously" "You cannot confide in such a man/lady."

What do such considerations do? They make us betray our loved ones and, above all, ourselves. The basic internal voice can make us antagonistic, neurotic, and superfluously dubious. It can likewise drive our sentiments of protectiveness, doubt, nervousness, and envy to undesirable levels.

One is occupied by his/her accomplice, subsequently no genuine connection and communication. After contemplating, one may begin to carry on either youthfully or in ruinous ways. For example, one may begin to manage the accomplice around, checking all his/her moves, offering pointless dreadful remarks, disregarding, or abusing the other.

Assuming your accomplice remains late busy working or passes by the nearby bar for a beverage before returning home. The basic inward idea will trigger contemplations, for example, "Where is he/she? What's going on with him? With who and why? Does she/he prefer to be away from home? Perhaps he/she doesn't cherish me any longer." These musings can go through your head such a great amount that when your accomplice returns home, you are feeling shaky, suspicious, incensed, and guarded. In this state, it turns out to be difficult to have a valuable discussion about his/her whereabouts. Therefore, this accomplice will feel misjudged and baffled. Moreover, he/she will likewise take a guarded position. Before long, the dynamic of the relationship shifts from delight and solace to silly and out of line medicines. Rather than getting a charge out of the remainder of the night, it gets squandered as everybody feels pulled back and upset.

Do you understand that in such a case, you have successfully made the separation you at first dreaded? Or you likewise understand that your accomplice may have had no negative aims? The truth of the matter is the separation you have made was not brought about by the circumstance itself or conditions. No, it was activated by that basic inward voice which may have been off-base. That voice hued your deduction with antagonism twisted your discernment and at long last, drove you to implosion.

The greatest test that drives us to implosion while seeing someone is self-question. If we evaluate the vast majority of the things, we stress overseeing someone and understand that we can deal with the outcomes. Lion's share of us is flexible enough to encounter heartbreaks and recuperate. It likely has occurred previously but you didn't kick the bucket from it. In any case, our internal voice will in general dramatically overemphasize things, particularly the negative ones. That voice threatens and catastrophizes everything, making it difficult to remain sound. Truth be told, it can trigger genuine spells of nervousness over some non-existent relationship elements that don't exist and bizarre, immaterial dangers.

Likely, separations would not be so agonizing if that we didn't have that basic voice. The investigations destroy us by calling attention to every one of our imperfections and the things we neglect to do. The contorted reality makes us imagine we are not solid and versatile enough to endure. That basic voice is the negative companion who is continually offering negative guidance "You can't endure a catastrophe, simply remain protected and don't get powerless."

We structure our resistances by relying on exceptionally beneficial encounters and adjustments. The inward voice obtains from those interesting encounters. If a previous accomplice said that he/she will leave you since you are overweight or underweight, the inner voice will utilize that line to twist reality. It will make you feel another accomplice is seeing similar defects and that he/she will leave as a result of them. When feeling uncertain or on edge, a few of us will in general become urgent or tenacious in our activities. Others become control monstrosities, needing to have the accomplice. Countless individuals begin to feel swarmed, as there is no breathing space in the relationship, in this manner deciding to remove themselves from their friends and family.

In outrageous cases, we isolate ourselves from the sentiments of want in the relationship. We can become reserved, cautious, or we can completely pull back. Such examples of connection and relating can emerge out of our initial educational encounters. In our youthful years, we create connection designs unwittingly, contingent upon our condition.

The examples become the model for our grown-up life. They impact how we evaluate our necessities and how we get them satisfied. These connection examples and styles are the primary determinants of the measure of tension one feels in a relationship.

CHAPTER 2:

Identifying Behaviors That Triggers Anxiety

Fear of Collapse

This is a sudden fall. It might occur due to peer pressure from close friends who are obvious in one's life, and mostly they always come with shocking words which can cause one to collapse and sometimes eventually die. It can also be caused by a lack of support from one's partner; good support encourages and strengthens love because it is also a bond that fulfills true love. Part of the support includes finance, food, and even closeness to your partner. For the best outcomes, one should avoid peer pressure and negative people.

Just like any other photophobia fears, fear of collapse freezes the heart. Your heart becomes. You are constantly thinking that this relationship is going to hit the rock any time, and if you do not do something about it, it will end up destroying your relationship. To recognize this fear, you will see the following.

Suspecting a Motive

When your partner tries to show you kindness, for example, take you out for a drink or buys a beautiful dress, all you think of is that there must be something he wants, or he has done so that is why he is behaving the way he is.

- Trust Issues

You cannot trust anything your partner says, you must go ahead behind his back to find out if he was saying the truth or talking about the exact thing.

- Sticking to the Old Ways

You only want to do things according to the times when you felt like it was working. You do not want to change and experience something new.

- Doubt

You are always in doubt, asking yourself whether it is going to work. You convince yourself that it might not work.

- Clingy

When you see your partner distancing himself or pulling away, you start being so clingy even after he tells you he needs some space. It is good to give someone space, and this does not mean he is leaving. Being clingy only shows that you have a fear of collapse.

Fear of Being Vulnerable

Vulnerability is not always a show of weakness. If you are vulnerable, it only means you trust easily, people can get to you faster; they can understand you better, understand your likes, dislikes, and boundaries, and be able to watch their steps when they are with you. It gives you an upper hand, unlike you thinking that it pulls you down. To face your fear of being vulnerable, you will have to point the following signs to know if indeed it is the fear of being vulnerable:

- Not Opening-up

You do not want to open up to your partner because you think he will see you as weak. You prefer to suffer in silence. For example, you have a problem concerning your parents' home that needs financial help, but you can't tell your partner because you think he will see you as weak. You feel he will think that you are working too, and you must be weak to get help from him.

- Avoiding Conflict

Each time there is a problem in the relationship, like a situation that is more likely to lead to a heated argument or other conflicts, instead of handling it, you let it pass by sugar coating it with fancy dinners, cocktails, or even movies so that it won't be a topic of discussion anymore.

- Overprotective

You do not want your partner to understand what is going on in your life. You have put up a shield that should be ventured through. There is a no-go zone in most of your doing even the least important things because you are afraid that if he finds out, he will capitalize on it and you will be seen as weak.

- Overthinking

You are constantly asking yourself a thousand and one questions every time you think of your partner knowing something about you. You are thinking so much about what he will say, how he will react, how he will see you, and so many others.

- Lashing out at Your Partner

This is a defensive mechanism. You do not want your partner to understand a certain thing about you, so the only way to make him stop and never be interested again is to lash at him. This will keep him at bay from anything that concerns you.

To avoid this in a relationship, partners should be faithful, honest, loving, caring, and stop exposing themselves to that possibility. Lovers should also respect their partner's gargets/devices (such as phones) so that they can acquire peace of mind.

Fear of Not Feeling Important

This is a situation where someone does not feel useful to his or her partner. The fear comes in when your lover does not involve you in his or her activities; the partner remaining silent in the house, infrequent communication, frankness, not having sex with your partner whereby sex is the only action that can bond the relationship, and unfaithfulness among the couples. It hurts due to unexpected changes in the relationship. Some problems might persist; one has to adapt to the situation while getting the time of viewing the other partner. In the process of viewing your partner, one should also be patient to give room for any change.

- Too Sensitive

You are taking things too personally. Your partner makes a comment, and you think it was aimed at putting you down. For example, your partner says, "Honey, I think your dress will look better if it is ironed." You take this statement super personally, and you sulk about it because you think that he meant you are useless by wearing a dress not ironed. You start thinking on behalf of him.

- Making a Catastrophe Where It Is Not Needed

You start making a mountain out of an anthill. Your partner calls to say he will be late for dinner and you go on a no-speaking spree for a week. Don't you think you are exaggerating things here? He called to inform you early; why are you sulking and not speaking to him? Because you are suffering from the fear of not being important.

- Perfection

Everything you touch or do; you want them to be so perfect in that he will see you as the most important person. You do not want to give him any reason to comment or think otherwise. You are afraid to make a mistake because you think he will see you as useless.

- Panic Attacks

Every time you are looking at your phone to see if he has texted you. If you find that he has not texted, you start panicking. You start feeling less important. You start feeling that you are not among the things he values in his life.

- Doubting Your Every Step

You always doubt what you are doing. You are not sure if it will be good for him so that he can see you as an important person. You are not sure he will like the idea because you want to be the most important thing that has ever happened to him.

Fear of Failure

Fear of failure comes in a person when one does not succeed in his or her plans and oaths of their bond. This discourages one from loving another partner; it is caused by things like long periods of sickness, hunger, bad company, idleness, and lack of job opportunities. This leads the partner to feel bored, and the true love disappears; the partner seemed to be losing the loved one. To avoid that fear and stress, you should not make it personal, seek advice, share your problem, and let it go.

- Expecting Him to Fix Everything

You are expecting him to be a hero, a Mr. Spider man. You want him to save every situation there is. You want him to walk in your mind and do everything you are thinking of, but if this is not happening, then you think this relationship is bound to fail.

- Aggressive Response to Passive Questions

The fear of failing is telling you that this must be heard loud and clear and never be repeated, and you answer aggressively to a simple passive question that he asked. The aggressive response only instills fear in your partner or anger or mixed ideas, and this might ruin your relationship.

- Feeling That the Partner is Un-Reliable

Feeling that you are investing a lot in this relationship than he is, you think he is not reliable; he is not supporting you in anything that matters to you. You feel and think that he is unstable, and he is going to lead this relationship on the wrong path. You think that he is slowly digging the drainage to drain the relationship each time he tells you he is not in a position to attend your exhibition. This is the fear of driving you, and it is important to handle it.

- Having Thoughts That He Will Leave

Each time you are seated, you picture him leaving. You are afraid that he is going to walk out of the door any minute. This is what all the fear of failure is doing. Maybe he has no plan of leaving, and it is the fear driving you.

Fear of Entering into Intimacy

If you are asked why you keep on dodging the idea of intimacy and you have no answer; this only communicates one thing. You are afraid to get into it. For you to understand that you have this fear, look at how you will know that you have it in a room in your head by checking these points below.

- Incompatible Schedule

Each time an intimacy topic is brought up and planned when to happen, you say your schedule is not compatible with his.

- Lame Excuses

You are always giving excuses that do not make sense. Like, I just do not feel like it, I do not think it is the appropriate time, and when asked when the appropriate time is or why you do not feel like it, you completely have no answer.

- Am Not Worthy Enough

A feeling of unworthiness has engulfed you. You think he deserves better, and that is another reason to not enter intimacy. This is all wrong, it is only in your mind and it needs to be corrected.

- Feeling Shameful

Why would you feel shameful to a partner you have been with for a long time? It is not shameful; it is the fear of intimacy.

Past Experiences Ended Badly

Past experiences leave wounds, which causes fear based on their experiences. If you want to realize that you are suffering from this fear, the following are the manifestations:

- Getting Very Angry

A small thing that doesn't need all your anger makes you so worked up because it reminds you of the same thing before.

CHAPTER 3:

Overcoming Anxiety in Relationships

A nxiety in connections is several, and also not unusual individuals locate themselves right here. There are lots of points you can follow to get rid of anxiety in connections. When you had made suspicious points in the past, your mind had a method of advising you to repent. Also, after you do repent, you could not completely get rid of the anxiety.

Anxiety in partnerships can additionally be triggered by individuals that have self-esteem concerns. Whatever factor you have, anxiety in connections can be conquered just by encountering your concerns. Bear in mind, this kind of anxiety can actually cost your relationship.

If you did something scandalous previously, it is no marvel you experience anxiety in connections. A lovely young lady discovered a terrific guy whom she fell in love with; however, she was constantly full of anxiety. Anxiety will certainly lead to stress, and also, clinical depression is the mother of anxiety.

How to Stop Feeling Anxiety in Relationships

Just how commonly do you put on standard masks as well as when? Exactly how numerous times are you running from your own as well as provide the individuals surrounding you an identity that also you do not think in?

I cannot also visualize how I have lived my whole life with a cabinet complete of masks up until just recently. I believe I was the queen of masks. They looked so lovely to me, or else I would not have been using them.

I think that the one mask we put on most regularly is a concern. This mask is incredibly stunning when seen from the exterior.

Because we are worried that individuals around us will certainly not like what they see, we put on masks. we hesitate that they will certainly see something that we do not, such as concerning ourselves. Because of our youth, we utilized to review ourselves with the viewpoints of moms and dads, family members, after that institution, peers, our enthusiasts, and more.

- What are the things that we might have listened to the most?

- You are also tiny to comprehend this.

- You are also fat.

- Your nose is also large, your face also little, your teeth also yellow.

- You can do a lot far better.

- You need to come to be an attorney or a physician, and these are genuine service providers.

- Your good friend has much better qualities; he/she acts. You are humiliating us.

- Oh, that guy will certainly never ever go out with you. He is also helpful for you.

- You fill out the spaces.

We begin placing on masks, and we attempt to be as we assume various other individuals desire us to be to feel approved, liked, preferred, and amazing. We neglect that we are what we are, such as what we do not like; even worse, we feel we are not qualified to reveal all these sensations.

We reveal concern in the direction of the guys we enjoy. You do not shed a guy since he is not your own in the very first area. We do not own guys or individuals in basic.

OK, so if we recognize that we cannot shed a guy since we do not have him, what are we worried to shed? I inform you what it is: the excellent sensation concerning ourselves when we are with such a guy. We feel we have something to state and we have a function as well as an objective in a guy's life. Suppose we could feel as great when we are with ourselves without always remaining in a relationship? Suppose we could feel liked and also valued by ourselves? We can reverse and also reduce the utter suffering that succeeds a feasible break up with a male.

It is unusual that among all the worries that we have, the anxiety to shed our originality is not extremely solid. As if we are not also terrified to shed ourselves. We choose to shield the male we are in a relationship with. I was speaking on various other days with one of my sweethearts, and also she informed me that she blooms when she is in a relationship with a guy. She feels energized, does her hair, nails and gets expensive clothing as well as attractive underwear, and takes treatment of her body.

I had a minute AHA! Since we like us, we do not take treatment of ourselves, yet as we like someone else to do it. We credit a male to pull all the right ideas in us while we can do so rapidly.

Below is a workout that I would certainly like you to do throughout the following week. If you remain in a relationship or otherwise, you can just as do it:

Every early morning when you get up, check out the mirror of your space as well as claim to on your own: "You are terrific Violetta (utilize your name, obviously!) I enjoy you simply the way you are!"

Dress like you are preparing for the essential day: Date yourself!

Go out on the roads, look individuals in the eye and smile. Do it, and you have absolutely nothing to hide about.

Go to a premium shop with quality clothing and take time to look around. Touch the smooth gowns, run the soft materials via your fingers, attempt whatever you like, and after that leave the shop with a smile on your face.

Do you feel awkward and uncomfortable? To go to a public place alone a while earlier was simply intolerable to me. I like to do that now whenever I have the time.

Isolation anxiety is just one of the biggest obstacles in our lives to draw in high-quality. Individuals would be drawn to you like a magnet until you figure out how to accept and support the process you are. All the power and also the great ambiance in you will certainly end up being infectious, and also males will certainly simply wish to be around you.

I understand you can obtain to like on your own. Because you simply should be liked the means you are!

How to Feel Happier

Allow yourself to commemorate your brand-new liberty! Liberty from what? Right here are several of the anxiety-producing occasions and also circumstances that lots of people would love to be without, and also maybe you can relate to some or every one of the products:

- Stress and anxiety over your marital relationship

- Anxiety concerning your household's wellness

- A basic feeling of fear and also anxiety

- Codependent connections in your home as well as in your job

- A sensation of being bewildered by way too many troubles

- Regrets for your previous blunders in connections

- Persistent heartache

Perhaps you have a work you do not like; however, given that you require the cash to pay costs, you maintain going to the function there anyhow, regardless of the reality that the ambiance is eliminating your spirit. Maybe you are in a relationship that is full of quarrels and also disagreements, as well as objections and blame.

Identifying the truth of your sensations is the very first action. You do not have to do a total overhaul of your whole life to begin feeling better.

It may appear initially that fixing a negative relationship, for instance, implies that you will certainly need to leave it or reduce the various other individuals out of your life. And also, yet if you do not transform anything regarding the method you connect to on your own as well as to other individuals, you will certainly quickly find yourself in an extremely comparable relationship with a beginner.

You might have acknowledged that sensation vis-à-vis a good friend when you observe that they keep dating people that are wrong for them. You ask yourself how can they be so foolish. It's a lot easier to recognize these errors in another person's life than in our very own. This is because that has nothing to do with just how wise you are. You need to discover the lessons that are existing to you in your present connections, as opposed to discarding them with the idea that doing so will certainly solve your dissatisfied as well as distressing sensations, since or else that very same lesson will certainly simply appear once more in the following relationship.

It can feel that your ideas regulate your sensations as well as you are powerless to alter anything at all when you are besieged by anxiety and also a concern. When you take an opportunity of opening your heart to others in your life and allow them to understand you, and be closer to you, and sustain them in their objectives, you may find that they would do so. However, they did not recognize exactly how to damage the pattern of communication that has ended up being a repeating cycle with you.

Currently, release the nervous sensations inside as well as praise yourself for having the maturation and also toughness to quit devastating actions. Appreciate your flexibility and also commemorate your brand-new lease on life!

Anxiety Insomnia Treatment

In this book, we're most likely to speak about the reasons as well as the treatments for sleeping disorders and anxiety. Since stress, anxiety, and fear can trigger anxiety, and anxiety and sleeplessness go with each other, they are additionally connected to sleep problems. Think of when you're stuck in bed and also bothered with whatever that might fail concerning tomorrow, you obtain an adverse assumption of the future, and also your body and mind are attempting to determine what to do regarding it, and they're hectic to sleep as well.

When you're an individual that generally rests well, yet all of a sudden you observe you exist in bed much longer than normal; early sleeping disorders. This is normally connected to something brand-new that is, your life, and also, it's most likely connected to tension or fear. Lots of people look to treat their anxiety as well as sleep problems with medicine, yet a few of them pick to attempt to treat it normally with natural herbs or by attempting to face the origin of the issue.

Treatments for sleep problems normally belong to doing away with stress and anxiety as well as just anxiety. If it's anxiety concerning a relationship or something else, you have to obtain to the origin of the trouble.

If the origin of the sleeplessness trouble is the trouble of your rest setting or rests' health after that, you might have to look right into transforming points concerning the means you prepare for your rest as well as the method you normally drop asleep. If for years or years, you have had a hard time with sleeplessness, you may be dealing with persistent sleeplessness.

CHAPTER 4:

What Makes a Healthy Relationship?

These are simple and easy to practice for a better and stronger relationship.

Talking Openly

Communication is an integral aspect of a stable relationship. Healthy couples find time for a regular check-in with each other. It's important to speak more than just parenting and household maintenance. Seek to spend a few minutes each day exploring deeper or more intimate issues to stay committed to your spouse in the long term. That doesn't say you can stop taking up difficult topics. Holding anxieties or problems to oneself will generate resentment. However, it helps to be polite when arguing about difficult topics. Research indicates that the way you interact with your spouse is significant, and the negative impact of communication may have a negative impact on the bond. Disagreements are part of any relationship. However, some types of combat are particularly harmful. Couples that use disruptive tactics during conflicts such as shouting, resorting to personal attacks, or withdrawing from the debate are more likely to split up than couples that clash constructively. To cope with conflicts, use positive approaches such as listening to the point of view of the spouse, and respecting their concerns is a better path forward.

Keeping It Interesting

It may be challenging to remain close to your spouse or be romantic between children, jobs, and outside obligations.

Many people schedule daily date nights to make things fun. Nevertheless, even dates will get stale if you still watch a movie or go to the same restaurant. Experts advocate stopping the norm and doing fresh things whether it's dance, attending a class together, or planning a picnic afternoon.

When Should Couples Seek Help?

Every relationship has ups and downs, so certain variables in a relationship are more prone to cause bumps than others. For starters, finance and parenting decisions cause ongoing disputes. One indication of a dilemma is repetitive iterations of the same clash again and again. Psychologists may help partners strengthen their trust in these situations and find healthier strategies to step past the dispute. You don't have to wait until there are indicators of problems in a relationship until you try to improve the alliance. Marital education programs that help to learn skills such as good communication, effective listening, and conflict management have been shown to reduce the divorce risk.

Know More about Your Partner

How much does your partner know you? Do they have the attributes to make you grow into a stronger person? Do the practices make you think of your relationship twice? Do you know all the positive and negative bits of them?

These are the questions that will make you know whether you are with the right person or not if you are answering them. Yet, you can always note that not all relationships are flawless, so it is necessary to have an open mind on which imperfections are worth your comprehension.

Here is the important stuff you should learn about your significant other.

Know Their Life Story, Both the Good and the Bad Parts

Upon first sight, many people believe in love and claim it can be the beginning of something wonderful. Most people, though, learned their lessons the hard way and discovered that love is not enough to keep a relationship going.

You will need other aspects, so one significant reason is to allow your spouse to realize who he/she is, so it doesn't end there. You must also completely embrace what you will find when you unravel the tale of their lives, particularly the bad bits.

Know the Things and Habits That Annoy Them

Everyone has a list of things that bother them, so it is very helpful to know every detail on your partner's list, and you can make the appropriate changes to prevent the typical trivial fights.

Try to realize as best as possible that you are two separate individuals with very different backgrounds, and reaching a compromise is one step closer to creating a deeper bond, particularly if you're new in the relationship.

Favorite Things and People

Create a list of things and individuals that could make them happy, and find it in your heart to value them as well. This is vital that you are conscious of these essential parts of the existence of your significant other as apart from demonstrating that you are very vigilant. It is a sensitive way to consider the fact that her joy will come from various places—not only from you and your relationship.

The Things That Fuel Their Temper

What's making them angry? Which are the things, incidents, or acts capable of causing them to erupt? Anger is a fairly normal emotion felt by any human being, so knowing what causes it is a helpful way to learn the other person. You will gain a lot about the way people convey their frustrations as well as their reactions to the triggering stuff.

The Memories That Make Them Cry

Understanding grief and how people are keeping painful feelings will help you get to know a person better. By understanding what makes your life's love cry, trying to reach out to them, and making that bond, you are building a sanctuary that they will still run to anytime they feel like breaking down.

Know the relationships are not just about love. Beyond being a lover, you're also a mate, a trustworthy confidant, and an ever-supportive partner.

Their Dreams and Aspirations

What are the things they hoped for? What are the goals and aspirations they set out to pursue? Learn your companion well and admire their strength and determination to tackle the future without any uncertainties.

Seeing how your partner sees herself ten or twenty years from now is an amazing thing because it's just a happy feeling when you're with somebody who is not scared of aiming big because of dreaming high.

The Jokes That Make Them Laugh Out Loud

Humor can play a very important role in relationships because aside from offering other people a pleasant smile, it can be a nice and quick relief from the unjust challenges in life. So, make your spouse laugh.

Find out all of her favorite lines, google the funniest stories, learn and go make this very precious person laugh out loud because it doesn't matter if you're negative at it.

Their Frustrations and Defeats

What are the aspects that reminded them that, even though they earn it, people will not always get what they want? Life challenges will bring down even the most hopeful individuals, so make sure to be present when it's the turn of your companion to be aware of that.

Enable them to do tasks they never wanted to attempt again just because they struggled the first time. Be a source of motivation and an undying belief that such losses and mistakes would fail to destroy their spirit.

The List of Their Favorite Food

This is more likely to be the most undervalued aspect of any relationship, and this needs more credit. How well do you know the favorite food preferences of your partner? What restaurant is their favorite? Are they in love with Japanese cuisine, or are they more like the spice queens and always wanting Indian food? Take her to an amazing experience with food as she deserves all the world's real food.

The People Who Broke Their Hearts

Accept their history and other people who have led to the way they currently see the world. It's a required move for your companion to grasp inside and out completely. Be careful, however, and make sure you have an open mind to consider stuff you can't alter. Only reflect on the fact that it took every phase of your partner's life to make her a happier, stronger human.

How They See Their Future with You

Last but most significantly, you ought to learn whether you are a part of the dream of the future with your partner. Five to ten years from now, what is your role? Would you still speak to each other about your life and how you want to live it with them?

Understanding your partner well and figuring out the issues, attitudes, and activities that lead to how they see the world will make a difference and help the relationship withstand the time check. Ask the right questions then and there, and don't be scared to hear the answers.

Be a Good Listener

Tips to Be a Good Listener in Your Relationship

"You can't listen?" You've heard this phrase pretty much at least once in your lifetime. Maybe only a couple of you learned that from your partner. Communicating is also an essential cornerstone in a secure and safe relationship, but communicating requires two elements: talking and listening. Talking is a basic thing that everybody does, but this time the emphasis would be on the listening side. Most people are chatting, so only listening to a bit. Yet, what does one do to be a great listener? Don't worry! Ten strategies below are to help you be one:

Listen More Often

Telling yourself how to become a good listener? The number one suggestion is to listen more often. You may be the person that always talks and forgets how to listen. It never hurts to lower one's ego for long enough to lengthen one's endurance and only listen to what your companion has to tell. When you teach yourself to listen most frequently, as you converse with your boyfriend or girlfriend, it should come automatically.

Communication Is a Two-Way Street

Communication, as stated earlier, is not one way: whether one talks the other listens. Those positions are interchanged from time to time. The dispute occurs where certain functions are not at all shared, and only one talks and the other listens. Keep in mind that you should know when to stop talking. Effective contact will never be accomplished if two people in a relationship do not routinely exchange such positions.

Drop Your Phone

You need to drop your phone while talking to your girlfriend or boyfriend, particularly if this is a significant problem. That means you appreciate the individual talking, and you're all ears on what he or she has to say.

This is disrespectful if, during a face to face talk, one continues checking the screen or fiddling with his or her phone. Turn your phone to a silent mode to be a better listener, because those emails and notifications can wait.

Don't Interrupt

Another significant note is never disturbing the one talking to become a good listener. Be all ears to what he or she is telling, and wait until the person is done, then share your thoughts on the issue. His or her opinion is just as important as yours on the topic. This shows rudeness if the person speaking is disrupted. Often people get so interested in the topic that they keep cutting off other persons. If you see yourself related to this, consider holding the horses and making others take turns.

CHAPTER 5:

Love and Relationship Advice for Couples

C ontrolling indignation isn't simple, however, it is conceivable with the correct technique and exertion. Significantly, you find a way to control your displeasure, perceive the signs that go before it, and converse the indications it makes.

Acknowledge That You Have a Problem

Like liquor addiction or any sort of compulsion, until you acknowledge you have an issue, you will never begin searching for arrangements or approaches to oversee it. Neither will you be set up to make a solid move. Consequently, the FIRST step is to acknowledge that you have an issue, and that issue is identified with outrage control.

Monitor Your Angry-Reaction Episodes

You will be shocked to realize that the vast majority won't comprehend what drives them mad. They would make statements like, "These days, I get extremely furious. Everything pesters me." or "I appear to have no persistence by any stretch of the imagination. I am irate constantly." But if that you ask what precisely rankles you, you would not have the option to state it solidly. As you have seen before, it would be massively useful if that you keep a log of the examples when you blew up, the motivation behind why blew up, and how you responded to the incitement. As prompted before, you have to make a note for each day record:

- About what drove you crazy;
- About how could you react;
- Regardless of whether the response to the indignation was advocated.

Record these components consistently for 1-3 months and study the examples that develop. What are the triggers that drive you crazy? What is your style of managing incitements? What sort of outrage do you anticipate? That it is so hurtful to you? How hurtful is it to the surrounding individuals?

Make the Best of Your Support Network

Nothing can be accomplished in seclusion. In this example as well, you have to enroll the assistance of your loved ones if you need to overcome your displeasure. Give quality opportunities to your loved ones and bolster them while they bolster you. It is exceptionally uncommon that individuals can battle major issues alone. This is the reason you have to enroll the assistance and collaboration of your darlings in your mission to vanquish outrage.

Systems to Short-Circuit the Anger Cycle

We have spoken before about systems that will help you director outrage. These techniques are intended to interfere with the pattern of outrage and forestall its acceleration to lamentable statures. You can work out your own 'outrage plugs.' Here are a few guides to make you go:

- Walk away when you feel your anger is mounting. This is maybe the best electrical switch. Expelling yourself from the scene will forestall warmed trade or doing whatever would boomerang on you.

- When you feel nearly losing it, holler as loud as possible, "STOP." This may get a couple of grins and leave your adversary speechless, yet it will likewise prevent you from stirring up a repulsive irate state of mind.

- Count up to 10 before you open your mouth to state anything. This typically works best for couples with the 'leave' technique. Sometimes you may need to count up to 20 or 100. The fact of the matter is that you have to accomplish something different until you can take a few to get back some composure.

- Breathe in profoundly and center on the breath in; breath out the procedure for a moment or something like that.

- Push your considerations towards wonderful occasions. Envisioning charming scenes, recalling soothing and upbeat occasions can toss cold water off your rising temper and chill it off practically in a moment. At the point when you feel outraged hurrying in, close your eyes quickly and review something charming. The adjustment in the state of mind will take your brain off the annoyance trigger and you will have the option to take a gander at the circumstance with a cool psyche.

- Retire to a sheltered, joy asylum. At work spot and home, have a spot reserved where you spend considering beneficial things, smelling relieving fragrances, and feeling better. This is the spot you could use for contemplation. At the point when you feel the outrage rising, go to your retreat room/put and ruminate for 5-15 minutes or more, if you have the opportunity or tendency. Only 5 minutes in contemplation would change your temperament by and large.

- Do something you like. Accomplishing something you like is intended to take your brain off your resentment. Nonetheless, be cautious that you don't make it as compensation to blow up. Do it as a short-circuiting system to your resentment, remembering that there is an exceptionally slender line between this objective and programming your psyche into accepting its award for your outrage.

Abstain from snatching a smoke, shopping, betting, Facebook, liquor, sex, erotic entertainment, and whatever such thing that may get you dependent on an off-base thing. It ought not to resemble bouncing from the griddle into the fire.

- Laugh aloud. It sounds off-kilter and you may get a couple of eyebrows raised at this odd conduct, yet chuckling out is so that anyone might hear an extraordinarily ground-breaking and compelling indignation electrical switch. Giggling out resoundingly—in any event, when you don't mean it and it is just the technician thing—brings down your pulse, helps to discharge poisons from the body, and quiets the psyche. Likewise, the responses you will see on the essences of the individuals around when you begin chuckling out loud will be adequate to change your disposition.

Put Forth a Conscious Attempt to Bring in Empathy

Sympathy is an incredible electrical switch. Take a stab at picturing what could be the explanation behind the other individual to carry on the way he/she does. It isn't in every case simple to expel yourself from your hurt sentiments and take a stab at seeing the other perspective, however, it is certainly justified regardless of the exertion.

Frequently, all you need is a concise break between the incitement and response to change the way of your activity. Likewise, assuming the best about an individual makes you a superior individual; simply realizing that you can meet people's high expectations will make it worth your time and energy.

Sometimes absolution is the incredible move you can make for the individual who irritated you and for yourself. At the point when you state, "Possibly this is a real mix-up. I pardon you. If you don't mind see that it isn't rehashed." The generosity of such a signal could completely change him and yours simultaneously.

Apply Life's TWO Most Powerful Rules

There are just TWO standards that administer human life:

Rule No. 1: Never sweat little stuff.

Rule No.2: Everything is little stuff.

It might make you grin as you read it, yet take a gander at these two principles intently. Taking into account that everything in life is changing, what could be the "huge stuff"? Quite often, it isn't the difficulty that breaks you; it is how you take a gander at the difficulty that does it.

If you can help what stresses you, by all means, do it and put your psyche very still. Pursue the answer to your concern with all you have. If you help it, extraordinarily; the issue is comprehended. If not, acknowledge it and proceed onward. Acknowledge that occasionally, a few things are not intended to be; and don't worry over it.

This needs some training, yet once you decide to take a gander at the positive side, you will have the option to control your indignation.

Weight on Building Mutual Trust

Trust is an extremely incredible feeling. It is extremely hard to encounter antagonistic feelings with an individual you trust. You have to contribute your time and exertion to manufacture two-route trust with your friends and family–family, companions, partners, colleagues, and so forth. Trust would set aside an effort to fabricate and set inadequately, however, once it is there, it turns into the best remedy for outrage.

Listen Twice as Much as You Talk

There is a joke regarding why individuals have TWO ears and just ONE mouth. It appears it resembles Mother Nature (or God–whatever you accept validly) was giving you a noisy and clear message, for example, "Talk less, listen more." It is a superb exhortation, regardless of whether you like the joke. Half of the occasions an irate quarrel could have been deflected if that one or both the gatherings guaranteed that what they heard was right; or the correspondence which was mean to be passed on. Supposition and miscommunications are maybe the most widely recognized explanations behind irate battles/fights/groundbreaking contempt.

Tune in to what the others are stating; tune in with riveted consideration. Revamp the correspondence and confirm whether you got the message right, particularly if that you don't care for the message. Try not to be reluctant to ask; you'd be astounded at how many occasions you will find that you misconstrued the message since you were taking a gander at it from an alternate edge.

Pick Assertion over Aggression

At the point when you don't care for something, you have two options: stand up for yourself and state, "NO" or blow up and hurt the relationship. It is anything but difficult to perceive any reason why being self-assured is the better decision. Next time you discover something irritating you, don't be neighborly and bear it while gritting your teeth; neither should you detonate into outrage, pouring the choicest affront on those individuals.

Rather, be confident. State what you need considerately yet solidly leaving no extension for wriggling around. "I don't care for this propensity for yours." Or "I am unquestionably not doing this since I don't care for it." Or "I discover this sort of conduct unsuitable."

Tell the individual that you don't care for it, won't acknowledge or endure it. Simultaneously, let the individual realize that you are eager to cooperate to locate an elective way that suits both.

For example, your companion never assists with the family tasks leaving you battling and tired. Let him know, "Let us isolate the family errands between us, so we both have some time together." This will work far superior to hollering at him, "You do nothing around this house, you bum. What was I thinking when I got hitched to a mountain man like you!"

Grin and the World Will Smile with You

Have you seen that the vast majority will in general be pulled into cheerful people? The tragic ones are generally the ones dodged and forgotten about. It sounds cold-blooded and brutal; however, this is reality. On occasion, you'd be glad to loan your shoulder to a companion, relative, or associate. It feels great to help other people.

CHAPTER 6:

The Basics of How to Connect in a Relationship and Why You Act Irrationally

Here you will find out about the nonsensical practices that accompany nervousness, antagonism, and desire. They and their ID are examined quickly and what to do as opposed to pursuing those silly practices.

A Misunderstanding of Emotions

The idea that ladies are nonsensical is constantly matched with an assumption that legitimate thinking is better than a feeling, that objectivity adds to positive decisions, and that feelings lead to frail ones. It couldn't possibly be more off-base; proof has exhibited that it's not simply that people are not sincerely included that they don't settle on savvy decisions; individuals can't settle on choices without feelings by any stretch of the imagination. While for viable activity, feelings are significant.

Savant Martha Nussbaum has composed feelings as a method for the basic idea, assessments of the current state of one's life regarding one's objectives. Along these lines, idealistic sentiments advise us that things are going better for us, and negative feelings illuminate us that something isn't right in our lives. This mindfulness gives a basic reference to a fruitful method of living.

That contrasts and a customary impression of feelings as clamorous, upsetting, and troublesome; they ought to be monitored in that capacity. With this outlook, regularly people do not have the longing to dissect their own or different feelings and along these lines have little mindfulness about their own or other enthusiastic procedures. The public particularly denies men of chances for enthusiastic expressiveness and comprehension.

'Irrationality' is a refusal to recognize the truth of another.

Typically, for a situation where the individual doesn't get a handle on whether this compelling feeling is worthy, what individuals mean by 'unreasonable' conduct is a presentation of a forceful feeling. What's more, just however the audience doesn't get a handle on the inclination doesn't mean it has no sensible avocation for this. Sometimes, the 'unreasonable' word legitimizes and looks after pessimism, since it infers the activity is the result of such a characteristically inadequate or harmed person that it opposes and doesn't merit any reasonable individual's thought.

Sentimental connections are a field wherein feelings go out of control, as do socially mistaken assumptions and ensuing nonsensical charges. Sentimental connections request exceptional emotions since they are connection connections. As young people and grown-ups center around solace and security and love subordinate connection connections, knowing the wants and powerlessness of each other second to second is the foundation of fruitful connections. At the point when one mate feels imperiled for relationship security (e.g., forceful conduct or apathy), the individual in question will react with a compelling feeling of disengagement, outrage, distress, and dissatisfaction, when experienced and voiced enough overwhelmingly. Such rehashed reactions may likewise seem nonsensical.

Enthusiastic changes are astute markers of one's course throughout everyday life, and the status of the hugest connections. Negating another's very own existence by blaming the person in question for being 'unreasonable' prompts abusing the individual's entitlement to self-assurance. Getting tied up with a depiction of oneself as 'silly' negates our abstract reality and comes up short on the favorable circumstances that our feelings have like a manual for carrying on with a more advantageous life.

The Relationship Scorecard

What's Going On Here?

The 'keeping track of who is winning' wonder happens when somebody you're dating proceeds to blame you for past slip-ups. At the point when the two accomplices do that in the relationship, it's what we consider the 'relationship scorecard,' where the relationship is a challenge to find out who gets the most wrecked throughout the months or years, and along these lines who is increasingly obliged to the next.

Why It's Toxic?

The Partnership Scorecard is a depleting one-two punch. You're not simply concentrating on past disappointments to get away from the current issue, yet you're aggregating past blame and disdain to control your companion into feeling regretful at this point.

If that this proceeds on sufficiently long, the two sides will at last burn through a greater amount of their effort trying to show that they are less dependable than the other, as opposed to understanding what made the current issue. People burn through their whole time attempting to be less off base with one another than being progressively exact with one another.

What to Do Instead?

Manage issues separately, except if they are genuinely related. It's a repetitive concern whenever somebody cheats constantly. However, the truth that she humiliated you in 2010 has nothing to do with one another, so don't bring it up.

It's essential to recollect that by choosing to be with your loved one, you decide to associate around the entirety of their past activities and conduct. At long last, if that you don't grasp those, you don't acknowledge your accomplice. At the point when you were messed with things a year back because you ought to have managed it around then.

Dropping 'Insights' and Other Passive-Aggression

What's Going On Here?

Rather than communicating it legitimately and obviously, a friend endeavors to bump the other individual the correct way to sift through it. You'll discover insignificant and unpretentious motivations to irritate your accomplice as opposed to uncovering what truly agitates you, so you'll feel qualified to grumble to them.

Why It's Toxic?

As it illustrates, the two don't convey transparently and plainly. An individual has no reason to be detached forceful if that they don't hesitate to communicate dissatisfaction or defenselessness inside a relationship.

An individual could never want to drop 'insights' if they think they are not being judged or accused of their trustworthiness.

What to Do Instead?

Express your musings and wants openly. To clarify that the other individual isn't dependable or qualified for specific feelings with the goal that you would like to be helped by them. At the point when they love you, they will have the option to give this help quite often.

Holding the Relationship Hostage

What's Going On Here?

If one individual has a particular objection or concern, he extorts the other individual by moving the whole responsibility to a relationship. To begin, if that somebody feels like you've been cold to them, rather than saying, "I feel like no doubt about it," they'll state, "I can't generally date someone who's cold to me."

Why It's Toxic?

Keeping the relationship prisoner is passionate coercion and causes a great deal of superfluous strain. Indeed, even the slightest hiccup throughout the relationship adds to a potential duty emergency. It is critical for the two individuals in a relationship to understand that undesirable musings and emotions can be shared easily without it influencing the entire eventual fate of the relationship. Without the opportunity to be completely forthright, a couple will contort their contemplations and feelings, adding to a domain of doubt and abuse creating.

What to Do Instead?

Getting agitated disliking something in your relationship is alright; that is called being a typical person. However, recognize that having a place with an individual isn't a similar thing as continually cherishing a person. You can be consistent with anybody, dislike them all. You might be everlastingly faithful to other people, and frequently they may trouble or mischief you. In the other option, two accomplices who can share counsel and input without judgment or weight will confirm their drawn-out dedication to each other.

Blaming Your Partner for Your Own Emotions

What's Going On Here?

Envision you're encountering a harsh day, and your buddy isn't excessively caring or steady about it perhaps they've been on the telephone the entire day with different companions away, or they've been occupied when you've embraced them. You choose to remain at home together and simply watch a film today around evening time, however, your buddy is planning to go out to meet companions.

At the point when your inconvenience with your day and your accomplice's response to it comes up, you'll discover yourself lashing out because he is excessively mean and unfeeling towards you. You have never requested good help, and your buddy will normally realize how to affect you better. They ought to have gotten off the line based on your horrible passionate condition, to discard their arrangements.

Why It's Toxic?

Reprimanding our accomplices for our emotions is narrow-minded, and an ideal representation of maintaining inappropriately characterized individual limits. This will rapidly become a mutually dependent relationship if you make a pattern wherein your companion is as yet subject to how you feel (and the other way around). Everything should be arranged just to peruse a novel or sitting in front of the TV. At the point when somebody starts to feel disappointed, your interests leave the window, and you have to support each other to feel great.

The principal issue with mutually dependent qualities is that they create disdain. It is ordinary because every so often one individual blows up at the other with an underlying reason that he/she has had a negative day and is baffled and needs consideration. Regardless of whether it's a dream that one accomplice's life should even now spin around the other's passionate prosperity, it effectively turns out to be extremely pessimistic and regularly manipulative about the accomplice's feelings and wishes.

What to Do Instead?

Assume liability for your sentiments, feelings, and expect your life partner will assume liability for theirs in return. There is a little yet significant hole between your accomplice being strong and your accomplice being submitted. It is to make certain penances by expectation and not because this is what is required.

CHAPTER 7:

Ways Anxiety Affects Your Relationships

Having generalized anxiety conditions (GAD) can adversely influence many facets of your life, including your partnerships.

Below are two certain methods in which your anxiety can result in issues preserving links with others, along with techniques you can execute (under the support of a psychological health and wellness expert) to assist you to browse these undesirable add-on patterns.

Being Overly Dependent

Some individuals with GAD have an intense desire for distance from their companions (or pal), depending upon them continuously for assistance and also confidence.

In addition to being excessively reliant, individuals with GAD might find themselves vulnerable to overthinking, preparing for all worst-case circumstances, being indecisive, being afraid of denial, and also seeking continuous interaction (and also being distressed if a companion or close friend does not react promptly). Individuals with GAD as well as excessively reliant connections might likewise have problem with their temper towards those they feel dependent upon, acting out in manners which are damaging to their partnerships.

Combating Problematic Dependency

If you find yourself creating extremely reliant accessories, creating means to deal with your anxiety and also depending a lot more on yourself for feeling far better can take the stress off your companion or buddy.

If you find your own ending up being questionable or mad in these connections, initially advise yourself that this might be sustained by your anxiety. Take a couple of minutes to assume, regarding any kind of difficult information (realities) that sustain your concern to restore some point of view and also attempt.

A specialist that concentrates on a sort of talk treatment called the cognitive-behavioral treatment can assist you design techniques on exactly how to comfort yourself and also take thoughtful activity by yourself, rather than requiring your companion for convenience each time you fear.

Being Avoidant

On the various other ends of the range, some individuals with GAD come to be avoidant of connections as a means of managing their anxiety. They might prevent adverse feelings (for frustration, instance, or irritation) by not exposing their sensations, opening, or being susceptible. An individual that is avoidant of close relationships might be experienced as chilly, psychologically not available, uncompassionate, and even stand-offish, although they might wish for distance.

Combating Avoidance

If you find yourself being excessively remote in your connections, cognitive behavior modification, likewise with various other kinds of treatment, such as psychodynamic psychiatric therapy, might be practical. A psychological health and wellness specialist can assist an individual in discovering existing as well as previous partnerships as well as the feelings bordering those social links.

Treating Your Anxiety as well as Relationship Problems

A specialist will certainly additionally discover exactly how GAD influences your partnerships. Discovering your feelings much more deeply might be a great approach for somebody that often tends to be avoidant in connections. On the other hand, for individuals who are much more dependent on others and also psychologically responsive, this technique could backfire. It is vital to keep in mind that for individuals with GAD, medicine is also typically an important part of therapy. While the drugs suggested for anxiety, like careful serotonin reuptake preventions or serotonin-norepinephrine reuptake preventions are not alleviative, they can aid reduce your signs as well as assist you to feel much better as you revamp your distressed ideas and also habits with your specialist.

Anxiety and Romantic Relationships

Seeking a charming relationship can often seem like a harmful video game. Dating calls for a particular quantity of susceptibility, and it also includes the threat of obtaining pain or being let down. Individuals can experience a reasonable quantity of anxiety concerning their present enchanting relationship or the obstacles of seeking a brand-new one due to the fact of the unsure result. Individuals with social anxiety problems might regularly stress just how they are being evaluated by others, so they might prevent enchanting connections or date in basic due to the worry of shame. It's vital to bear in mind that you do not have to have a detected anxiety condition for anxiety to cause conflict in your charming relationship.

- Do you have fears that stop you from dating or seeking partnerships?

- Do you experience raised anxiety around sex-related affection?

- Do you depend greatly on your companion to guarantee you or tranquil nervous ideas?

- Do you stay clear of significant discussions with your companion because you hesitate to address the problem?

- Are you frequently afraid that your companion is most likely to leave you?

- Do you experience anxiety when your companion is away?

- Do you persuade yourself to believe your companion betrays without proof?

Activity Steps for Managing Relationship Anxiety

- ### Request for Aid

Never think that you need to take care of your anxiety in connections on your own. Just think about how private therapy can assist you in handling your anxieties concerning connections or take actions in the direction of a better dating life. Pairs therapy can likewise aid individuals to discover each other to boost interactions as well as develop analytic abilities in their relationship.

- ### Develop Your Very Own Passions

If you are placing every one of your concentrates on a charming relationship, options are that you will most likely feel distressed. Individuals that have strong partnerships with friends and family, as well as placed concentrate on their very own individual objectives as well as passions, are most likely to make better companions. They are less likely to experience splitting up anxiety or unpredictability concerning the relationship.

- ### Analyze Your Reasoning

Anxiety makes it tough to fairly analyze whether a concern is reputable. If you are feeling a lot more distressed in basic, after that, you could encourage yourself that your companion is intending or ripping off to leave you when there's no proof. Take into consideration whether you require working to handle your anxiety via healthy and balanced practices, connecting much better with your companion, or addressing concerns of worry in the relationship.

- **Share Your Worth**

Sometimes individuals in partnerships are so concentrated on making one more individual like them that they fail to remember to defend their very own worth as well as demands. Concession belongs to any kind of relationship. However, that does not imply you should not share your reasoning or be assertive when something is necessary for you. The earlier you can establish the criterion for sharing your requirements in a relationship, the less likely you are to feel resentful.

- **Do Not Stay Clear Of**

People that feel unstable in a relationship might be lured to sidetrack or prevent the problems from creating troubles. Establish a requirement for resolving problems head-on in the relationship, also if it feels awkward.

Opportunities are, you currently have a suggestion of exactly how to boost the relationship and also your very own capability to take care of anxiety. Take into consideration today whom you can hire to assist you in handling your relationship anxiety.

Depression with Anxiety and Relationships

Clinical depression not just influences the patient; however, it influences all connections in some means or an additional. Largely, the relationship with your companion can be deeply influenced. Whilst attempting to be encouraging, they can come to be annoyed because they do not recognize exactly how to aid.

Your companion can aid you to begin to stroll once again; there is light at the end of the passage because one day quickly, your actors will certainly be eliminated, and also point go back to typical. Your companion might see you sobbing and also desires to take away the discomfort from you. However, they are incapable of assisting.

You might have the sensation of simply desiring to be left alone and also be disturbed at the consistent activities of your companion. Your companion, in turn, might feel irritated as well as 'not excellently sufficient' to aid you.

This is an extremely delicate part of the relationship you have with your companion. The secret below is interaction, which will allow your companion to understand that you like it.

The paradox is the distance between having sex assists and taking away many of the anxiety. It's the power of human calling, and you might also want to recommend to your companion that while you're not feeling like having sex, you'd like it if you could have a discussion and embrace it. It might not be suitable, from your companion's factor of you, yet if they like you and also are attempting to sustain you, the scenario might succeed in avoiding the failure of your relationship.

How Can A Relationship Coach Help?

Specialists such as these can supply assistance, analytical abilities, and also boosted coping techniques for concerns such as anxiety, relationship problems, unsettled childhood years concerns, despair, anxiety monitoring, body photo problems as well as imaginative blocks. Numerous individuals additionally discover that trains can be a significant property to handling individual development, social connections, household problems, marital relationship problems, as well as the inconveniences of everyday life.

A few of the benefits available from relationship coaching include:

- Achieving a far better understanding of your worth as well as objectives

- Establishing abilities for boosting your partnerships

- Searching for a resolution to the concerns or problems that led you to look for treatment

- Discovering brand-new means to manage tension and also anxiety

- Handling temper, pain, clinical depression, as well as various other psychological stress

- Improving interactions and also paying attention to abilities

- Altering old habit patterns as well as creating brand-new ones

- Finding brand-new methods to fix issues in your family members or marital relationship

- Improving your self-worth and also enhancing confidence

Do I Truly Require Training? I Can Generally Manage My Troubles

You are taking an obligation by approving where you're at in life as well as making a dedication to alter the scenario by looking for training. Training offers durable advantages and also assistance, offering you the devices you require to stay clear of triggers, re-direct harmful patterns, and also conquer whatever difficulties you deal with.

Why Do Individuals Look For Mentoring, And Also Just How Do I Recognize If It Is Right For Me?

Some individuals require aid handling a variety of various other concerns such as reduced self-confidence, clinical depression, anxiety, dependencies, relationship troubles, imaginative blocks, and also spiritual disputes. Training can assist to supply some much-required motivation and also assistance with abilities to obtain them with these durations. In brief, individuals looking for training are all set to satisfy the difficulties in their lives and also all set to make adjustments in their lives.

CHAPTER 8:

How Knowing the Secret Love Language of Your Partner Can Help You to Handle His Anxiety and Make Him Feel Loved

Tension can be challenging to oversee. However, there are solutions, and when you are seeing someone, those solutions can be worked through altogether. Although some anxiety in a relationship is ordinary, having it rule your relationship can make it harmful, regularly harming the individual you love the most. For some people who suffer from anxiety, bouncing from relationship to relationship helps to ease their anxiety only for a short period till the insecurity creeps in again. They are regularly left inquiring as to why their connections consistently come up short, never entirely understanding that it is their anxiety that is pushing individuals away.

Studies have indicated that individuals with low confidence have far more elevated levels of insecurity, especially in their relationships. It keeps them from making a profound and significant association with their accomplices.

Individuals with low confidence do not just need their partner to see them in a superior light than they see themselves. Still, in moments of self-doubt, they experience difficulty, in any event, perceiving their accomplice's confirmations. Acting out their insecurities pushes their partner further away, creating a self-fulfilling prophecy, and because this struggle is internal and goes on most of the time, the anxiety compounds. It is essential to manage your weaknesses without involving your partner in them.

You can do this by taking two steps:

1. Uncover the real roots of our insecurity.

2. Challenge your inner critic that sabotages our relationship. You should set up where your uncertainty originates from, regardless. Nothing stirs inaccessible damages like a cozy relationship and being open to somebody. Our connections work up old sentiments from our past more than all else. Our brains are even flooded with the same neurochemicals in both situations. Our first example can shape our grown-up connections. Your style of connection impacts which kind of accomplices we pick and the elements that happen in our relationships. A safe connection design encourages an individual to be progressively sure and aloof. At the point when somebody has an on edge or engrossed connection style, they might be bound to feel shaky towards their partner. There is a mystery to overseeing and conquering the obstructions that reason you to experience the ill effects of your uneasiness. The secret is recognizing that the hindrances that scare you and make your negative musings are the way to carrying on with a reliable and secure life. When you grasp these impediments and choose to work through them, you will have the option to begin to build up more profound attention to where and when your frailties are originating from. The minute you start using your anxiety as a mindful reminder that your insecurities and mistrust are rearing their ugly head; you are better able to manage the consequences positively. Furthermore, here is the uplifting news; all frailties are an opportunity to benefit some work in bettering yourself. When you begin to focus, and you are never again determined by your uneasiness and your uncertainties, you will have the option to take a shot at some incredible strides to reinforce your relationship. These steps are:

They Forgive Your Past

Since the more significant part of your insecurities has been formed by a family member or authority figure reprimanding you, recognize this and try to identify who they are. Begin to excuse them gradually. Defend and comprehend that they were driven by their frailties, battling, and were in all likeliness battling with their very own evil spirits. People are not great, and given that they carry on incompletely, we as a whole do. This doesn't mean they were directly in what they did, but instead that you can comprehend, they were also battling through their very own fights. To forgive them for their bad behavior will be healing for you because holding on to resentment isn't helping you. When you let go of the past, you can start to mend, slowly and carefully.

Acknowledge Yourself, the Great and the Negative

Pause for a minute to respite and take a self-evaluation of your life and how you are living it. Notice the pieces of yourself, both your body and your internal identity that you don't care for or might want to change. Presently, investigate these pieces of you, and attempt to imagine the love for yourself. Consider yourself to be a whole individual made up of large and flawed parts. Recognize that you are meriting love as an accomplice since everybody, paying little respect to their flaws, has the right to be adored. If that you are combating, attempt to imagine why you love your companions, in any event, realizing they are flawed. In the same manner, you love your companions; you should show love towards yourself.

Start to Rehearse Self-Approval

Insecurity drives an individual to look for others' endorsements. If you see yourself needing another person's applause and consideration, attempt to stop for a minute and supplant that requirement for support with self-approval. When you remove the intensity of others' approval and begin to give your endorsement, you move the power of certainty working to yourself. Having another person's consent is decent to have; however, having your very own support is ground-breaking. Try not to misunderstand us; this doesn't mean you are dismissing or don't need association with others, or love from your partner. You can, in any case, be adored by your accomplice while additionally rehearsing self-approval.

Stop Comparing Yourself

Comparing yourself and what others look like, what they're doing, how fruitful they are, or the amount they have is never a significant correlation. This conduct effectively hurts you, so as opposed to getting desirous or contrasting yourself and another person, change your point of view. Understand that you are unique and comparing yourself with someone else is like trying to compare an apple with an orange. Attempt to be cheerful for them and happy in their prosperity, understanding that they are on an alternate way to you and that they also have their very own issues. When you wish everyone well and embrace the path you are on, you take away your anxiety's power over you and can be joyful for yourself and others. In all honesty, there is somebody who might be listening who is most likely contrasting themselves with you as well.

Figure Out How to Be Trustful at the Time

By using the devices and rehearsing them, when nervousness raises its head as well as does it consistently, you will confide in yourself. At the point when you can create trust at the time that you can support, you can appreciate the minute without nervousness dominating. Figuring out to be trustworthy at the time sets aside some effort to create. Recollect that figuring out how to believe yourself is indistinguishable from figuring out how to confide in another person. In any case, when you can tell in yourself and trust that you will know the distinction between tension and genuine indications of threat, you and your partner will have the option to start to appreciate each other's conversation again.

While strolling your way to mending and joy, you will consistently discover things that will incite your nervousness, yet the more mindful you become, and the more you practice the methods in this, the simpler it will be to haul yourself out of full tension. Before long, you will end up getting all the more tolerating of yourself and your accomplice's love. Together you will have the option to fabricate your relationship to a reliable spot that both of you can appreciate without dread or hatred.

After perusing the parts above on connection type, you should realize your connection style. This is useful because it can assist you with achieving ways you might be reproducing a dynamic from quite a while ago. It can help you with choosing better accomplices and structure more advantageous connections, which can change your connection style. It can make you increasingly mindful of how your sentiments of frailty might be lost because of something old rather than our present relationship. By changing your connection type, you can battle tension with actual conduct and a caring, steady accomplice to you.

Your weaknesses can likewise originate from the essential inward voice that you've disguised dependent on negative programming from quite a while ago. This inward pundit will, in general, be exceptionally vocal about the things that truly matter to you, similar to your connections. Connections challenge the center emotions you have about yourself and drive you out of your customary range of familiarity. They drive up the volume of your inner voice and reopen unresolved wounds from our past. If you are already negative or have a tendency to be self-critical, relationships will amplify your anxiety, often forcing negativity to the surface.

Here is a recap of how to deal with your tension in your relationship through every situation and help you in recuperating and pushing ahead.

1. **Think About What Is Causing Your Jealousy**: You can think about what sentiments, individuals, and sensations cause you to get desirous and flood your brain with envious musings. Is what you are feeling connected to a past occasion? Perhaps it a family relationship or an existing negative perception from your childhood. When you can associate your feelings and eruptions to the things that occurred in your past, you will have a more precise way on the most proficient method to work through those feelings in the present.

2. **Remain Vulnerable And Stay Calm In The Present**: It doesn't make a difference how envious you are, there is continuously an approach to discover your way back to your

actual self and to mollify your viewpoint. This should be possible by tolerating that you are human and by managing your sentiments mercifully. Recall that desire and tension travel every way in waves; they will step-by-step construct and die down after some time. You can acknowledge your envy and recognize your sentiments without responding to it. Learn devices that assist you with working through your jealousy without overcompensating. Alleviating breaths and long strolls are only a portion of the strategies that will help you with calming yourself. Recall that it is simpler to quiet down when you do not endure or tune in to the negative words and thoughts that originate from your inward critic. Getting the hang of quieting procedures can be troublesome; however, it is a theoretical apparatus to assist you with facing your essential musings.

3. **Stop Acting Out**: The internal voice that makes you blow up and guide you to lash out at your accomplice and companions causes long haul harm in your connections. If you allow it to spiral out of control and you are stuck in a look of jealousy, it may even wreck your relationship. This is a form of self-sabotage because jealousy causes you to lash out or punish someone you care for without it being their fault.

CHAPTER 9:

How to Defeat Negative Thoughts Without Using Drugs

Negative reasoning examples make life less agreeable when they keep you stuck in the middle of what's up and what's correct. Negative reasoning regularly meddles with what you need. It causes you to feel miserable, discouraged, and despondent.

If the glass is half unfilled, it is practically troublesome in each experience to see the positive, potential, or silver linings and life exercises. In an association, it is incredibly hard for you or your accomplice to be content with this outlook. If your accomplice feels the individual in question can't satisfy you and amplify your fulfillment. For instance, the individual can feel less, frail, insufficient, and so forth. If you accept that your accomplice does nothing sufficient, there might be connections of rubbing, stress, and dissatisfaction. This dynamic, shockingly, can without much of a stretch become an endless loop of cynicism.

You procure the vitality you bring into the universe with the goal that when you harp on the negative, you can see and get into your connections. While accidentally or intentionally, you may have grown deceptions to shield yourself from harm or dissatisfaction, the time has come to make a positive change to keep up a solid, adoring relationship. I comprehend that it might feel simpler not to get your expectations on another relationship (particularly if that you were already devastated), yet is it not one of your needs to discover somebody who is stunning and flourishing as a couple? If you have addressed truly, this is a chance to transform your cynical focal point into an increasingly discerning and inspirational demeanor.

How to Overcome Negative Thinking

This is the secret:

1. Honestly evaluate your convictions about yourself, your relationships, the world, and what you wish for in your everyday life. Do you accept ideas like "nothing works for me," "men (or ladies) consistently hurt me," or "the world is a terrible spot"? If your words sound like these, your thoughts are negative.

2. Take control of your negative thoughts. Let us utilize the example, "Nothing works for me," that feels overwhelming, conclusive, and perpetual. Modify this thought inside to make space to make sense of stuff for you and to value everyone that has done well for you. Discuss your recollections and note that life has worked out in a good way for you commonly. Attempt different positive contemplations and see what feels right. For instance, "I am available to significant communication in my life and love," "I am grateful for," or "I can deal with my life."

3. Rewire your cerebrum. Perceive and change a negative idea or conviction into one of the best contemplations you have created. This is an incredibly significant alter in your perspective. So it requires some investment, vitality, and constancy to get the thought you need in a more secure, new way. Nonetheless, when you continually write it, you will see that your negative contemplations disperse, and more advantageous ones emerge. This is the way you bring down the negative focal point and take a gander at the world all the more sincerely and with more expectations.

A couple of different tips to make your dating and relationship life all the more fulfilling as you alter your perspective to accomplish the affection you wish for.

- Never forget that dealing with your desires is essential to your relationship's prosperity. Inconsistencies and clashes are unavoidable in the realm of relations, so recall that it is regular and good. The most significant thing is how you and your accomplice oversee and create troublesome occasions.

- Remember, your accomplice is also an individual. Not all your accomplice does is 'correct' or 'acceptable.' However, you fight the temptation to change your basic focal point when you are disappointed. Don't attempt to sum up the whole relationship in a second when you feel hurt.

- Consider the accomplice purposely in a positive light. Express gratitude towards him/her for the easily overlooked details and empathy that your accomplice appears. State, bless your heart. It propagates a pattern of idealistic and caring connections.

- Don't think about things literally. There will be helpless dates, troublesome discussions, and times that can be baffling. Try not to add these encounters to your negative heap. Take life exercises, rather envision yourself moving towards your objectives. Draw in yourself to be glad on your excursion to marriage.

Keeping Toxic Thoughts from Affecting Your Relationship

There are extraordinary quantities of things that can demolish a completely decent relationship. Cheating and inconsistency, for instance, are two significant issues. As per researchers, there is one thing that can be more than everything else that ruins a relationship.

The greatest enemy of the relationship can be negative contemplations, says Bustle, authorized analyst Nicole Issa, Psy. D. "There is a nearby input connection between the feelings, emotions, and activities. Having negative contemplations will bring you down the bunny gap." It is essential to know from Dr. Issa that your reasoning propensities will add to significant issues with your connections. For instance, youth experiences with your folks can cause you to feel disgraceful of affection. That is the reason you may get into all connections accepting that at some stage, your accomplice is going to desert you, and you might be hesitant to make some noise.

"Truly we are making our world," Joann Cohen, relational arranger, and dating mentor say to Bustle. "If we accept we have a decent relationship, we work through things that accept that things are in every case alright. In any case, when you come to associations with a negative idea, you generally expect the most exceedingly negative for your accomplice as well as for the result of your relationship." You have to discover approaches to make them positive to forestall negative musings. Recorded underneath are a few things you can do to stop harmful thoughts, as indicated by specialists, which are attacking your relationship.

1. Think About The First Occasion When You Have Begun To Look All Starry-Eyed At Your Spouse

When you pass an unpleasant time, it is anything but difficult to let that cloud judge you. Discussion about the 'genuine' sentiments of your accomplice when you begin attacking yourself mentally, the first occasion when you went gaga for them, and discussion about how you felt. "Closing your eyes and seeing the brilliant eyed individual with whom you became hopelessly enamored will make things look substantially more positive and possible," says Cohen. On occasion, we need just a little token of great occasions to determine poor people.

2. Letting Go of the Past

Truly, relinquishing the past is more difficult than one might expect. To be reasonable, "We as a whole have a bit of our history with us to 'shield' us against getting injured once more," says Cohen. "Also, if you keep on bringing your old relations damage to your new relationship, you disrupt and make a reality that things simply don't or won't work." Then, attempt to isolate your past from your present, to forestall your past from making poisonous contemplations. Regardless of the amount they look, talk, or carry on the equivalent, your ex isn't your present accomplice. If that you can isolate your past relationship from your new one, being progressively included is a lot simpler for you.

3. Find Different Approaches To Channel Your Vitality

Poisonous reasoning will make you do absurd, relationship-damage stuff like hack into your accomplice's telephone or harm. To counter this wonder, Dr. Issa says that he realizes what your contemplations are doing. For example, for what reason do you believe you have to simply 'register' your accomplice multiple times in succession? You would likewise need some certification or affirmation that your accomplice cares. "When you realize that you can do (these) stuff, set aside some effort to rehearse those aptitudes to assist you with counting to ten and unwind," she says. Discover approaches to lessen the extreme emotions you have with the goal that you won't act in manners that you will lament later.

4. Stop Assuming That you Know What Your Partner Is Thinking

Negative musings are as a rule dependent on discernments that don't generally exist. "If that we put our pessimistic emotions on another person or spot them on someone else, the resentment of the other individual is the thing that you are perusing," Cohen says. The significant thing here is never to assume. Try not to form a hasty opinion. Try not to cook it yourself if that you can't resist. Get to the edge and talk with your companion. "Attempt or request explanation, take the words on face esteem," she says. "You should never trust you know how they feel."

5. Have That One Person You Go To, To Vent Your Outrage

If you are distraught about your accomplice, it's normal to put every one of your issues to any individual who's tuning in. However, as indicated by Cohen, "When you do that, you make a hole between your significant other individual and your reality, making more antagonism than you know." If you need to let yourself down, pick one individual, and remain with them. "Saying it to everybody isn't useful to your appalling business and will just empower increasingly negative sentiments," she says.

6. Create A List Of Your Toxic Thoughts And Come Up With Positive Ones

Keeping harmful contemplations from obliteration takes some self-reflection with helpful other options. In any case, one best activity while reflecting is to work out all the run-of-the-mill thoughts that lead to battles and divisions. Make it a stride further and compose hard verifications possibly in support of an idea. From that point forward, concoct an increasingly brief and versatile elective reasoning ability. For example, if that you think your accomplice is not, at this point, keen on you since they didn't answer your content, list every single thing they could do. "Consider different events to which they replied late to show that they're included despite everything," says Dr. Issa. "Here the elective idea might be as basic as similarly as I haven't known about them, yet it doesn't mean they couldn't care less." Then, the more itemized you are, the more viable it will be.

7. Take Breaking-up Totally Off The Table

Whatever the harmful contemplations are, as a rule, they are from a similar area, dread. Specifically, the dread that your accomplice will leave. "I utilize the similarity, you'd consume the boat when you remark," Cohen says. "It's impossible to escape the island when you consume the boat, so cooperate to endure." If there is no arrangement, you begin seeing one.

CHAPTER 10:

Signs of Anxiety in a Relationship

While it can stem from many things, even a combination of several things, you need to understand how it happens for yourself. You are going to learn about the basics and have a better understanding of where these feelings start. By having this knowledge and this perspective, you should be able to swiftly avoid these things to prevent becoming anxious again in the future. Taking a look at the given examples, you will likely find that you can identify a lot of them, if not most of them. Don't think about this as a negative thing. Instead, you can think about all the progress that you are about to make.

The Root of the Problem

Before you work on fixing the problem, you must be able to identify it. While it is often a bad choice to be critical of yourself, in this case, it becomes necessary. To deal with the issues that you are having in your relationship, you must be able to identify exactly what is causing them. Turn inwards to see if you can get to the root of your problem. Ask yourself why you are choosing to behave the way that you are. There are no right or wrong answers for this step. No matter how you are feeling, even if it is extreme, you must have a reason for it. Know that this might not be the healthiest choice, but it will soon become a curbed behavior.

If you try to apply all the different fixes that you know, this is only going to be a waste of time and energy. Don't become frustrated because you aren't seeing an improvement in yourself or your relationship. Take a more targeted approach. See if you can get down to the very bottom of your problems, identifying them, and seeing them for what they are. It can be scary to face your problems in this way, but this is the way that you are going to be able to fix them. Know that you need to have trust in yourself and that you need to have trust in the process. Problem-solving is difficult for a reason, but you will be happy with the result. When you only solve the surface layer of problems, the rest of them are bound to come up later. It makes sense to get down to the root of things.

Previous Relationships

If you have ever been in a relationship in which you were mistreated, you are naturally going to be cautious of this in the future. It is a defensive mechanism that is normal for any abused individual to take on. However, it becomes a problem when you start to place this role on your partner, even when they are not abusive. Your constant fear and judgment will eventually lead your partner to many negative feelings, from insecurity to anger. It doesn't feel great to be accused of being controlling or manipulative when you aren't. Make sure that any fears you have surrounding this issue are grounded in reality. If you have ever been broken up with unexpected, cheated on, physically or mentally abused, or lied to, then you are more likely to develop this kind of anxiety. When you are wronged so badly, it often can shake you to your core and change you as a person. What you must learn is that you need to heal from the past instead of comparing your present relationship to something that could end up the same way.

To convince yourself that you are being mistreated again, you will often go out of your way to look for 'signs' that your partner is not good for you. Whenever you have to search for these things, they are likely not based in reality. You will know if your partner is doing something wrong from the actions that they present to you. Understandably, if you have been manipulated in the past, this can give you trust issues. Again, you need to keep these fears under control instead of taking them out on your partner. If you doubt your partner so strongly, this could be a sign that the relationship is not healthy for you. If your partner is late to get home from work, and the first thing you think is that they were cheating on you, then you should be able to see this as a sign of your anxiety taking over your way of thinking.

Low Self-Esteem

When you have low self-esteem, this can present itself in many ways. Having low-self-esteem often comes with many insecurities. Whether you are insecure about the way you look or your ability to please your partner, you will find that you will start projecting your issues. For example, if you feel disappointed in yourself, you will also start projecting this feeling and will start to believe that your partner is also disappointed in you. The way to tell if you are projecting it or not is if your partner has expressed this to you themselves. If they have not indicated their disappointment, then this feeling is coming from your anxiety and being projected.

As you can imagine, it becomes very unfair when you start to accuse your partner of feeling certain ways when they insist that they do not. It can become a very exhausting battle to fight, one that often proves that it isn't worth it. You will know when you are projecting feelings onto your partner when they constantly feel that they have to prove to you how much they love you or how they see you. Reassurance is important in a relationship, but if they are constantly spending their time reassuring you, this can become exhausting. No matter what answer you receive from them, it likely won't be enough to fix your low self-esteem.

You need to work on bettering yourself, not only your relationship. Realize that you are a person with individual needs. You need to be able to look at yourself in the mirror and be happy with what you see and the person that you are. When you feel anything less than this, there will be a risk of you projecting the negative feelings onto your partner. Make sure that you prioritize self-care. Understand that it is not selfish or excessive; it is necessary for your mental health.

Attachment Style

An attachment style is something that develops when you are a child. Depending on how you are raised, you can either have a healthy sense of how to bond with someone or you might feel that you constantly need to receive reassurance to know that you are cared for. This is something that can end up being projected as you reach adulthood and get into serious relationships. Even though these decisions were made by your parents, they will impact you for the rest of your life.

If your parents were cold and withheld affection, you might have developed a habit of hiding your emotions and needs. Babies who are left to cry for extended periods learn how to self-soothe. This can be a difficult process, as they are taught that no one is going to come for them when they are in need. As translated into adulthood, you might feel this way about your partner or you might even believe that your feelings are not important.

Having an anxious attachment means that you are living in fear that your partner could leave you at any moment. These abandonment issues usually stem from having a parent do the same thing during childhood. Children who come from broken homes can often grow to believe that every person in their life is not permanent. If you feel this way, you are never going to feel secure with your spouse because you will be constantly waiting for them to abandon you.

Alternatively, there is an avoidant attachment style. This occurs when you are the one who keeps your partner at a distance, not revealing too many feelings or providing reassurance. This attachment style can make you appear to be cold or not as invested in the relationship, even when you want to be. No matter what kind of attachment style you have, if it is unhealthy and impacting your relationship, therapy will become very beneficial to you. Being able to sort through your issues and understand why you feel this way will provide you with clarity.

Loss of Trust

You can lose trust in your partner for a variety of reasons. It is the way that you handle this feeling that will ultimately determine if it is a problem or not. Typically, when someone loses their trust in another person, that person will have to prove themselves trustworthy again. If you feel that you are too disappointed by their actions to forgive them, or if you choose to live your life while constantly punishing them for what they did, this is an indication that you are being led by your anxiety. If you constantly feel a sense of disappointment or negativity, it might be possible that you entered the relationship with this mindset. Not having any faith in your partner can be devastating as the years go on. Both of you will feel that your efforts do not matter. By constantly expecting the end of your relationship, you are going to develop a very apathetic mindset. This can form a defense mechanism, but it is not the healthiest way to deal with your trust issues. When you can work together with your partner on these trust issues, your relationship is going to stand a fighting chance. Are there concrete reasons why you no longer trust your partner? If you cannot think about factual reasons for your partner being untrustworthy, you might have to turn your focus inward. What is making you feel this way and why? Before you react to the surface issues, it is important to get down to the deeper meaning behind the problem. Allow yourself to explore these feelings and realize that they might be stemming from a warped perception of the relationship that you have created. Even if you want the relationship to last, it is going to be difficult when you cannot set aside your negativity. These anxious thoughts are going to eat away at you constantly, providing a distraction. This won't be fair to either of you.

Misunderstanding

Fighting is a normal part of any healthy relationship. Couples should not get along 24/7, even if they are very similar or have a strong bond. By disagreeing, you are showing that you are still individuals. Being able to stand up for what you believe in is important, even if you are standing up to your spouse. When two adults that love each other get into a disagreement, they should also be able to communicate through the issue. This does not signify that the relationship is doomed, but that can often be what your anxiety leads you to believe.

There are certain types of fighting that can be dangerous. This usually happens when anger becomes physical.

CHAPTER 11:

How to Help Your Anxious Partner and Yourself

Loving a Person with Anxiety

This part is dedicated to partners of people who struggle with anxiety. Relationships and love demand that we get involved in our partner's life and this means we always have to be supportive and loving. If you have a partner with one or more types of anxiety, you are already aware of how it can influence not just the relationship, but your life too. Anxiety comes in many forms, and there is no magic pill that can help. Anxiety is also an individual experience that can differ in many ways. The list of things we can do to help our partner when they are having an anxiety attack differs from person to person.

Acute Anxiety

Acute anxiety happens out of the blue. It can be caused by different things, certain situations, or other people you and your partner meet. It happens suddenly, and there is no time for planning and taking it slow. You need to be able to react at the moment and to know how to assess the situation. Understand what is happening, what your partner is going through, and come up with the right way that can help neutralize the anxiety. There are four steps you can take to be supportive and helpful in case of acute anxiety:

1. Be calm, be compassionate. If you are not, you won't be able to support your partner's needs at that moment. If you give in to anger, frustration, or anxiety, it won't help. It can even make things worse. You also need to remember not to give in to your

partner's anxiety and accommodate it. In the long run, this is not helpful. Instead, offer understanding, not just solutions.

2. Assess your partner's anxiety. What level is it? What are the symptoms and signs of an anxiety attack? An anxiety attack can hit with a different strength each time. You need to be able to recognize it to choose actions appropriate to the given situation.

3. Remind your partner of the techniques that helped with anxiety attacks. Whether it is breathing or exercise, your partner is probably aware of their success in neutralizing anxiety. But in the given situation, maybe he or she needs reminding. Once they are on the right path to dealing with anxiety, your job is to provide positive reinforcement. Give praise and be empathetic once your partner executes techniques that will help with an anxiety attack.

4. Evaluate the situation. Is your partner's anxiety attack passing? If it is, be supportive and encourage your partner to continue whatever he is doing to lower his anxiety. If it stays at the same level, or increases, you should start the steps from the beginning and come up with different techniques and strategies to help your partner with an acute anxiety attack.

Chronic Anxiety

To address chronic anxiety, you might have to try out exposure therapy, as it is considered the golden standard of treatment by many people. Usually, it takes the guidance of a professional therapist to try exposure therapy. But, if the level of your partner's anxiety is not severe, you might feel comfortable enough to try it on your own. In this case, you have to act as a guide and learn how to be a supportive person for your partner.

You have to start with the least challenging situation and progress slowly and steadily towards more challenging ones. If anxiety isn't decreasing in the first challenge, it's not time to go to the second.

For example, let's say your partner has a fear of heights. He or she wants to overcome this fear and be able to climb the building's last floor. How will exposure therapy look in this case?

1. Tell your partner to look out the window from the ground floor for exactly one minute.

2. Climb to the second floor together with your partner. Remember that you are not just an exposure therapy guide; you also need to act as support. Make them look out the window from the second floor for one minute. In case of anxiety showing up in its first symptoms, remind your partner to do breathing exercises to lower its impact.

3. Once your partner feels better, they should try looking out the window again.

4. If no anxiety presents itself, you should leave your partner's side. They need to be able to look through the same window, but this time without you.

5. Climb to the third floor and repeat steps three and four. When your partner feels ready, continue to the fourth floor, sixth, and so on. If your partner's anxiety is too high, don't hesitate to stop. The first session doesn't need to take longer than 30 minutes.

6. Each new session needs to begin with the last comfortable floor your partner experienced. You don't need to always start from the ground floor, as your partner progresses, feeling no anxiety when looking through the window of the second, third, and even fourth floor.

7. Take time. Your partner will not be free of the fear in just a few days. Be patient and continue practicing exposure therapy in this way until your partner can achieve the goal and climb the last floor.

8. The goal of exposure therapy is not just to get rid of fear and anxiety. It should also teach your partner that he or she can control and tolerate discomfort. Your partner will have an opportunity to practice anxiety-reduction techniques in a safe and controlled environment, with you in the support role.

Specific Disorder Interventions

Under the guidance of a trained therapist, the two of you will learn how to approach it in the best possible way. Your partner's therapist might ask you to join in a few sessions, and he will teach you how to better help your partner in situations that elevate anxiety. If your partner is not diagnosed, but both of you suspect he might have a certain disorder, advise your partner to visit a doctor. Self-diagnosis can lead to mistakes, and you will make the wrong choices in how to approach your partner's anxiety.

Panic Disorder with Agoraphobia

If this is your partner's diagnosis, you two probably already have a pattern of behavior that is designed to accommodate your partner's anxiety. You probably follow your partner to social events, and you are the one who is in charge of running errands outside the house. This accommodation is counterproductive in the long run. You are showing that you care, love, and support your partner, but it prevents him or her from experiencing a full life. Your partner needs to learn how to overcome anxiety. You may approach a panic disorder with exposure therapy, so your partner becomes less dependent on you:

1. Choose an errand that your partner thinks he can handle himself. It can be shopping, going to a doctor's appointment alone, walking a dog, etc.

2. Plan what errands are more challenging for your partner and add them to the list. Write them down as *To be accomplished in the*

future.' It is important to work slowly but keep a clear vision of what needs to be accomplished.

3. Work together on slowly accomplishing the first task on your list. If it's going shopping alone, accompany your partner a few times, so they are accustomed to the environment. When he or she feels confident enough to go alone, let them. Encourage and support their decision.

4. Once your partner accomplishes the task, be there to discuss his experience with it. Listen carefully and address any issues that might arise. Encourage your partner and keep track of his progress.

Obsessive-Compulsive Disorder

When it comes to OCD, what you can do for your partner is not to engage in his behaviors. Also, encourage him not to give in and repeat their compulsive behaviors. If you give in and comply with your partner's OCD, you will not be helping. Although it will surely elevate the tension made by your partner's OCD, complying will reinforce the fears. For example, if your partner asks you to go to the kitchen and make sure all appliances are off, you shouldn't comply. But you should also not argue or call your partner irrational. It is ineffective, and it will only deepen the anxiety.

Discuss with your partner how is it best to approach anxiety and agree on a strategy. This is where a professional therapist will be of most use to both of you. A professional can guide you through this conversation and help both of you feel comfortable discussing the delicate topic of your partner's disorder.

You will need to learn how to change from saying things like:

"I will not go to the kitchen again, you are imagining things, and being irrational" to "I appreciate your concern about the kitchen appliances, but we agreed that the best thing we can do is to help you learn how to manage the feelings you are having right now."

Your partner will agree for their benefit that the best thing you could do is stay by their side, not check the kitchen, and help them work through the anxiety. This can be done with breathing exercises that will help your partner calm down. In time, your partner will show less fear. The OCD will decrease, and you will feel less frustrated.

Generalized Anxiety Disorder

The behavior of people with GAD is similar to that of people who have OCD. They have fears about certain things, and these fears are not comforted by reassurance. GAD usually creates concerns that we all have. It can be about finances, health, and school. But people with GAD will blow these fears out of proportion and they will influence their daily life. If your partner is diagnosed with GAD, you are aware of how simple problems we face every day can sound like total catastrophes. Your partner probably assumes the worst possible end of certain situations.

It often happens that people with this affliction develop a constant feeling of inadequacy. They believe they are not good enough for their partners, and that they never will be. When this happens, they usually try to overcompensate and make everything perfect so their partner can love them. On the other hand, some may feel that there is nothing they can do and that there is no point in trying. They underperform reinforcing their feelings of inadequacy.

Social Phobia

Social phobia comes in many forms. It can make going to work a very difficult task, or it can make maintaining relationships impossible to achieve. A therapist uses this technique of testing the hypothesis of a patient. This is a very successful way of bringing realization to the patient that their fears and anxieties do not have a foundation. A therapist can teach a person with a social phobia the basic communication skills to prepare them for situations they might encounter in their endeavors to overcome anxiety.

CHAPTER 12:

Common Anxiety Disorders

S o many people wonder how anxiety and depression are interconnected. Well, one thing that you need to understand is that when anxiety reaches a certain clinical level, it stops being just anxiety, but a disorder that could potentially result in depression. When anxiety persists for longer durations, the chances are that it will impair normal functioning. In other words, anxiety disorders become a habit that affects one's life seriously. It is important to note that anxiety must be diagnosed as early as possible. When it is better accounted for, it becomes very easy to control and treat. However, to avoid misdiagnosis, you must start first by ruling out hyperthyroidism, ADHD, or cocaine abuse, among others, that often share similar symptoms as an anxiety disorder.

That said, some common types of anxiety disorders include;

Generalized Anxiety

This is often anxiety that persists for too long and is characterized by extreme worry about something. For instance, one may worry too much about failing an exam, what happens if they were to die, or their inability to sleep, among others. What you will notice about people with generalized anxiety is that they are often described as being 'worried well.' Although it is often counterintuitive at the first glance, people with generalized anxiety often use their mental act of extreme worry to distract themselves temporarily from the emotions linked to what they are worried about in the first place.

Unfortunately, this extreme worry is what eventually results in excessive stress and anxiety.

Panic Disorder

When someone has panic attacks, this is often defined as having a sudden surge of extreme fear and anxiety that can get to optimal levels within minutes. This kind of fear is often characterized by symptoms associated with flight and fight responses. These symptoms include; an elevated heart rate, feeling light-headed, sweating, and chest tightness, among others. When you find yourself experiencing repeated panic attacks, then the chances are that you are persistently anxious about having those panic attacks or the results of panic attacks as the death of madness.

Specific Phobia

This is often referred to as anxiety that is specifically linked to something. For instance, you may be anxious about such things as flights, enclosed spaces, oceans, snakes, among others.

While true specific phobias are very rare, it is something that is commonly observed in people with panic disorders. In other words, you will find someone being irrationally afraid that a certain thing or situation could lead to panic and not that the specific situation or thing is dangerous in itself.

Social Anxiety

This is a condition in which one is fearful of social situations or gatherings. Typically, when one is exposed to real judgment or public scrutiny, they tend to coil up and freeze. This is often characterized by excessive worry and concerns about how others will evaluate or perceive them. In other words, they are worried about their public image/outlook.

Obsessive-Compulsive Disorder

This is a condition that is characterized by continued obsession, compulsion, or both. The thing with an obsession is that they are often thoughts, urges, or even images that keep recurring in an intrusive manner leading to distress and anxiety. For instance, you could be obsessing seeing your house on fire because you forgot to turn off the stove; however much you try to ignore or suppress the thought of it happening.

Compulsion, on the other hand, refers to recurring behaviors or rituals that one performs in an attempt to alleviate anxiety linked to their obsession. For instance, you could wash your hands as many times as possible before drying them, or you may count the number of steps in each building construction you get into, among others.

The thing with OCD is that people often focus on the intrusive mental activity and treat it as something dangerous or bad. This is mainly because they think that they are responsible for it or believe that it means something.

Post-Traumatic Stress Disorder (PTSD)

This often occurs when one is exposed to a real threat. This could be such threats as rape, murder, earthquakes, and floods, among others. Because of this exposure to in the past, they end up having recurring intrusive and distressing memories of their trauma. They may also try to avoid objects or certain situations that are linked to their trauma.

In other instances, people with PTSD often change their moods and thoughts associated with their trauma or may suffer increased arousal.

Think of PTSD as fear of memory. This is because one ends up having a fear of something that is in the surroundings that could trigger them to remember their traumatic events along with the sensations, thoughts, or feelings of the trauma. Because of this, they tend to get pre-occupied with avoiding anything that could trigger their trauma. The worst thing is that this attempt to avoid it often leads to depression, isolation, and substance abuse. It also is associated with increased levels of anxiety.

Separation Anxiety

This is age-inappropriate distress that is linked with separation from someone, a person viewed as an attachment figure. In most cases, this often refers to a parent. This explains why it is typically observed in childhood with children refusing to go to school. However, this has also been seen in adulthood. For instance, a spouse may suffer separation anxiety when their partner leaves town for business meetings.

How Does Anxiety Work?

However, the next most important thing is for us to discuss why it happens at all. Why is that that one can get irrationally afraid of something and then stay afraid?

This brings us to how anxiety works in the first place and how can we leverage this knowledge to benefit us.

Well, one important thing that you need to bear in mind at all times is that the only important concept as far as anxiety is concerned is avoidance. To be more specific, the main reason why so many people experience persistence in the clinical levels of anxiety is that they try hard to avoid their anxiety.

While this may sound counterintuitive at first, one thing that you must understand is that at the core, every anxiety disorder is the same. Although they may look and feel different for some reason, they share similar dynamics. This means that people with anxiety disorders often have learned to train their minds to be afraid of their sensations, thoughts, and emotions. And all that has been done by accident.

It is interesting to note that the very thing that they try in an attempt to make their anxiety better is avoiding it altogether. This is exactly what makes it even worse! To understand how it works, it is critical that we start with the little chunks of neurons located at the center of the brain, referred to as the amygdala.

Your Amygdala

The main role of this part of the brain is to ensure that you are safe from danger or other forms of physical threat. It is the part of the brain that helps you stay alive. To achieve this, the amygdala tells you to look out for any potential threat. This explains why you keep scanning your surroundings for any suspicious object or event.

If it finds something that it perceives as a threat, it sounds an alarm that tells the body to get ready to deal with the threat. It does this by stimulating the secretion of adrenaline and activating the fight and flight response. This is when you start experiencing faster breathing rates, muscle tension, increased blood pressure, and supply to the head and the torso, and other body extremities for efficient delivery of oxygen in readiness for fight or flight.

Well, all this is superb if a real physical threat is confronting you, like someone holding a gun to your head in a dark alley or a venomous snake jumps and coils around your body. In such situations, your hope would be for that amygdala to stimulate as much adrenaline as possible to help you get out safe and sound.

However, this comes in when the amygdala is confused about what is a real threat to your survival and what is not. Is it worthy of stimulating full-blown adrenaline for a fight-or-flight response, or is it something not worth it at all because they are not a threat to your survival?

To illustrate this, let us consider an example.

How Avoidance Contributes To Fear Learning and Increased Anxiety

We would all agree that hiking is not all that dangerous an activity, right? While there are risks that are associated with hiking, such as falling off a cliff or being attacked by wild and dangerous animals, the truth is that in most cases, hiking is a very safe outdoor activity.

What is interesting is that so many people are very anxious about going out for a hike, but choose to turn down an invitation to go hiking irrespective of who is asking them. They choose to go for walks in paths that they are well versed with and try as much as they can to avoid hiking by all means possible, including watching movies about hiking and nature trails.

You may be thinking, "But how is that possible? How can she/he be afraid of hiking when it is one of the perfectly safe activities?"

Well, one thing you need to understand is that the issue does not lie in what they believe. Instead, what matters most is what the amygdala tells them to believe. In most cases, the amygdala will strongly believe in the things we teach them.

According to research, it is evident that people with anxiety have likely triggered a process referred to as Fear Learning. This process has, in turn, taught their amygdala to be extremely sensitive to anything that could be potentially dangerous and afraid of things that may not be a threat in the first place.

To better understand this concept, consider yourself an average Joe going out for a hike in the foothills. After half-an-hour, you see something dark and curly on the trails. Immediately, the amygdala fires up, and you become alert to a potentially venomous snake. Your heart starts beating fast, muscles tense up, your heart rate is elevated, and you start to sweat.

But, what is most important as far as anxiety is concerned is the step you take after that. While the amygdala alerts you to scan your surroundings for threats and stimulates the release of adrenaline in readiness for flight or fight, what you need to bear in mind is that this part of the brain has an error correction mechanism. This mechanism is what allows you to verify whether the flag raised is correct. It also goes a long way in gauging how you respond to the potential threat. It uses that behavior to confirm or deny the initial threat evaluation.

CHAPTER 13:

How to Talk to a New Partner About Your Anxiety

Being involved with somebody with issues of uneasiness can be horrendously upsetting. Once in a while, it can seem as though dread, somebody who wobbles among you and your companion, is a third individual in the relationship. This individual consistently plants questions and vulnerability.

In any case, there is no requirement for nervousness to demolish the relationship or to make it hard to appreciate. As a matter of fact, you can adore each other all the more profoundly by understanding apprehension all in all and how it influences both your accomplice and your relationship. Instruction can likewise diminish a lot of pressure.

The book separates all you have to learn and do when somebody is restless to discuss: how to support your accomplice, how uneasiness can affect your relationship, looking for your emotional well-being and that's only the tip of the iceberg. Continue perusing if you need to guarantee that your organization doesn't turn into a third individual.

Nervousness Filled Conversation

If you ask or conclude it after monthly gatherings, there will be a moment that your accomplice uncovers that they need to manage dread. It is a crucial time in the relationship, along these lines be touchy and don't pass judgment. He will be much obliged to you for confiding in you with this information, which you presumably didn't impart to numerous individuals. Consider it to be the beginning of a discussion that you can regularly reemerge.

Getting Anxiety and Knowing What It is doing to Your Partner

Learning dread and what your accomplice is doing will assist you with understanding and help them collaborate with some fundamental realities about uneasiness. Clinician Dave Carbonell, Ph.D. therapist Dr. Helen Odessky, among others, recommended remembering these:

- Anxiety is typical. Everyone has it. It turns into an issue or turmoil just if that it is not kidding.
- Anxiety is a genuine issue, not a composite. It's an issue in psychological well-being.
- Anxiety can be a devastating condition that keeps individuals from working and carrying on with an ordinary life.
- Anxiety makes individuals experience flight and fights reactions and stress over dangerous issues, including whether an accomplice may cheat or leave.
- You can't "fix" anxiety.
- Many individuals who have nervousness issue wish they never had it. They are worried that their uneasiness is a weight for other people.
- Many individuals have incredible connections and are cheerful regardless of managing uneasiness.
- Symptoms of uneasiness, reliably or both may happen in waves. Individuals with a nervousness issue or issues can have timeframes when they have no side effects.
- Anxiety isn't balanced or legitimate. This makes the individuals stress over something even when there is no proof or when it does not merit stress. It likewise makes them act nonsensically in some cases. Your accomplice presumably realizes that.
- Anxiety isn't a shortcoming.
- Anxiety can be dealt with. Psychotherapy can reduce manifestations and show individuals how to treat them better.

A great many people have a portion of these stressing considerations in any event. They are a typical piece of a relationship, especially another one.

Be that as it may, individuals with nervousness issues or an uneasiness issue will in general have this tension many times and all the more seriously.

"Our musings are dominating and heading straight into the direst outcome imaginable," said Michelene Wasil, a specialist who comprehends both individual and mental tension.

Uneasiness causes physiological impacts, including brevity of breath, restlessness, and tension. On edge, individuals can respond to worry with the battle or flight reaction, as though stress were a physical assault.

In some cases, troubling musings persuade your accomplice to act in manners that pressure and stress the relationship. For instance, therapist Jennifer B. Rhodes stated, individuals with tension frequently check their accomplice's association with unbound methodologies. These procedures for the most part address one of their on-edge feelings.

Let us state that your accomplice is on edge to be the first to start correspondence. You don't care for him as much as he needs you to, he starts to stress since you don't send the primary content as frequently as he does. Nervousness strengthens and he begins to feel that if he didn't connect first, you would never converse with him.

He concurs that it's a smart thought to fantasize about you some time to fix this dread. This powers you to convey first. Maybe a few times you'll contact him before he feels great, realizing you'd put forth the attempt. The confirmation urges him to question his absurd and apprehensive conviction that you won't hit first. However, it's unmistakably not a decent methodology.

Tragically, there are numerous practices of seeing someone persuaded by tension. Here are a couple of more models:

- Being controlling
- Perfectionism
- Passive forceful conduct or being avoidant
- Being excessively basic
- Being bad-tempered and furious
- Having trouble centering and being occupied

If you are involved with somebody with social tension issues, the nervousness is probably going to influence your public activity, forestalling, or showing hostile conduct. Perfectionism is meeting someone with social uneasiness. You will be unable to carry your accomplice to all the get-togethers or gatherings you need to join in. Like different sorts of tension, this may offer ascent to contradictions or prompt both of you to become separated.

CHAPTER 14:

Causes of Anxiety

D ifferent unreasonable practices emerge because of tension in a relationship. Some of them as referenced before incorporate pulling back from the relationship, acting unapproachable, remaining protected, etc. As we think about our past, we promptly acknowledge there is an assortment of impacts in our past affecting our present life and choices. The connection designs obvious in our grown-up life have their foundations followed back to our youthful ages. The data passed by the pundit inward voice and the mental protections we apply are because of the assortment of life encounters.

Tuning in to the negative inward voice can make us to:

1. Become Tenacious

In specific situations, nervousness emotions can make us act urgent and bug our accomplices. Nervousness can make an individual quit feeling as free and solid as he/she did before getting into the relationship. Therefore, he/she may discover him/herself self-destructing effectively, acting unreliable, getting desirous, or staying away from those exercises that require autonomy.

2. Control

Our human instinct requests that when we feel compromised, we endeavor to control or rule the circumstance. If we feel undermined in a relationship, odds are, we will attempt to recover control of the circumstance. What we neglect to acknowledge is that the sentiments of danger are not genuine; rather, they are because of the inward basic voice that is contorting reality.

When taking control, we may begin setting rules on what an accomplice ought to and ought not to do, who to visit, converse with, connect with, and whatnot. This is a frantic endeavor to ease our sentiments of uneasiness and instability. This controlling conduct can raise hatred and distance our accomplices.

3. Reject

If that a relationship is causing us to feel stressed, a typical and out of line protection instrument is dismissal. We begin to act standoffish, that is, unapproachable. We become some way or another segregated and cold. This guarantees if the accomplice out of nowhere leaves, we won't feel torment. At the end of the day, we are securing ourselves by getting the best of our accomplices. These activities of dismissal can either be inconspicuous or obvious. In any case, they are a certain method of making a separation between two accomplices by working up uncertainty.

4. Retain

Now and again, rather than unequivocally dismissing our accomplices in light of tension, a few people will, in general, retain from them. For example, when things have gotten extremely cross and an individual feels worked up, he/she withdraws. Individuals who use retaining strategies to manage tension in a relationship keep down either a piece of their fondness of an entire portion of the relationship through and through. Retaining may appear to be innocuous since the accomplice isn't confronting dismissal of tenacity and control, however, note; it is one of the gentlest and calmest enemies of fascination and enthusiasm in a relationship.

5. Retreat

Tension prompts dread and fearing a relationship you are in can be truly pushing. To keep away from such pressure, countless individuals decide to withdraw, that is, abandoning the genuine demonstrations of affection and supplanting it with a dream bond. By definition, a dream bond is a bogus deception that replaces genuine emotions and demonstrations of affection. In this condition of imagination, an individual spotlights the structure rather than substance. He/she abandons the genuine and imperative piece of the relationship and remains in it to have a sense of security. In a dream bond, individuals take part in numerous dangerous practices, for example, retaining or participating in non-indispensable exercises. The subsequent separation prompts the finish of a relationship. As much as the retreat will shield you from sentiments of dread, it will give you a misguided feeling of wellbeing and you will lose a great deal of valuable time living in a dream. What a great many people neglect to acknowledge is that by the day's end, they should confront reality.

Love is a delightful thing, however, believe it or not, it has its requests and results. Truly, love is an exceptionally confounded thing. Why so? Since, while we are occupied with searching for it (Because it is a delightful thing), we additionally realize that it is one of the fundamental drivers of misery on the planet. We don't know about a thing that can make an individual urgent how love does. Love is our primary purpose behind living and a significant due to torment in our lives. It is the main feeling that can divert anybody over the world from being a sort and delicate individual to a harsh and angry person. Also, it couldn't care less about status, sex, or age.

Strikingly, as individuals search for this two-fold edged blade called love, they likewise experience something different; Relationship tension. We as a whole encounter uneasiness seeing someone either quietly or strongly. It is entirely expected to be on edge about things, particularly love. Be that as it may, for this situation, we are concentrating on the sort of nervousness that shakes the establishment of a relationship so hard that it breaks. This sort of tension makes an individual uncertainty of love. Relationship tension is apparent when two individuals invest a large portion of their energy being restless about the relationship and agonizing over it as opposed to tending to it strongly.

Anyway, if that it isn't unexpected to have worries about a relationship, how might one tell that he/she is encountering relationship uneasiness? The following are a few signs that one can search for showing that one is having extraordinary or pointless relationship uneasiness.

a. Over-investigating

This is the inclination to overthink things, and even actually search for shortcomings or negative angles. There is a satiating that goes, over-investigation causes loss of motion. Here is the thing; there is nothing amiss with utilizing rationale. Indeed, it is alright to be basic or suspicious in any event until you make sense of things. The capacity to consider things completely before tolerating them can assist you in telling the difference between fiction and reality: what is a negligible dream and what is the truth.

Be that as it may, there is a drawback to over-analyzing a relationship. You will never be happy with the appropriate response. Everything that is said or done is dependent upon investigation and increasingly questioning. A genuine case of over-investigation and its results is the point at which an individual starts to overthink things and therefore makes situations in his/her brain, thus putting together their activities concerning nonexistent occasions that have not occurred at this point.

Picture this; you are on a first or second date. Your garments, shoes, and language give a decent early introduction. Everything about the imminent relationship looks brilliant. Be that as it may, when the accomplice shows up, you begin bombarding them with a gazillion inquiries regarding their previous connections. "Have you been in another relationship? What number of ex's do you have? For what reason did you leave them? Was there conning included? Who started the separation? Are your folks still together? Do they have a decent relationship?"

Perhaps you have been to a date where the other individual was asking you these sorts of inquiries. Do you realize why individuals do this? It is because they are searching for security. They would prefer not to come up short but then they are exceptionally terrified of allowing everything just to be as it is. It is more about security than affection. "Is this individual liable to say a final farewell to me?"

On the more brilliant side, it is thoroughly fine for an individual to communicate his/her stresses over affection and being harmed. In any case, it is completely off-base to pose an individual a few inquiries that are excessively close to home for the sake of ensuring yourself. It isn't right on all levels to constrain somebody to review a few things that may be difficult for them. Try not to ask individuals inquiries that cause the individual to feel cross-examined. Also, if you find that you can't prevent yourself from posing these inquiries, it may demonstrate that you are experiencing relationship uneasiness. You can't control your feelings of trepidation about connections and responsibilities, accordingly, searching for approaches to approve your reasons.

B. Dread of Being in a Genuine Relationship

To what extent would two individuals be able to take before choosing to be in a genuine relationship? To what extent can individuals know each other before consenting to take things to the following level? There is no particular duration. Everything relies upon the individuals in question and how well they know one another. Some take three dates, others one month while others may take a very long time before being prepared.

If that an individual has relationship nervousness, his/her response to each demand for duty will be "Never" or "I am not prepared." Regardless of whether the individual is infatuated or not, he/she won't focus on the relationship. The genuine purpose behind this absence of duty is the profound situated dread at the rear of the person's brain. This individual is worried about the possibility that he/she is going to wind up alone, once more. Along these lines, he/she stays away from those circumstances that may set him/her up for double-crossing.

Experiencing passionate feelings includes confronting genuine dangers. It is tied in with permitting yourself to feel powerless. The crucial step of adoration is setting a monstrous measure of trust in another person and permitting him/her to form our hearts. You can't be 100% sure that the individual will deal with you. You are not yet sure if the individual is the one for you. Thus, nervousness will make you think "If that I am not 100 percent secure with this individual, is there a need for reality?" Then excusing somewhat more, you will find a solution like, "If you don't get submitted, you won't get injured." Now, that is a thought brought to you by tension.

All things considered, this is what's going on; you are feeling apprehensive in this manner, hesitant to focus on an individual. Subsequently, you will never learn through understanding. If that you are continually dismissing the odds of adoration. In what manner will you know the genuine article that may assist you in managing the relationship's uneasiness?

C. You Have a Terrible Temper

The most terrible thing about relationship tension is that it influences the two individuals in a relationship. Indeed, it harms you and your accomplice, unjustifiably.

CHAPTER 15:

How Does It Affect Actions and Thoughts?

When one person in a relationship suffers from anxiety, this can have a lot of negative effects. This is especially true if the one who suffers from the disorder doesn't get understanding or support from their partner. Since anxiety involves fear, stress, and excessive worrying, these may develop into irrational thoughts. In turn, these thoughts can have an impact on how your partner perceives you and your relationship.

Because of your partner's disorder, you need to work extra hard to maintain your relationship through avoidance, dependence, and other challenges. Even if your partner starts sabotaging your relationship, you should try to understand why they are doing it while helping them overcome their insecurities and negativities. When it comes to helping a partner with anxiety, focus on understanding, support, and love. All of these things can help you weather any storm to keep your relationship intact. Of course, this journey is easier said than done. Sometimes, even if you know what to do from what you learn within these pages, taking action when faced with real-life situations can be very difficult, especially when negative feelings emerge within you. Therefore, you should learn how anxiety may affect your relationship so that you are prepared for what may come. This will help lessen the impact, thus allowing you to think and respond more appropriately.

How Can Anxiety Affect Your Relationship?

If you have ever been extremely anxious about something in the past, then you know how debilitating this feeling can be. Now try to imagine how your partner feels when anxiety comes knocking, but this time, it doesn't go away. This means that your partner would be in a constant state of fear, worry, and anxiety. Unless your partner does something to deal with these feelings or you do something to help them, they might start taking a toll on your relationship. Anxiety is truly a debilitating condition, not just for those who suffer from these symptoms, but for those who love them, too. Here are some ways anxiety can affect your relationship:

Anxiety May Break Down Your Connection and Your Trust

Relationships are built on trust and as time goes by, this trust builds an unbreakable connection filled with love. However, when one of you, in this case, your partner, develops anxiety, it will start eating away at the trust you have worked so hard to build. When this happens, your connection may break down, as well. As your partner battles with their anxiety, they will feel differently about you and your relationship.

If you don't notice what is happening with your partner, their condition may get worse. Then, your partner will feel ashamed or even afraid of their anxiety which, in turn, may cause them to pull away from you. Your partner might start doubting how you feel about them, how much they mean to you, and even whether you still love them. When your partner surrenders to these doubts, they might also lose their trust in you.

Anxiety Might Cause Your Partner to Reject You

The opposite of anxiety is acceptance, therefore, if your partner suffers from an anxiety disorder, they might reject you. Of course, this would be very painful, even if you know that your partner's disorder is the major cause of their rejection. In such a case, try to hang on and continue helping your partner. Giving up or accepting their rejection will just bring your relationship to an end.

As you can see, anxiety can wreak havoc on your relationship. This is why you must help each other so that you can defeat the disorder instead of allowing it to defeat you. One of the most important ways to do this is by communicating.

Anxiety Might Take the Joy Out of Your Relationship

If all the other effects above happen in your relationship, you both might end up unhappy. Think about it: if your partner behaves irrationally and you react by arguing with them or losing patience, how can joy remain a part of your relationship? Sadly, this is a common thing that may happen, especially if you don't work with your partner to help them manage their disorder.

Anxiety May Cause Your Partner to Become Avoidant

While some people become too dependent on those around them, especially their partners, others cope through avoidance. To deal with their feelings, your partner might start avoiding you and the other people around them. You may notice your partner becoming distant, aloof, or even cold. In some cases, they might even become emotionally unavailable. Even if you had a strong relationship in the past, anxiety can destroy this by causing your partner to become avoidant.

Anxiety May Cause Your Partner to Procrastinate and Panic

An anxious person may feel worried or fearful of the surrounding people. Because of this, they might think that they need to hide their true self. If your partner's anxiety causes them to feel this way, you might see a different side of them emerging. Since your partner doesn't feel like they can be themselves with you, they start panicking and procrastinating. This is when you might see them avoiding chores, making excuses, coming up with distractions, and doing other things that aren't like your partner at all.

Anxiety Might Make Your Partner Overly Dependent On You

Sometimes, people who suffer from anxiety might yearn for an intense closeness with their partner all the time. The reason for this yearning is to seek regular feelings of reassurance or support from their partner. Unfortunately, when you have a partner who is overly dependent on you, you might not be able to separate yourself from them. Even if you convince your partner to spend some time apart (like if you need to travel for business or you want to go out with your friends), your partner might end up overthinking. They might begin catastrophizing about worst-case scenarios, and when you finally get home, they start an argument with you. If this keeps happening, it will affect your relationship.

Anxiety May Cause Your Partner to Behave Selfishly

Anxiety often causes people to act irrationally. If your partner becomes overly fearful, they might only focus on their problems or concerns. Everything will become about them, and this causes them to act only for their benefit. To you, these actions will seem selfish, especially when your partner doesn't seem to even consider your thoughts or feelings. But they are only doing this as they try to deal with or overcome their anxiety.

CHAPTER 16:

How Excessive Attachment and Jealousy Hinders the Well Being Of the Couple

Jealousy can unfortunately ruin even the best relationships. It can be a powerful signal that it is time for you to change or risk losing an otherwise fulfilling relationship. Jealousy can be a good checklist to better understand your underlying feelings, taking immediate action, and protect your relationship from experiencing the disastrous fallout of your jealous thoughts or behavior. Here are some of the most foolproof techniques to help you tackle jealousy and insecurity in relationships with ease.

Question Yourself Each Time

Each time you find yourself feeling even remotely jealous, question the underlying feeling behind the complex emotion of jealousy. Is jealousy a consequence of my anger, anxiety, or fear? What is it about this situation that makes me jealous? When you question you're jealously critically, you are a few steps away from taking constructive steps to convert a cloud of negativity into a bundle of positivity.

Be Open About Your Insecurities

Discussing your insecurities with your partner will help you create a frank and open communication channel. Rather than doing and saying crazy things to your partner, be upfront, and share your feelings. Say something similar to "I apologize for bothering you regarding your friendship with ABC, but it is not my lack of trust in you. I simply feel insecure about it."

Admitting it is you and not the other person who goes a long way in resolving your relationship issues over hurling accusations at your partner. Together, you can work better on your insecurities if you both acknowledge it and take active steps to eliminate it.

Learn to Trust People

Learn to get into the habit of trusting people more. Choose a trusting disposition over a distrustful attitude. Unless you have concrete evidence about someone, take their word for it. Going around snooping, stalking your partner, and behaving like a suspicious maniac only harms your relationship further. Rather, if there is no reason to be suspicious other than a feeling of insecurity or jealously, let it go.

Get to the Root of Your Feelings

It can be hard to objectively assess why you feel pangs of jealously every time someone compliments your partner, or he/she speaks warmly with his/her colleagues. It can be highly tempting to blame another person for your emotions. However, getting to the root of your jealousy by being more self-aware is the foundation to free yourself from its shackles. Take a more compassionate and objective look at the origination of your jealousy. Think about the potential causes of feelings of insecurity.

For instance, if you find yourself being increasingly jealous of your partner; know why you feel it. Is it because you don't want to lose him/her? Is it because your relationship ended due to a similar reason? Do you suffer from a false sense of self-entitlement that your partner's time belongs only to you? Do you feel what you feel because of a sense of inadequacy that constantly makes you think "you aren't good enough?" Once you identify the underlying reasons causing feelings of jealousy and insecurity, it becomes easier to deal with your behavior.

Write Down Your Deepest Thoughts

Journaling is known to be one of the most effective techniques for bringing to the forefront your deepest feelings and emotions. It helps you discover multiple layers of your personality to achieve greater self-awareness. For instance, you may constantly harbor feelings of insecurity because you were raised by neglectful parents or you may never feel you are "good enough" because you were raised by parents who had extremely high and unreasonable expectations of you.

People who have been neglected in their childhood often feel they aren't worthy enough to be loved. This, in turn, causes them to think that their partner is seeking someone more worthy or deserving of love than them, which creates feelings of insecurity. Writing down may help you discover certain events, circumstances, and facets which may directly be responsible for your irrational behavior. Once you've nailed down underlying feelings behind the jealousy, it is way simpler to manage it.

Learn From Your Jealousy

Jealousy can be converted into learning or inspiration if you channelize it productively. For instance, if your partner plays the guitar well and finds himself/herself the cynosure of all eyes at a party, you can up your skills, too, by learning from him/her or signing up for guitar lessons. Instead of wallowing in defeatist self-pity, you have transformed your negative feelings into something positive.

Jealousy Doesn't Mean Something Will Happen

We need to understand that our jealous hunches do not necessarily mean the act is occurring. Just because we fear something is going to happen doesn't mean it will happen. A majority of the time, our fears are unfounded and not even remotely close to coming true. Just because your partner is somewhere else, and you fear he/she is with someone else, doesn't mean he/she is proposing marriage on a date. Understand the difference between thoughts and actual events. The make-believe imaginations of our destructive minds are often far from reality.

Paranoia or replaying a worst-case scenario is common among people suffering from jealousy or insecurity. They imagine things that have no basis in reality. For instance, your partner may call or visit an ex to express his/her condolences when the ex's mother passes away. This doesn't in any way imply that your partner is still hooked to the ex.

However, you may find yourself imagining terrible things that may be the result of sheer jealousy and paranoia. Rather than imagining negative things, try shifting the focus of how wonderful your partner is to be considerate and pleasant with an ex. This might be the very reason that made you fall in love with him/her. See what you did there? You shifted your feelings from insecurity to pride, from untrue suspicions to a positive reality.

Get Rid of Past Relationship Garbage

A strong reason why you are always paranoid about your current partner cheating on you can be traced back to an earlier relationship. You may have had an ex-partner cheat on you with your best friend. The betrayal may have had such a severe impact that you view every relationship in a similar distrustful light.

However, understand that your current partner has nothing to do with your relationship. He/she should not have to bear the brunt of what someone else did. Painting everyone with the same brush can be a disastrous mistake in any relationship. There is a solid reason your earlier relationship did not last, and you should leave the baggage of your earlier relationship where it belongs—in the trash can.

Focus Your Energies Elsewhere

Rather than obsessing over who your partner is cheating you with, try to develop interests outside of your relationship.

Do not make it the nucleus of your existence even if it means a lot to you. Pursue your hobbies, be a part of local clubs, volunteer for good causes, be active in the local community, play a sport, learn different languages, take fun dance/aerobics sessions, be a part of a local book club–anything that shifts your focus from overwhelming jealous thoughts to productive channelization of energy.

Surround Yourself with Meaningful Relationships

People are often so wrapped up in their romantic relationship that there is a tendency to distance ourselves from all other relationships. We believe in spending every waking minute of our lives with our partners. This only leads to a greater feeling of fear and insecurity because we realize that once this relationship ceases to exist, we have no other meaningful relationship as our safety net. We tend to develop greater feelings of insecurity and jealousy when we have no one to fall back on.

It helps to not make a single relationship in the center of your universe and develop several meaningful friendships. Do no distance from your close friends after getting into a relationship. Talk to them, spend time with them, do fun things together (that you probably did in school or college), have lunch dates, travel with them, and more. This will give you a life outside of your and your partner's time together. Once you have a momentous life outside your relationship, you will be less likely to wallow in self-pity and self-induced sulks. You will always have someone to talk to if you are surrounded by family or friends who understand and love you unconditionally.

Mindfulness for Managing Your Emotions

Mindfulness is a great way to calm your nerves and manage runaway emotions. Tune into your physical and mental self by identifying your feelings, thoughts, and emotions by taking deep breaths. Try to detach yourself from overpowering negative emotions such as jealousy and insecurity. Every time you find yourself overcome with thoughts of jealousy or insecurity, practice mindful meditation.

Find a quiet corner that is free from distraction, sit in a comfortable position, and clear your mind by eliminating all thoughts and take deep breaths. Focus only on the present and your deep breathing without allowing your mind to wander. If you find your mind drifting, gently bring it back to the present by concentrating on your bodily sensations. Daily meditation sessions can help you break free from ugly thoughts and behavior patterns.

Do Not Judge Others Based on Your Past Actions

Ever notice how suspicious people are always suspicious of others? Or how liars think everyone around them is lying? Our perceptions of people and their motives are often a reflection of who we are. Stop using your past or present behavior as a yardstick for perceiving your partner's actions. For instance, if you have a history of being involved with married men/women, do not assume that no married man/woman can ever be trusted and start mistrusting your spouse. Just because you did or are doing something does not mean he/she is indulging in it, too. People who often have loyalty issues themselves constantly attack their partners for being unfaithful or immoral. There is a greater need to shift the blame from their inability to cope with issues related to unfaithfulness. Acknowledge that there is a problem, talk to a therapist about it and try to treat it rather than making your partner bear the brunt of your follies. Sometimes people fail to understand why despite giving their partner no reason to feel insecure or ever being unfaithful to them they are still made to feel like lying scums. The problem often lies with the person suspecting them and not the person at the receiving end of these unfortunate suspicions.

Avoid Being a Victim of Relationship Games

People often try to feel great about themselves by purportedly getting their partner to feel jealous. Do not fall into the trap. Displaying any signs of jealousy will only encourage your partner's behavior. Tell your partner firmly that indulging in a jealousy/insecurity inducing behavior only demeans him/her and won't make him/her feel any better about himself/herself. Even if you feel jealous, try to keep a stoic and unaffected demeanor, which should eventually stop these excruciatingly uncomfortable, attention-drawing tactics.

CHAPTER 17:

Techniques for Eliminating Stress

Each person deals with stress in their own way. This is not to say that these are voluntary reactions. These are *in*voluntary responses our bodies make to compensate for the effects of the causes of factors of the stress. Our bodies respond to the effects of stress differently. Some people may experience shortness of breath and exhibit trembling and tremors. Others may exhibit stress physically, getting stomach aches, headaches or they may get sick frequently. It is impossible to eliminate stress given the demands of your life, the society we live in, your job, your relationship, and of course, yourselves.

With stress being a part of most societies, with a set of different commonalities and variances, making it a point to identify individual and specific stressors, can allow the individual to take back some control by employing stress management techniques to lessen the stress effects on one's overall health. Knowing what demands the most of your energy, identifying what depletes you of the energies your body needs to function optimally, is one manner how you can overcome the negativity brought about by those situations. Read about some ways one can help cope with stress below.

Taking care of your health is vital to not only your physical health but your mental stability as well. Taking care of your health means that you will need to be mindful of what you eat. Sticking to a balanced diet is not only beneficial to the body but the mental balance as well and is a healthy step towards combating stressful situations. When an individual exercises regularly, even if it is just a quick 30-minute brisk walk around the block or a regular bike ride to work, it is invaluable. Getting a proper and moderate workout for your health is essential to curbing the effects of stress. Having the proper amount of sleep at the correct time is a catalyst for a clear head. A good night's rest allows for better decision making.

Sometimes, a good ear is all you need to blow off some steam and avoid further stress from progressing and worsening. Support is usually found from friends and or family by talking about the source of the demands on your person. It is easy to isolate oneself under stressful situations or when going through a difficult spell, avoid staying away from being around the company which may lead to more serious mental issues like depression and suicide.

Learn to remove yourself from a stressful situation. Sometimes, stepping away from the situation which causes you stress can help you clear your head of the cause of your anxiety. Taking the high road can also mean turning away from the situation that causes you stress. It is also good to be reminded that using drugs and alcohol as means of escaping the realities of a stressful event may help on a short-term basis but can cause bigger and worse problems in the long run. The ill-effects of the use of illegal drugs, self-medication, and excessive alcohol consumption during stressful events in one's life leads to dependency on substances that first does not help us in facing the situation, thereby learning how to make decisions on future responses.

Every person is bound to deal with stress in one way or another simply because stress is a part of life. What we need to keep in mind is that not all stress is bad because it does give us the ability to assess a situation and make calculated deductions about the best response to any given situation. Concern does creep in when stress is prolonged because of the impact it has on our overall health.

With more than a host of stressful situations waiting around the bend with each day we traverse, it is more than ever important to accept the stressors that can trigger off stress hormones. From minor everyday incidents that come along with the birth of each day to the more long-lasting, more chronic forms of stress that are less prioritized of our everyday lives tucked away and not dealt with by us. Proactively finding ways for you to deal with the underlying, tucked away stressors in your life will empower you to better deal with the everyday challenges. To manage stress means to maintain a fulfilling and healthy life.

If we could see that there are thoughts that are creating more stress and not our situation we would be better able to manage stress. Being able to recognize this is good news to you because then you would be equipped with the right skill set to recognize fact from supposed thoughts in your current situation. Keep in mind that you don't have to change your situation to be stress-free, you just have to change the way you think about the situation.

To be free of what is creating stress, we first need to identify what specific thoughts, stories, or beliefs spawn the stress. Do this whenever you feel stressed. Ask yourself an honest question: "What outcome am I afraid of?"

For example, let's say you have a report that you need to submit to your boss and you worry about whether the report is accurate good enough, and acceptable to your boss or perhaps you might be going out on a date you and you might be worried that the person you are going out with will not like you or perhaps you are preparing for an exam and you are worried that you might fail this test.

The next question to ask yourself after you've determined to answer for the first is what outcome I think is the best. Your answers may be, "It would be best if I prepare the report we had of time and check that everything is in order." And perhaps for your date, you might say, "I'll just be myself and see where it goes from there," and for the exam, you might give yourself an answer like "I need to learn to study more efficiently." When you determine the best outcome, you set yourself up to succeed. How you may ask is this? Asking yourself what the best outcome is allows you to better prepare yourself. You are essentially avoiding the worst possible outcome to be free from your thoughts to be free from that specific stress.

Once you understand that your thoughts are creating your stress and want to identify the specific stress, the next thing you have to do is not believe that thought. This sounds like a radical and difficult step to manage the stress, but it is your way of helping yourself to eliminate unnecessary, unmerited, and stressful thoughts.

When a person believes words to be true, there is a corresponding emotion that goes along with the words you hear or think. Notice that, on the other hand, when you don't believe that there's any truth to the words you hear, no emotions are involved. Asking these questions and giving real, honest answers yourself enables you to identify what it is that is causing your stress.

When you answer these questions honestly, then you have set yourself up to understand what it is you can do. Perhaps it's just a matter of being more prepared for a job interview. It could also equate to you studying harder for an exam.

Hence, you eliminate the supposed thoughts that cause you stress. Stress and anxiety are only created by what you know. Stress cannot be created when you know that you are free. Uncertainty does not create stress but the nagging thoughts of supposition.

Once you realize that you don't know which outcome is better or worse, once you understand that uncertainty is a given, you allow yourself to be free of the stress and anxiety that is paving the way for you to do what is rightful. Knowing that uncertainty is evident, gives you the tools to prepare and look inward. Realizing that uncertainty will always be present allows us to put the best versions of ourselves into action.

If you come to realize the idea that good or bad could happen given a particular scenario (and be inventive with the scenarios) and give logical answers to these supposed bad outcomes, you will be able to understand that there are so many possible outcomes.

Take, for example, a person who feels unrecognized by their boss. One person may not find your worth in what you do, but other people find you to be indispensable. Take a bad break up. Say you got hurt from a bad split but this separation paved the way for perhaps a new and more fulfilling relationship with another person or maybe you discover that you are presently better off without the taxing relationship that ended. In other words, mindset is vital to managing stress.

We have been "programmed" by the demands of society to work under stressful conditions. Preparing for a test, or a job interview, submitting a report are just some realities we all experience. We don't know any other way of operating unless it's under circumstances of pressure and demand. Operating under pressure and fear (of rejection or reprimand) as the way to getting approval or success has been the norm for many of us.

When you are stressed while doing something, there is no fun or pleasure in the task at hand. You may procrastinate and put it off till the last minute because it does not give you the uplift of doing something you enjoy. Procrastinating only heightens the stress factor because, now, you're on limited time.

On the other hand, if what you were doing gave you pleasure, if you enjoy what you do, you would spend more time on this task, and it wouldn't bother you one bit. You look forward to doing it, and you carry out the task the best way possible because there is no accompanying stress to what needs to be done.

It is easier to be focused and creative when we are free from stress and anxiety. When we are free from stress, we can be more comfortable and authentic. Identify the source of stress. Eliminate stressors by asking yourself logical questions about the root of the stress and answer them just as honestly.

Stress makes us unhappy. It prevents us from being accessible to people. Stressed people are not pleasant to be around, and this is manifested through the interaction between people. So this is another vicious cycle in which we are trapped by the grips of stress. How you may ask?

Through isolation; when we are not pleasant to be around, our response (under stress) is to withdraw. We isolate ourselves from the company of others, thereby giving more way to the stress of insecurity. This becomes a lonely cycle unless we recognize and break the cycle! When you are not stressed and happy, you are better primed to help you get what you want.

CHAPTER 18:

Loving a Person with Anxiety

A nxiety comes in many forms, and there is no magic pill that can help. Anxiety is also an individual experience that can differ in many ways. The list of things we can do to help our partner when they are having an anxiety attack differs from person to person. You should know how to recognize the symptoms and learn how to neutralize an anxiety attack by relying on previous experience.

Your involvement in your partner's journey of learning how to live a life free of anxiety is of great importance. When it comes to sudden panic attacks, you can do several things to help distract your partner and ease any suffering. When it comes to chronic anxiety, you are the one who will get involved in exposure therapy. There are specific strategies you can take into consideration when it comes to each type of anxiety.

Obsessive-Compulsive Disorder

When it comes to OCD, what you can do for your partner is not to engage in his behaviors. Also, encourage him not to give in and repeat their compulsive behaviors. If you give in and comply with your partner's OCD, you will not be helping. Although it will surely elevate the tension made by your partner's OCD, complying will reinforce the fears. For example, if your partner asks you to go to the kitchen and make sure all appliances are off, you shouldn't comply. But you should also not argue or call your partner irrational. It is ineffective, and it will only deepen the anxiety.

Discuss with your partner how is it best to approach anxiety and agree on a strategy. This is where a professional therapist will be of most use to both of you. A professional can guide you through this conversation and help both of you feel comfortable discussing the delicate topic of your partner's disorder.

You will need to learn how to change from saying things like:

"I will not go to the kitchen again, you are imagining things, and being irrational" to "I appreciate your concern about the kitchen appliances, but we agreed that the best thing we can do is to help you learn how to manage the feelings you are having right now."

Your partner will agree for their benefit that the best thing you could do is stay by their side, not check the kitchen, and help them work through the anxiety. This can be done with breathing exercises that will help your partner calm down. In time, your partner will show less fear. The OCD will decrease, and you will feel less frustrated.

CHAPTER 19:

Fear of Abandonment

A fear of abandonment is a complex phenomenon in psychology that is believed to originate from childhood loss or injury. This worry has been examined from a variety of perspectives. Concepts behind why anxiety of abandonment occurs to consist of disturbances in the regular advancement of little ones' social and mental capacities, past connections and life experiences, and direct exposure to certain norms and also concepts have been studied.

Although it is not the main phobia, the fear of desertion is probably among the most common and most damaging worries of all. Individuals with the fear of abandonment might tend to display necessary actions and also thought patterns that affect their connections, inevitably leading to the abandonment they dread becoming a reality. This anxiety can be ravaging. Recognizing this worry is the very first step towards solving it.

The worry of abandonment is the frustrating worry that individuals close to you will undoubtedly leave. Anyone can create anxiety of abandonment. It can be deeply rooted in a stressful experience you had as a youngster or a stressful relationship in the adult years. If you fear desertion, it can be virtually difficult to keep healthy and balanced relationships. This incapacitating concern can lead you to wall surface yourself off to prevent getting hurt. Or you may be unintentionally undermining partnerships.

The first step in dealing with your anxiety is to recognize why you feel in this manner. You should be able to resolve your issues and problems on your own or with treatment.

But the fears of desertion may additionally be part of a personality disorder that requires treatment. Continue the analysis to explore the reasons and also long-lasting effects of a worry of abandonment, even when you ought to seek assistance.

Signs of a Fear of Abandonment

Numerous people have a problem with anxiety. Nearly 10% of individuals in the U.S. have some type of phobia. When it involves connections, its resulting habits consist of:

- You are fast to affix, also to not available partners or relationships.

- You are reluctant to commit fully, as well as have had very few long-lasting partnerships.

- You aim to please. For some ladies, a study has also located an increase in the desire to have undesirable sex.

- As soon as in a partnership, you stay, despite how undesirable the relationship is.

- You are often hard to please as well as nitpicky.

- Emotional affection is hard for you.

- You feel insecure and unworthy of love.

- You locate it tough to rely on individuals.

- Being jealous of everybody you satisfy is not an odd sensation to you.

- Feelings of separation anxiousness are extreme.

- Feelings of underlying stress and anxiety and also clinical depression are very common to you.

- You often tend to overthink points and also work hard to identify the concealed significance in everything.

- You are hypersensitive to objections.

- You have quenched anger and also control issues.

- Self-blame prevails for you.

Sorts of Concerns of Abandonment

You may be afraid that someone you like is going to leave and not come back physically. You may fear that a person will undoubtedly desert your psychological requirements, either can hold you in relationships with moms and dad, a partner, or a good friend.

Fear of Psychological Desertion

It may be less apparent than physical truancy. However, it's no less stressful. We all have psychological needs.

When those demands aren't fulfilled, you may feel unappreciated, hated, as well as separated. You can feel quite alone, even when you remain in connection with somebody existing. If you've experienced psychological desertion in the past, primarily as a youngster, you may reside in continuous fear that it will certainly take place once more.

The Anxiety of Abandonment in Children

It's regular for babies as well as toddlers to experience a separation anxiousness phase.

They may sob, howl, or refuse to allow when a parent or critical caregiver needs to leave. Children have a hard time understanding when or if that person will certainly return. As they begin to understand that enjoyed ones do return, they outgrow their anxiety. For a lot of kids, this takes place by their third birthday celebration.

Desertion Anxiousness in Partnerships

You may be frightened to let yourself be susceptible to a company. You may have depended on issues as well as stress excessively regarding your relationship. That can make you suspicious. In time, your anxiousness can cause various other people to drawback, bolstering the cycle.

Signs and Symptoms of Fear of Abandonment

If you fear desertion, you may recognize a few of these signs and also indications:

- Overly conscious criticism

- Problem trusting in others

- Trouble making friends unless you can be confident they like you

- Taking severe procedures to avoid being rejected or separation

- A pattern of unhealthy connections

- Problem dedicating to a relationship

- Functioning hard to please the other individual as well

- Blaming yourself when things do not exercise

- Remaining in a connection even if it's not healthy and balanced for you

Abandonment Problems in Relationships

If you fear desertion in your present partnership, it might result from having been physically or emotionally abandoned in the past. For example:

- As a teen, you may have experienced the fatality or desertion of a parent or caretaker.

- You might have experienced parental forget.

- You might have been turned down by your peers.

- You experienced a prolonged health problem of an enjoyed one.

- A charming partner might have left you instantly or behaved in an undependable fashion.

Such occasions can result in a fear of desertion.

CHAPTER 20:

Toxic Relationships

A nxiety isn't always the element that affects a relationship. Sometimes it's the other way around, and the reason you have anxiety is that it is a toxic relationship. But what exactly does toxic mean? We refer to a relationship as toxic when it isn't beneficial to you and it's harmful in some way. The building blocks for a healthy relationship are made from mutual respect and admiration, but sometimes it just isn't enough.

However, there is a difference between a problematic relationship and a toxic one, and that is mainly the noxious atmosphere that surrounds you. This kind of relationship can suffocate you with time and prevent you from living a happy, productive life. Many factors lead to toxicity. It is most often caused by friction that can occur between two people that are opposites of each other. In others, nothing specific is to blame, and the toxic relationship grows from the lack of communication, the establishment of boundaries, and the ability to agree on something, or at the very least, compromise.

Take note that not all toxic relationships develop because of the couple. Sometimes there is an outlier seeking to influence conflict because they will benefit from it in some way. This type of individual preys on other people's insecurities, weaknesses, or manipulates his way inside a relationship from which he has something to gain. In some cases, a toxic person seeks to destroy a relationship to get closer to one of them. He or she may not even be aware of their damaging behavior because of a self-obsessed focus that does not extend to anyone else. Personal needs, emotions, and goals take priority over anyone else's wellbeing.

With that in mind, let's briefly explore the characteristics of a toxic relationship:

1. Poisonous: A relationship that is extremely unpleasant to be around as it poisons the surrounding environment. It makes anyone around the couple anxious, and it can even lead to psychological and emotional problems such as anxiety and depression.

2. Deadly: Toxic relationships are bad for your health. In many cases, it involves risky, destructive, and abusive behaviors. Some people end up harming themselves with alcohol, drugs, or worse. Injuries and even death can become the final result.

3. Negative: In this kind of relationship, negativity is the norm. There is no positive reinforcement, even when children are involved. The overwhelming lack of approval and emotional support is standard.

4. Harmful: Toxic relationships lack balance and awareness. Those involved are never truly aware of each other and lack the most positive principles that a healthy relationship needs. Toxicity also promotes immoral and malicious acts that harm a romantic relationship.

While it is true that some of them are, that's not always the case. However, psychopaths are expert manipulators due to their ability to mask their true feelings and intentions. These people have a psychological disorder that makes their personalities imposing, pretentious, and even impulsive. Many aren't aware of their behavior and the effects it has on others. They tend to be self-absorbed and expect a great deal from others while being narcissistic and deceitful. In other words, they lack insight as well as empathy. Psychopaths are people who seek attention, admiration, and acceptance, but they will need to accept their responsibilities and the needs of others.

Why and how would anyone end up in a relationship with someone who displays psychopathic traits? The answer lies in their ability to maintain appearances and manipulate others. If they realize you see through their charade, they will do anything to convince you that they are a good person. They may start doing good deeds, not out of empathy and love, but out of the need to redeem themselves. In many cases, these people can recover if their psychopathic disorder isn't too severe. With help, they can gain control over themselves and their toxic behavior, so they can live a productive life without hurting others in the process.

As mentioned earlier, toxic relationships don't always involve psychopaths or those who display similar traits. In many situations, these relationships are the way they are due to decent people that are terrible decision-makers or lack social skills. Taking a wrong turn in life happens to everyone, and many people change but not always for the better.

Warning Signs

Now that you can better identify toxic relationships and the kind of people that are involved let's see if you're in one or not. Some underlying issues and disorders can make people behave negatively. However, they can still be excellent partners. With that said, here's a list of questions you can ask yourself to learn more about your relationship:

1. How do you feel in the company of your partner?

2. Do you feel happy, safe, and nurtured in the presence of your significant other?

3. Are all the other people involved in your relationship safe and happy? For instance your children (if you have any), parents, and friends, and so on. As mentioned earlier, people tend to avoid toxic relationships instead of being in contact with them.

4. Do you experience anxiety or panic attacks when you are about to discuss something with your partner?

5. Can you think of any scenarios in which you were manipulated to do something that wasn't for your best interest?

6. Is your partner pushing the limits of what you would consider ethical? Is he or she even crossing the line of what is legal?

7. Does your partner push you to perform challenging tasks that you consider entirely unnecessary? These challenges may seem pointless, and that you need to resolve them just because it's what your partner wants.

8. Do you feel emotionally strained and exhausted after interacting with your partner?

If you can answer a few of these questions, you are likely in a toxic relationship that may be making you anxious and damaging your health. You then need to decide for yourself whether you wish to stay in this kind of relationship to repair it or leave. If you do decide to stay, you need to make some decisions. For instance, you need to feel in control with the idea of resisting all the negativity that comes with a toxic partner, because you will need to endure feelings of anxiety and stress. You need to ask yourself whether you are gaining enough from that relationship and whether it's worth sacrificing yourself for it.

Handling a Toxic Relationship

As mentioned, a toxic relationship can be a powerful source of anxiety. It doesn't have to be a romantic relationship either. Some of them you can avoid by cutting contact with some people to feel relief. However, there are certain people you simply cannot break away from, whether they are romantic partners or your mother-in-law.

The first step is to accept the inescapable situation. When your options are limited, you cannot achieve relief by avoidance, and acceptance leads to a decrease in anxiety. You may be tempted to be hostile towards that person, but it won't help. Instead, it will just add to your worries and stress. At this point, your only alternative is managing your anxiety by admitting to yourself that you may never be able to get along with that person. Also, you can attempt to ignore him or her completely by never going to spend time together and ignoring any contact. However, none of these tactics usually work. Resistance can help in the short term, but it will continue generating anxiety and stress because the toxic person knows how to get under your skin and take advantage of you. Accept that this relationship is difficult and challenges you, but you are doing your best to make it better. That doesn't mean you should completely surrender. By accepting your situation, you will allow yourself new possibilities and new options instead of repeatedly punishing yourself.

Take note that for the process of acceptance to take hold, you need to be consciously aware that you are not responsible for anyone else's emotions and reactions. Toxic behavior often makes people blame you for their situation and feelings. Do not accept any of that, as you are not the reason for their suffering. They need to take responsibility for their thoughts and actions instead of blaming others. The second step is telling the truth. If a toxic relationship is creating stress, likely, you often lie to avoid conflict, which causes even more anxiety. The problem is that when you lie to such a person, you enable them and become partially responsible for the reality they create, leading to the toxic environment surrounding them. For instance, let's say you intentionally didn't invite the problematic person to your birthday. When confronted about it, you may be tempted to say that you sent an invitation but used the wrong address, or it went into the spam folder. Lying isn't easy, especially if you are an anxious person. People can tell, especially if you tend to make excuses for yourself often enough. Instead of lying, you should tell the truth and the real truth. This means that you shouldn't use an excuse. Just say they make you uncomfortable and extremely anxious, that is why you didn't invite them. Telling the truth can be difficult and even painful because it affects others. It takes a great deal of courage and once you get through the experience, you will feel a powerful sense of relief. In the end, it's better to get something off your chest instead of carrying it.

CHAPTER 21:

The Diamond Inside of Anxiety

To the vast majority, fear strikes like power from the depths and draws them into an infernal world in a blast of panic from their highly functioning everyday lives. Where they were once excited to move into a healthy married life, now they are so concerned about it that it hampers their ability to feed, sleep and work properly, let alone to plan a wedding. You would like the anxiety to disappear, thinking incorrectly that it is an indication that you are in the wrong relationship and that the only solution is to leave. That's when they find their way to Google's "engagement anxiety" or "marriage terror."

It is a challenge to make; nobody would want to live with the demon of fear, so you should understand why you want the demon to vanish. Yet there can be no real healing without the ability to discover its origins and heights.

It is a strange and counterintuitive assertion, but what all my clients realize eventually is that the fear-based thoughts and repetitive questions contain great information. This will help you reach this knowledge by dressing like a hero or heroine embarking into what Joseph Campbell calls the "Hero's Journey." Then you can have the ability to dive into your psyche's darkest areas and keep a light of reality about what you are seeking in them. And here's a nugget of confidence to combat the fear of looking inside. There is an unharmed warehouse of sadness, a soft space of vulnerability, a shy person, a river of terror, a warehouse of myths about love, marriage, romanticism, and intimacy. And when you learn to take care of your difficult feelings and to substitute false assumptions with the truth, you will find a degree of harmony, confidence, and healing, which you had never learned. The uncertainty you feel about your relationship is not new, and you have not felt insecure in your life for the first time. If you, like most people who find me, have frequently or continuously suffered from anxiety throughout your life, now is your chance to repair it.

The magic of this deep soul research shows what the soul is trying to express. The soul wants wholeness, peace, and serenity, but it does not always know how to fulfill these wants. Instead of specifically requesting more life, for instance, we prefer to project the will into our partner in the form: "He's not interesting enough." If we stick to that concept and assume it's real, we lose the chance to mine for the diamond within anxiety.

I've always told you that the purpose of concentrating on the negative attributes of our partners is to shield or protect yourself from the hard feelings caused by transitions: the remorse of letting go and the dream of the ideal mate, the uncertainty of jumping into the unknown, and the insecurity accompanying the danger of love. But I realized recently that, while the thoughts defend against painful feelings, they are also gates to expand our consciousness and to deepen our emotional and spiritual development.

To break through the nervous barrier and hit the inside gem. It is important to understand which questions lead to diamonds. I have grouped the most common issues according to their positive role to promote this process.

Finding Your Way through the 'Mirror Maze' of Emotions and Relationships

It may also feel like a day-to-day life for those with shyness and anxiety. If you are an insecure or shy guy (or woman), you probably have smart, talented, funny, affectionate, and interesting friends, but you are still so unsure about yourself that you are lost in trying to find out who you should be rather than who you are. You think your true self is "too isolated" from those around you. And when you care about others, lead and take responsibility, you doubt your worth and how you make a difference for others. You certainly have worked hard to be a member of the community or, more frequently, to avoid being insulted by a lack of attributes that will make you attractive or appealing to others.

You may be married or have relationships and are involved in caring for others, but you feel you've never been able to express your thoughts, emotions, dreams, and interests directly. You could doubt whether anyone would hear or care, even if you spoke out. Your days and hours are full of tasks and events, but despite what you are doing, you find very little satisfaction.

Relations and social interactions can be a labyrinth of reflections and dead ends to us, shy men, like this hall of mirrors. When you obey one rule, you will never know how to find your way out, keep your eyes on your feet, and know where you are. You will concentrate on placing every foot carefully before you if you are not disturbed by flashing lights, changing colors, and tenting views of the exit. You can check your way and move forward with each stage.

Fear and anxiety work best when disturbed and unsure. The confounding wind of interactions, talk, and movement around you may become daunting if you feel that you are responsible for following these sometimes-conflicting currents and reacting to them. When you concentrate on knowing yourself and being attentive to yourself, your values, perceptions, emotions, and awareness, you can start the journey out of the stormy labyrinth.

Money and Finance: The Cause of Anxieties for Most Families

Martha had a night of restlessness. The next day she got a credit card company billing statement telling her she was behind schedule on her monthly charge. Each time a debt collector called her at the office and home, at times, even in odd hours of the night, she always felt threatened. They have had trouble paying the mortgage and the monthly rates for the new vehicle. Their financial struggles are partially due to her husband Ben, who admits himself to be a major donor. Ben is a passionate driver who invests a great deal of time, "spicing up" his Japanese car and making it look like the street racer in the movie "Too Hard, Too Furious." Both Ben and Martha have been subjected to tremendous stress and anxiety each day. Despite their financial problems, they are struggling a lot and sharing the blame for slipping into the debt pit. It is not shocking that money is now a big cause of divorce.

Money or, better, lack of money is one of the key causes of marriage tension and anxiety. In the United States, the average household has a credit card debt of at least $9,200. Bens and Martha have no experience in financial growth methods and techniques. The common mistake hard-pressed couples make is that they invest more than they can return.

We are all faced with various obstacles and money pressures. Facing these financial challenges can be very daunting if nothing is done about them early. Owing to the relentless demand for our everyday living, it is also the leading cause of stress and anxiety that can destroy your mental and physical well-being.

However, money should help us better our condition and not make our lives miserable. To raising the burden created by financial difficulties, the following financial management advice should be read and taken into consideration: First, create a practical budget. It is the very first step to gaining control of your finances. Create a list of all the money or bills you have to pay. Then choose to pay them one by one based on your fixed payment power. It is also important to mention all other revenue sources. The next move is for all of your "fixed" expenses such as mortgages, rent, car payments, fuel, credit card, and insurance premiums to be written down. Then calculate how much money you have left to know exactly what you spent on other things. Before you finish paying for priority accounts, it is necessary to adhere to your payment schedule and not build any other payable. You can track where your money goes with a small notebook. Moreover, using a budgeting system for your computer can be a helpful method to manage your checkbook.

The second step is to teach your children money. Children are now easily tempted by advertisements and marketing gimmicks. With peer pressure and the relentless blockade of fads, children can lose their interest in something they don't need. They have to be told how difficult it is to raise money, and that they cannot purchase anything they see in a toy store, on TV. Children about eight years of age can already be taught to handle and start saving allowances.

Another step in the direction of financial freedom, whether you believe it or not, is to contact your creditors. Explain your condition and ask them to reorganize your loans. Ask them to offer a debt reduction solution but ensure that interest rates are reasonable and regular payments can be made. Seek to persuade the creditors to build a new payment plan, which would lead to a win-win financial situation.

If you want to regain financial independence, cost reduction initiatives should also be an automatic undertaking. You can save money by actually doing stuff like turning off the lights if you don't need them, scheduling your journeys or grocery store orders, and only cutting back on sales of fast food. Both of these helps to reduce your monthly expenses. You might, for example, avoid subscribing to the magazine or select a cheaper cable with fewer channels.

You should consult a financial planner on investment options and securities such as bonds and inventories if you have enough savings.

CHAPTER 22:

Strategies to Improve Existing Relationships

If you've found someone you want to spend the foreseeable future with and would like to either start on the right foot or work to improve the connection you already have, consider some of the following points:

1. Have Common Visions and Values

If one person is a spendthrift and the other is thrifty if one is watching their diet and the other eats only junk food if one is on the right and the other on the left of the political spectrum, etc., chances are high that battles will take place frequently.

For your relationship to last, you must have a set of commonalities for which you come together and a vision that allows you to project yourselves into a bright future.

All of this helps to share dreams and a good understanding of each other!

2. Gratify The Other and Give Recognition

Whether you're married or not, much of what destroys couples and relationships comes from taking each other for granted. How does this translate into daily life?

When you refrain from putting in the effort, when you do not do your part to nurture the relationship, when you criticize too much and too often, when you don't take their feelings to the heart or acknowledge their struggles, and when you naively believe that your partner will love you forever, regardless of what you do.

Relationships do not work like that.

For each person in a relationship to feel loved and appreciated, both must express gratitude and recognition for the other regularly.

This attitude nurtures collaboration, encourages a strong connection, and helps us appreciate our partner. They do not owe us their affection, so knowing that it is freely given is gratifying.

3. Be Proud of The Person With Whom You Are In a Relationship

How can you live happily as a couple if you do not admire, at the very least, the person you are with?

There's no need to have received a Nobel Prize, cured cancer, or solved world hunger. If you do not appreciate at least one trait of the other person (intelligence, beauty, determination, courage, humor), you do not appreciate their place in your life. People gravitate towards those who express love, acceptance, and fulfillment. Make your partner feel loved and accepted all the time.

4. Have Realistic Expectations

Some women are continually looking for an impossible Prince Charming and believe that love must resemble a fairy tale, while men may be influenced by the unreasonable standards set by the media.

Whatever these unfounded expectations are, if they are unrealistic, by definition, they will generate disappointment.

Research into positive psychology has shown that it is better to have realistic and modest expectations as much as possible, even in your relationships.

If you are happy with what you have, you will find satisfaction.

If you are always looking to replace your partner with someone "better," without seeing their true qualities, you will condemn yourself to an eternal search for an illusion that exists only in your imagination.

5. Give Regular and Ample Affection

Research has also shown that long-lasting couples are those who have been able to gradually replace love and passion with attachment.

We are not aware of it, but a lot of our behavior is determined by our hormones and our neurotransmitters. Cuddling, affection, and tenderness stimulate the production of oxytocin, the hormone of attachment.

If you want to feed the well-being of your partner, you must not forget the power of showing affection.

6. Do Not Let The Sexual Flame Go Out

After the passion at the beginning of your relationship, as time goes on, the frequency at which you make love might reduce. This can be for many reasons, none of which should be used to assign blame.

If this tendency continues, sexual desire may end up being extinguished. Without (necessarily) bringing out the whip and the handcuffs, it is possible to continue to spark the sexual flame.

Yes, some clothes and toys can help, but the real key is to devote enough time to intimacy in your relationship, despite the tumult of everyday life.

Eating well, exercising, and staying healthy can help keep the flame alive despite the passage of time. But, it also depends on your taste and your partner's. This fits into a more general vision which also comes from your personal development and health.

7. Be Open To Improving and Working On Yourself

If you or your partner constantly live in a state of pride and self-denial, it is clear that the relationship is preparing for doom.

Being in a partnership or relationship means working on yourself, making compromises, acknowledging shortcomings and mistakes, and working to correct them.

Proud people usually avoid this subject carefully: themselves, and more particularly their mistakes and faults. It will be difficult for you to live with such a person unless you dream of sharing your life with a manipulator.

8. Stay Faithful

To be faithful implies getting out of the excessive egotism that makes us prioritize our pleasure while ignoring that of the person we love.

A minimally empathetic person will quickly realize that if they would not want the other person to cheat on them, it is not acceptable behavior for themselves either.

If you claim to love the other person, deceiving them becomes the last thing on your mind.

Love is one of the richest experiences we have to live by through happiness and hardship. Why sully that with lies and unfaithfulness?

In short, romantic relationships are dynamic, like life, like those who live them. To live these enriching relationships, you must first come to recognize that your point of view is not the only point of view.

Only by trying to understand others do you come to build more fruitful relationships.

Respect, empathy and communication lead to more satisfying partnerships than the need to constantly be right.

Conflicts cannot be avoided in relationships. Two people who bring different life experiences to the table will inevitably have disagreements.

But when you strive to achieve your goals regardless of what the other person wants, you engage in behaviors that can only lead to a break-up. The challenge may be to bring different motivations together through common values, but you have a big tool to meet this challenge: communication.

To share your life with another person, basic wisdom requires you to make some sacrifices. When you do not communicate with your partner, even if the goal is to avoid conflict at all costs, you will only achieve even more disastrous results.

Regardless of whether you've been dating your partner for a short or long time, strong connections are formed when you accept the responsibility of making an effort and considering your partner's point of view.

While each relationship is unique, no relationship is impeccable. By doing these 9 things to improve your bond, you won't just guarantee a quality connection with your partner, you'll also demonstrate that you're resolved to work for one.

1. Ask Your Partner Something New

Communication is the measure of togetherness in a relationship. It's pleasant to ask how your partner's day went, yet it's exhausting when you ask again and again. Communication must not be boring or redundant, so it is your joint responsibility to keep yourself engaged with dialogues that are engaging and meaningful at the same time.

2. Assign A Month To Month Night Out On The Town

Despite your busy schedules, ensure that you plan a night when the two of you will spend time together. Be consistent and be devoted to it once you have agreed on a date with your partner. If you're hoping to zest up your relationship or want to try something other than Netflix, leaving the house is a far more promising endeavor. More memories are made out in the world than on your couch.

3. Express Your Appreciation

The solace that a relationship offers is the reason we will, in general, ignore what our partner does and treat their demonstrations of affection as mandatory. To put it truly, your partner doesn't need to fill your gas tank or purchase your preferred frozen yogurt. They decide to because they love you, and your recognition and appreciation of the gesture will strengthen your relationship and inspire your partner to continue to be attentive and make you feel appreciated.

4. Change Your Timetable

We know you're autonomous and don't anticipate ceasing your life for anybody (and you shouldn't need to). Even though you have different responsibilities outside of your relationship, it's a nice thought to check your calendars and see if conflicts are preventing you from spending time together.

5. Keep In Mind The Little Things

Another approach to add importance to your discussion is to genuinely tune in to what your loved one is saying and talk about it later on. If you need to, make note of something you talked about that you want to remember, or an event your partner mentioned that you want to follow up on. It's often the little things in conversations and relationships that make the biggest difference. Also keep in mind that everyday things, while being small, can contribute to the happiness in your relationship. Reminders that you love the other person, have listened to them, or are thinking about them all seem like small gestures, but they are powerful.

6. Demonstrate Your Love

Apart from appreciating your partner, you need to let them know the extent of your love for them. You express your love through different gestures, from holding your partner's hand at a café to hitting the hay together toward the night's end. These gestures do not only show how you feel about your partner, but they also indicate that you are proud and appreciative of them.

7. Get Familiar With Your Partner's Behavior

Does your partner wish to be left alone when they are vexed? How do they react in some specific situations? These inquiries are basic, however, the responses to them will enable you to comprehend the behavior of your partner and prevent you from offending them accidentally. The way your partner views the world is not the same way you do, so the way they act in situations will most likely differ as well.

8. Learn When To Apologize

You need to realize that being correct isn't as significant as being empathetic. Though clashes occur in a relationship, few arguments are a test that should be won. What I am trying to pass across is simple: know what is worth fighting for and when you need to accept the blame. It is better to say sorry than turn a small argument into a relationship-breaking crisis.

CHAPTER 23:

Healing Scars

Old Wounds Still Hurt

Everyone has a past, so, inevitably, some things that hurt us when we were younger will continue to do damage us regardless of how much time has passed. These wounds often represent times when we weren't in control of our situations, which sends a feeling of helplessness through us. These pains are dynamic and will hurt more during certain parts of our lives and less during others. Those hurts that once hurt you so deeply may be distant, but every so often, there's a pang of pain to remind you what happened. This pang of pain is often triggered by your fears and worsened if your hurts are unresolved. You have to learn about what still hurts you and how to address these things to find inner peace.

Trauma is something that happens to everyone at some point. Not everyone experiences debilitating trauma, but everyone is traumatized, at least mildly, by something, but what is trauma? The word gets thrown around a lot colloquially and because of this, it is often hard for people to identify what trauma is and if they have it.

Trauma is a broad term that refers to the emotional, cognitive, spiritual, social, and physical reactions to an event that felt threatening to one's well-being or that of a loved one. It can be caused by a single event such as a car accident, but that's not always the case. The trauma results from the body's nervous system reacting to these potential threats, which can cause a change in how we respond to other events that resemble the trauma. Because of what you experienced before, your body unconsciously reacts in ways it didn't before, which can be the difficulty with trauma: your body thinks it is protecting you when sometimes it's working against you.

There are three types of trauma: acute, which stems from a single event; chronic, which is from a repeated event that is endured over a long period; and complex trauma, which is a series of traumatic events of various natures. Some major types of trauma can include bullying or living in a violent environment. You do not have to have a condition like Post-Traumatic Stress Disorder (PTSD) to have trauma, but such conditions may result from trauma.

Unfortunately, lots of people experience some sort of traumatic experience before they reach adulthood, showing how childhood experiences can result in the formulation of pathological fears and anxieties. Many people experience additional trauma in adulthood. This trauma can include things like the death of someone close to you, violence, natural disasters, accidents, and anything that causes enduring distress and fear in a person. The first place to look for old wounds is in your childhood. Childhood trauma is all too common. According to the National Center for Mental Health Promotion and Youth Violence Prevention, before the age of four, twenty-six percent of American children have experienced some type of traumatic event. Additionally, among adults in the United States, sixty percent have said that they were victims of abuse or had dysfunctional families. Thus, it's indisputable that conditions during people's most developmental years will influence what they bring into future relationships. Those who experience abuse, for example, may end up in abusive relationships or themselves being abusive based on learned behaviors. Abuse victims also may not have learned how to communicate healthily in relationships. Further, those who are bullied in childhood, for instance, may suffer from increased anxiety and self-esteem issues that become part of their romantic relationships. The possibilities are endless. Even a parent dying when a child is young can create trauma that results in issues such as a fear of abandonment. For each anxiety listed, a childhood trauma could easily be at the root. Look at your family's role in who you are now.

Contemplate how your family dynamics have influenced your life. See how you are like your parents (or other parental figures). Identify the areas in which you strive to be unlike your parents. Doing so can give you insight into how you may be repeating your parents' mistakes in some ways but also how you are an individual and have the power to be your person apart from how you were raised. It's okay to carry on things your parents taught you and to love where you came from, but it's also okay to pick and choose what you want to keep as part of you. You get to decide how big of a role your family has in determining who you are. Use that power wisely and in ways that help you rather than hurt you. Consider past relationships, both romantic and platonic, but especially romantic. Think of all your failed relationships. If you're currently in a relationship, think of that one simultaneously and compare it to your past relationships, picking out how it is the same as past relationships and how it is better and worse in various respects. Evaluate all the things that have gone wrong in the past and the things that have gone right. Don't just blame the person you were with or take credit for all the good things that happened. Consider your own mistakes in those relationships and ask yourself how you could have done better. If you can, link your past relationships to your traumas. Journal about how you think your past has influenced the patterns you see in failed relationships. Take this knowledge and try to do better in your current relationship or future relationships. Reflect on your grudges. Keep in mind all the grudges you hold. Who are you most angry with? What parts of your past have created bitterness that you can't get over? Whatever grudges you have, there's a reason that you can't or won't let go. Those grudges can show you what triggers the trauma you've experienced in the past the most. For example, if your mom always yelled at your dad for not being a good enough provider and you've never forgiven her for that, being told that you're not a good provider may be extra painful for you. Alternatively, you may use those same words against your partner when you want to be extra cruel. Either way, your grudge is a sensitive spot for you, and knowing what makes you sensitive helps you control it and thereby protect your relationship.

Emotional Scars and Romance

Whatever your past is, it's bound to have an impact on your romantic relationships. Now that you've looked back and dredged up some of your past traumas and hurts, it's critical to look at how these things influence present relationships because they do have an influence. Sometimes, your past will have a good influence on your relationships. Lots of experiences create positive engagements with your partner, but for this purpose, we're going to focus on how emotional scars can cause dysfunction in relationships.

One of the most enduring influencers on future relationships is your attachment style. Your attachment style is often defined by childhood experiences. An attachment style is a way that you respond to your needs and the way you attempt to have those needs met. These attachments have a major impact on how people enter into relationships and are defined by past relationships, especially those from when you're very young. Try to determine your attachment style and your partner's for better communication and understanding between you both.

There are several styles of attachment. A secure attachment style suggests that a person feels safe to be independent and true to themselves without fearing abandonment. Meanwhile, an anxious preoccupied attachment usually represents people who are clingy and require their partner to make them feel whole. This person can easily come needy and will feel insecure about their partner's love. The dismissive-avoidant attachment type, conversely, will often become emotionally distant and push away their feelings. To protect themselves, they will detach rather than clinging to their partner; they seem apathetic, but they are merely trying to protect themselves from hurt. Finally, fearful-avoidant attachment is a blend between dismissive-avoidant and anxious-preoccupied; this type of person cannot keep their feelings away no matter how hard they try to be detached. They tend to be moody and unpredictable. They are ruled by their emotions and can swing between behaviors such as being clingy one minute and distant the next. Whatever your attachment style, be sure to understand your common behaviors and those of your partner so that you can address the negative qualities that could otherwise pop out and ruin your relationship.

Furthermore, your foundational experiences shape what your model romance looks like and the type of person you will seek out. If you grew up in a household where people didn't talk about their feelings or much at all, you might subconsciously seek that out. You may find a partner who doesn't like to say how they are feeling and end up frustrated by this behavior. It's very common for people to end up in relationships with people like their parents, which again has a connection to attachment styles and the formational attachments people make. Thus, while you aren't doomed to follow in your parents' footsteps, be aware of this tendency to repeat the love (or lack of love) you saw between your parents.

Moreover, trauma impacts your ability to fully engage in a relationship. Trauma can cause serious mental health issues such as depression, clinical anxiety, PTSD, substance abuse disorders, and eating disorders. With so much mental dysfunction that can result in trauma, trauma can make it hard to appreciate or enjoy the things that make you happiest. The cloudy haze of trauma shouldn't rob you of being committed to a person or make you unable to be a full participant in your relationship, but it can very easily do those things and leave you struggling to put your   life   together.
Even if you don't feel traumatized by your past, there's surely something that has shifted the way you enter and continue your relationships. Even if you're "over it" and have addressed your trauma, those things don't just go away. Hurts of whatever kind leave scars and change how you react to certain situations. Don't assume that just because you've forgiven people who have wronged you or moved on from the pain that the scared part of you is gone. That scared part will always be there and emerge when you least expect it. Know that it's okay to feel hurt every once in a while over things that you think you've moved on from. It's okay to have scars that never fully heal even if you can barely see them.

CHAPTER 24:

A Theory of Change

Conceptions of Human Personality

There are three distinct concepts of the human personality, that is, the autonomous, the verbal, and the social entity. All of these means different relations between the person and the group and different causality theories.

Change in a person is a logical reordering of human thought processes from the autonomous individual perspective. The cause of any personal improvement is a reasonable individual effort. That viewpoint is expressed in clinical psychology and psychoanalysis. A growing person has an inner desire to self-actualize from an articulate perspective, which is the cause of change. That view is based on humanistic psychology. The person is a cultural being from the perspective of social individuals, necessarily dependent on others, who grow a mind only in contact with others. From this viewpoint, it is difficult to distinguish individual change from a change in the groups to which an individual belongs.

Some defined the cycle of transition as the mechanisms of change that reflect a mid-level distinction between a full psychotherapy framework and the theory of the techniques. This description appears to describe more of what was called the treatment process.

Wanted: A wise and humble Counselor

The best counselors in the profession are not always those who are well known, but instead, those who still achieve perfection and flat out to work harder than anyone else. These counselors are actively asking what they are doing and why being brutally frank about their research and its outcomes. They also receive input from their clients and friends, asking for the most honest evaluations of what works and what doesn't. Most of all, they are always so modest that they don't seek recognition or the limelight but go about their remarkable dedication to peacefully helping others.

What, overall, makes a great counselor?

A truly great counselor combines all facets of successful therapy through masterfully establishing a relational relationship, instilling optimism, rapidly concentrating on realistic objectives, choosing evidence-based interventions wisely, optimizing incentives for out-of-session on improvement, and encouraging commitment and follow-up to care to ensure that recovery results are sustained long after termination.

A successful counselor is also an individual who is completely dedicated to the clients or students they represent. We know that professionally and socially, we have to be engaged in continuous development to become the best resource. They have the opportunity to see beyond the spoken word and understand what is happening in the life of a client or student in even the unheard words. A great counselor is someone who loves helping those they represent to get motivated by encouraging their clients and students to become problem-solvers for their lives. Finally, a great counselor works out of a position with a client by helping [that person] learn how to handle life by themselves through some daily mental health check-ups.

Great counselors also have a passion for supporting others. We have respect for those we support, and they understand their positions in the therapy process. Good counselors are always committed to the practice of therapy and recognize the value of professional unity. Concomitantly, excellent experts understand each other. We know their core values and beliefs and foresee precisely how their core values and beliefs impact the therapy process. Superior counselors always have fun and use good-natured and kind humor. Finally, excellent counselors show a degree of tenacity that fosters sustained client engagement, even when the therapy process is challenging.

The most useful skills to possess as a counselor are described below.

The ability to genuinely listen to the spoken and unspoken and an ability to build partnerships with a diverse clientele is highly valued.

Any other valuable skills or qualities that a counselor should possess are as follows:

a. Self-Awareness: Self-awareness, including behaviors, beliefs, and emotions, and the ability to consider how and what factors can affect you as a counselor

b. Empathy and Comprehension: The ability to put yourself in another's position, even if that person is different from you

c. Versatility: The ability to do so as a counselor to meet clients' needs so that a counselor can establish and maintain a therapeutic relationship and clients' benefit.

More than ten keys to being a better counselor:

1. Knowing what works in therapy research
2. Understanding what counseling is
3. Knowing how to intervene adequately
4. Capable of using the body as an instrument (the key weapon in the arsenal of the counselor)
5. Comprising your own emotions
6. Understand the main value of mourning and properly doing so
7. Proper self-disclosure (it's not about you,)
8. Silence is used and tolerated (especially for those who prefer extraversion)
9. Understand breathing's role in therapy
10. Trusting and feeling respect for yourself

The most overrated and underrated skill to have as a counselor:

Relationship-building skills are significant, but Freud has identified much of the link that leads to a successful marital relationship as transference. It is one of the toughest things new counselors can endure:

the conundrum of why they couldn't communicate with the client. Often the question of communicating has more to do with features (e.g., "You remind me of ...") than any ability or actions. Experience is what you receive when you unsuccessfully try something. Good advisors have much experience.

A fully Sensible, Tested, and Effective Approach to Helping Couples

The effectiveness of marital therapy is directly linked to the level of motivation and timing of both partners. Marriage therapy is divorced therapy for certain couples, as they have already thrown in the towel. For example, one or both partners may already have agreed to end the marriage, and he/she uses therapy as a way to disclose it to their spouse. The issues in a marriage can often be too deep and long-standing to be successful in therapy. For others, they aren't genuinely expressing their problems with the therapist.

Furthermore, finding a therapist who has experience working with couples and is a good match for both you and your partner is important. When the therapist may not feel secure with both participants, this can have a negative effect on progress; or one participant can drop out prematurely.

Timing is an important factor in the workings of marital therapy. Unfortunately, most couples are waiting too long to reach out for assistance in fixing their marriage. Couples are waiting for an average of six years of unhappiness before seeking support, according to some research. Think for a few minutes about the figure. Couples have six years to build up frustration before they start the essential work of learning to effectively overcome differences.

For starters as an example, Rachel and Jeff sat down on the sofa and started discussing their longtime feud over how to handle money and whether or not Rachel could go back to college and graduate from education so she could change jobs. They have the same dispute with no resolution over and over again, tell by Rachel, she has been working in the insurance business for ten years and hates her job, but Jeff is blocking her attempts to join a profession that would make her happier.

When it's Jeff's turn to offer his opinion on things, he says that they just bought a house and have two young kids. For Rachel, this is not a good time to get a degree. He helped her get through her undergraduate degree in her mid-twenties when they were first married, and she doesn't even know if she's going to enjoy becoming a teacher.

So the first step to helping Rachel and Jeff strengthen their relationship is to allow them to come to terms with identifying the biggest issue in their relationship and for both of them to take their actions on their own so that they can do better. They need to have reasonable expectations, though, as negotiating can be a challenge when both partners have busy careers and kids.

Partners must see conflict as an unavoidable part of a romantic partnership dedicated to it. After all, there are ups and downs in any relationship, and conflict goes with the territory. But couples may avoid confrontation because it may have meant the end of the marriage of their parents or led to bitter controversies. In romantic relationships avoiding conflict backfires. Bottling up uneven thoughts and emotions doesn't allow the partner the ability to improve their behavior. One of the secrets of a successful marriage or romantic relationship is learning to carefully select fights and to differentiate between small and important problems.

Others describe 'marital masters' as 'People who are so good at coping with conflict that they make marital squabbles look enjoyable.' Research shows significant disparities between couples whose relationships were successful and those heading for misery and/or divorce. It's not that some people aren't getting angry or disagreeing. That is why they can remain linked and communicate with each other when they disagree. They pepper their disagreements with displays of love, genuine curiosity, and mutual respect, rather than being aggressive and hurtful.

Tips to help deal with differences between you and your partner:

- Establishing a comfortable environment and frequently spending time with your partner so you can talk about your interests and goals is important.

- Don't give up on personal ambitions and stuff like hobbies or activities you want to do. This can only create frustration.

- Foster each other's passions. Agree that you are not always expressing the same desires. Value the need for space for your companion if they want to go on holiday without you, etc.

- Learn how to skillfully manage disputes. Do not set aside resentments capable of ruining a partnership. Couples seeking to avoid conflict run the risk of forming dysfunctional relationships, which can put them at high risk of divorce.

- Facilitate an open dialogue. Listen to the questions your companion has and ask for clarity on vague issues. Avoid threats and do not say things that you will later regret.

- Keep away from the "blame game." Take responsibility for your role in the issues and recognize that in some way all human beings are flawed. The next time you're angry with your partner, find out what's happening inside you, and pause and reflect before you accuse them.

- Be honest about changing timescales. It takes more than several sessions to shed light on the dynamics and initiate the change process.

How can marriage counseling help couples?

- Where dysfunctional relationship dynamics can be recognized early and decided upon, the actual change process will begin.

- With the resources offered by the therapist, an empowered couple may begin to discuss their issues from a different view and discover new ways of understanding and resolving disputes.

CHAPTER 25:

How to Handle an Insecure and Anxious Partner and Build a Healthy Interdependence

Being involved with somebody with issues of uneasiness issue can be upsetting. Once in a while, it can seem as though dread, somebody who wobbles among you and your companion is a third individual in the relationship. This individual consistently plants questions and vulnerability.

No one has set you up for it, and you can't decide for whom you fall. There is no secondary school dating class, considerably fewer chances of meeting somebody who is intellectually sick.

In any case, there is no requirement for tension to destroy the relationship or to make it hard to appreciate. You can cherish each other all the more profoundly by understanding apprehension when all is said in done and how it influences both your accomplice and your relationship. Training can likewise ease a lot of pressure.

The book separates all you have to learn and do when somebody is on edge to discuss: how to support your accomplice, how uneasiness can affect your relationship, scanning for your psychological well-being, and that's just the beginning. Continue perusing if you need to guarantee that your organization doesn't turn into a third individual.

Uneasiness Filled Conversation

If that you ask or reason it after month-to-month gatherings, there will be a moment that your accomplice unveils that they need to manage dread. It is a crucial time in the relationship. In this manner be delicate and don't pass judgment. Much obliged to you for confiding in you with this information, which you most likely didn't impart to numerous individuals. Consider it to be the beginning of a discussion that you can regularly reemerge.

How Anxiety May Affect Your Relationship

At the point when you are managing somebody who is anxious, your accomplice most likely invests a ton of energy stressing and ruminating over everything that may turn out badly, or as of now turn out badly. Recorded beneath are a few instances of musings and inquiries in the mind:

- What will happen if he doesn't adore me as much as I love him?
- What if he's concealing something from me?
- What will happen if she is misleading me?
- What will happen if he misleads me?
- What if he's going to swindle me?
- What will happen if she loves another person better?
- What will happen if we separate?
- What will happen if he phantoms on me?
- What if he doesn't answer my messages?
- What if uneasiness ruins our relationship?
- What will happen if I am just the first to connect?

A great many people have a portion of these stressing contemplations, at any rate. They are a typical piece of a relationship, especially another one.

Nonetheless, individuals with tension issues or an uneasiness issue will in general have this nervousness all the more, much of the time and all the more seriously.

"Our contemplations are dominating and heading straight into the direst outcome imaginable," said Michelene Wasil, a specialist who comprehends both individual and mental tension.

Nervousness causes physiological impacts, including brevity of breath, restlessness, and uneasiness. On edge, individuals can respond to worry with the battle or flight reaction as though stress were a physical assault.

At times upsetting considerations inspire your accomplice to act in manners that pressure and stress the relationship. For instance, clinician Jennifer B. Rhodes stated, individuals with uneasiness regularly check their accomplice's contribution with unbound methodologies. These procedures for the most part address one of their on-edge feelings.

Step By Step Instructions to Deal With It

Tension doesn't need to risk your relationship. You can have a sound relationship through the correct adapting methodologies and maintain a strategic distance from uneasiness by reducing the excessive pressure.

Urge your companion to meet with a specialist. At the point when you take care of somebody, you are enticed to help them by attempting to go about as a specialist. The issue is that you are not an advisor. It will be genuinely depleting to attempt to have that impact. It could cause your accomplice to loathe you.

You are not obligated to your accomplice's advising. That is the reason the accomplice ought to be deliberately coordinated to meet with a specialist. An advisor can assist them with improving their treatment of uneasiness all through a relationship.

If you have a genuine, long haul relationship, look for a treatment for couples. A portion of the issues of uneasiness can rely upon your relationship.

Meeting with two or three advocates will alleviate your accomplice from the strain. Rather than pushing them to accomplish something for themselves, you urge them to participate in directing.

If that your accomplice acknowledges or opposes your recommendation to go to treatment, you ought to do it without anyone's help. This causes you to build up the aptitudes expected to comprehend and manage the uneasiness of your accomplice. An advisor can likewise show you how to help your on-edge accomplice all the more viably.

It's anything but difficult to neglect to deal with yourself if you meet somebody with uneasiness. You can generally think about your psychological well-being by going to treatment.

Figuring out How to Communicate Better About Anxiety

Tension can be terrifying. You should ensure you don't consider it.

Notwithstanding, one of the best approaches to manage nervousness in a relationship is to converse with your accomplice transparently, truly, and legitimately about it.

"It is pivotal to have genuine discussions together about what they feel and to approve those emotions," says advisor Daryl Cioffi.

You have to urge your accomplice to open up to show their tension. Attempt to tune in, go to bat for yourself, or think about your dread literally.

Dealing with Your Reaction to Relationship Anxiety

It is anything but difficult to pay attention to it and blow up when your accomplice discusses their feelings of trepidation in your relationship. According to advisor Michael Hilgers, tension can be handily comprehended as selfishness, refusal, or a longing to isolate itself.

"You're going to need them to get over it," said Hilgers. "You'd like them not to consider it."

You can transform this inadequate default reaction into something progressively positive by rehearsing your adapting aptitudes. Here is a guide to enable you to rehearse: expect that your accomplice is anxious about the possibility that she will sell out you. At the point when you pay attention to this, possibly you feel that she has this instability since she loathes you or because she believes you're the thoughtful one who might swindle.

When you do it, you can start to feel disappointed. You may react protectively and state something important.

"You will possibly intensify the issue if you can't twist without tormenting," said Hilgers.

You're going to strike once more. Avoid forward one hour later, and you battle. The fact of the matter is gurgling. Maybe you don't have a clue why you battle.

Rather than causing the pressure race to up, pause for a minute to unwind. Note that most probable, the dread isn't about you. You're not the source. It's your accomplice. It's your accomplice.

Ask consciously what your accomplice feels. Something like, "I'm so sorry you feel like this. That must be extreme. Would we be able to effectively assist you in feeling progressively certain about that?"

It's more essential to deal with your responses than to deal with your accomplice," said Talkspace specialist Marci Payne. It can assist you with being there and defined limits for your accomplice. If that the dread of your accomplice makes you blow a gasket each time you bring it up, it won't help you.

CHAPTER 26:

Parenting with an Anxious Partner

Being in a relationship while affected by anxiety is difficult but having children under the same circumstances can be genuinely challenging. Keep in mind that children can make parents, however, those who are naturally anxious or suffer from a disorder will obsess over the safety of the child before it is even born. It is normal to feel a certain amount of concern for your children, whether it's for their health or security reasons. Many parents continue worrying about their kids even when they are fully matured and starting families of their own. Relationships change when children enter the picture. Various relationship anxieties may start developing, even ones that were never there before.

The term "helicopter parent," refers to parents who are always worried about their children and come to their aid at the first sign of distress. These parents usually experience intense anxiety because of all the fears that manifest when children are around. These parents obsess over their kids' safety and will aggressively seek to control every aspect of their lives to keep them safe and feel nurtured. However, there are other parenting-related anxiety symptoms out there, such as:

1. Criticizing your children no matter how well they do. This issue can even continue into the child's adult life, as the parents will continue criticizing his decisions and lifestyle. Keep in mind that "normal" parents will be critical regarding their children as well, but not on the same level as those who suffer from an anxiety disorder.

2. Some parents fail to display enough affection due to their anxiety. They don't smile as often as they should, and they always expect something to go wrong, which leads to even more worries and more stress.

3. They are more inclined to ignore a child's opinion or completely disrespect and even mock his or her point of view. These parents sometimes fail to encourage independent critical thinking.

None of this means that only parents suffering from various anxiety disorders are anxious when it comes to their children. There are many reasons to be worried, and most of them are due to the lack of control parents feel. If you find yourself worrying about your children all the time or stress over the future of your children, you could limit the kind of activities your family participates in. Many such parents think that they protect their children by excluding them from potentially dangerous situations when they are on average, in safe social settings. Behavior like this can be caused by anxiety, in some cases, and it is incredibly damaging for the parents and child. Now let's take a look at how parenting anxiety can even affect your romantic relationship.

How It Affects Your Relationship

As already mentioned, anxiety can severely impact your approach to parenting and the development of your children. However, your partner may also be affected if you are displaying overprotective behavior. Preventing your children from participating in social events with other children, allowing them to explore their surroundings and interests only inhibits their growth and ability to learn. Your partner may have a different view on child upbringing or education and disagree with what you find acceptable. This conflict in your relationship can ultimately affect your parenting and the child's development.

If your anxiety is causing so much friction between members of the family, think of the age-old words of letting kids be kids. Don't forget that anxiety is all about the dangers you perceive and imagine, and this doesn't automatically turn them into reality. The threat of your child getting hurt may seem real, and you may think you couldn't handle your emotions if something happened to them. It's fairly common for parents to overreact after a child gets hurt during an activity. Imagine your kid is playing soccer with his friends and he breaks his leg in the process. After such a high energy event, you will be tempted never to let him play soccer with his friends again because it's too dangerous.

Now let's discuss the conflict between you and your partner when one of you has a different opinion on parenting due to anxiety more. Imagine the following scenario: Your child wants to take his bike and go to his best friend's house, which is around half an hour away. He wants to go alone, of course, without a parent escorting him. Your partner knows where the friend lives and the route is perfectly safe, so he says yes and lets the kid go on his own. However, your answer to his wish is a resounding "No." He then goes to the seemingly more "reasonable" parent to get another confirmation and leaves. At this point, the child has established that one parent is much easier to convince and is more accepting of his plans, opinions, and wishes. The problem, however, is that you are now probably feeling anger or resentment towards your partner for not agreeing with you and going against your decision. Besides, you may also be experiencing even more anxiety because the thought of your child leaving on his own is frightening.

While always being on the same page with your partner is hard, they should be aware and understand your anxiety can impact decision making, especially when it comes to parenting. Both of you need to invest additional time in communicating with each other and learning how to compromise in various situations. You need to work together despite your anxiety because you're on the same team no matter what. If the two of you already are parents, you should take a step back and figure out all the differences and similarities you find regarding your parenting methods.

As an exercise, you should think about the upbringing of your children and the way you are going to raise them. You need to decide how willing the two of you are to allow your children to explore new things and how much freedom you offer them to be independent. Both of you should write down a list of all the situations you can think about and then write down how you would handle them. Once you have the answers, you can compare them to see the differences between your partner's parenting style and yours as well. You should pay attention to which parent the child seeks permission from when it comes to risky activities. For instance, if you are very anxious and protective of the child, he may seek your partner's approval when it comes to sports or going camping. Think of any such examples and write them down to discuss things with your partner.

Lastly, you should think about the way you react to any situation that involves your child and write down your behavior. You should then compare your actions to those of your partner's. Pay special attention to the circumstances that led to your child being hurt. Whether it's physical while playing a sport, or emotionally by being embarrassed or bullied at school. Write down everything you can think of and discuss it with your partner. Communication is key.

CHAPTER 27:

Avoid Blaming and Criticizing

I magine you're sitting down to a private conversation with a trusted confidant. The topic turns to your partner and all the things they do to annoy, hurt, and even infuriate you. When you launch into a long speech full of blame and criticism, you probably feel like you're talking about the failings of your partner.

However, psychologists and other professionals believe that listening to a person criticize and attach blame says more about the psychology of that person than the person they're talking about. Some psychology professionals even choose to listen to people who criticize others to help them form opinions on that person's potential psychological diagnosis. Even as far back as the late 1800s, Oscar Wilde said, "Criticism is the only reliable form of autobiography."

How Criticism and Blame Affect Your Relationships

No one likes to be criticized, and no one likes to be blamed for everything, especially things that aren't truly their fault. When your relationship is characterized by excessive levels of criticism and blame, it can only suffer as a consequence. Your partner will soon learn to become wary of sharing their thoughts, feelings, and experiences with you so they can avoid the blame and criticism that is likely to follow.

In many relationships, criticism starts as small, insidious comments, building swiftly over time to repetitive, ongoing, large-scale criticisms of the person as a whole. It does not take any stretch of the imagination to see how healthy relationships cannot survive in a cloud of blame and criticism.

How Criticism and Blame Affect Your Confidence

When you're criticizing someone, it may feel like you are voicing your complaints about a certain act or behavior exhibited by the other person. Instead, when these complaints come out in the form of criticism or blame, what you are doing is expressing how the other person's behavior made you feel devalued. In this way, criticism is a form of ego defense and is usually performed by people with low levels of self-confidence who are easily insulted. By constructively communicating your feelings rather than resorting to criticism and blame, you can bolster your sense of confidence while still letting your partner know how you feel about their behavior.

The Difference Between Shame and Guilt

People often use the words shame and guilt interchangeably, yet psychologists recognize that the two words refer to entirely different feelings. In simple terms, guilt is a feeling associated with acknowledging how our actions have affected others, while shame relates to how we feel within ourselves. The two words are often used interchangeably because there are many instances when one experience can bring up both feelings. However, there are important distinctions to be made between the two. For example, imagine you deliberately say something hurtful to your partner. Your words have the intended result, and your partner becomes upset. You will probably feel guilty when you see how your words have affected your partner. If you simultaneously feel bad when you realize that you intended your words to be hurtful, you might also experience feelings of shame from realizing that you're the sort of person who would seek to deliberately hurt your partner.

In psychological studies undertaken with young children (Drummond et al.), it was shown that children who felt guilty after breaking a toy were likely to act positively by trying to fix the toy. However, children who felt shame from breaking the toy were more likely to try to stop their parents from knowing what they had done by hiding the broken toy.

The Difference Between Criticism and Feedback

Seeking to avoid criticizing and blaming your partner doesn't mean that you should keep all of your feelings to yourself. The trick is to find ways of communicating your feelings to your partner without resorting to criticism and blame.

We know that guilt refers to feelings about other people, and feelings of guilt can cause a person to try to proactively fix what they have done. We also know that shame refers to feelings about oneself, and feelings of shame can cause a person to withdraw socially or try to hide what they have done.

With this in mind, it becomes important to communicate feelings of dissatisfaction to your partner in a way that focuses on their behavior rather than themselves as a person. For example, imagine your partner turned up late to an important function, causing you embarrassment. To criticize and blame would be to comment on your partner as a person. "You're always late. Why do you have to be so lazy and inconsiderate?"

A healthier way of communicating is to focus on the behavior and how it made you feel. "I felt embarrassed when you showed up late. Can you please try to be on time next time?"

The first example may cause your partner to feel shame, which we now know could lead them to withdraw or try to defend what they have done.

The second is a more respectful way of communicating and may cause your partner to feel guilty for what they have done, but not to feel bad as a person. With this approach, your partner is more likely to own up to their mistake and recognize how it made you feel. They are more likely to change their behavior if you communicate your concerns in a respectful way that helps them avoid feelings of shame.

Break the Blame and Criticism Habit with Confidence and Compassion

Blame and criticism can damage any relationship and can oftentimes prove fatal. However, it must be acknowledged that when you blame and criticize your partner, you are doing so usually as a misguided attempt at either creating a better relationship or protecting yourself from harm. Understanding that the underlying reason for your tendency to criticize and blame is a positive one and can help you to feel compassion towards yourself.

Remember that you are now in the process of building your self-confidence and trust that with increased levels of confidence you will be able to communicate with your partner in healthy ways without resorting to criticism and blame. By improving your confidence and increasing your compassion towards yourself, you will, in turn, increase your ability to communicate effectively without falling back into old negative habits.

Conclusion

A nxiety can feel like an additional individual in the relationship, an irritating element that pushes among you and your accomplice. The tension appears to perpetuate uncertainty and disarray in the relationship continually. Regardless of whether you are telling your accomplice that you experience the ill effects of nervousness, or getting some information about their tension, how the subject is examined can represent the moment of truth in a relationship. Individuals who experience the ill effects of nervousness invested a great deal of their energy stressing and envisioning situations in which everything without exception could turn out badly.

They over examine their connections, posing negative inquiries, and enabling the responses to reflect terrible results. While it is typical for individuals to have these sorts of considerations and questions now and again, nervousness intensifies them. Those with a tension issue consider these inquiries regularly and with power. Individuals with anxiety envision the direst outcome imaginable, enabling their psyches to assume control over their sound point of view. Musings cause physiological manifestations in the body. Uneasiness doesn't just influence the individual experiencing it. It can put anxiety on your accomplice and can pulverize a relationship.

Tension doesn't have to risk your relationship. At the point when you overcome your feelings and utilize the correct adapting systems, you can have a healthy relationship. These adapting systems will prevent uneasiness from also causing anxiety in your relationship. The duty regarding assuming responsibility for your feelings lies with you as the sufferer of uneasiness. You are seeing a specialist who can show you solid methods for dealing with stress that will improve your satisfaction in and outside of your relationship. If you are in a long-haul submitted relationship, you may consider heading off to a few couple's sessions to work through any nervousness that is present in your relationship. By doing this, you are easing the heat off of your accomplice and your relationship.

At the point when you have negative musings, anxiety takes steps to crush you and makes them cry that your life is loaded with misfortune. Be that as it may, the fact of the matter is your very own negative musings make you the cause of all your problems. At the point when you enable yourself to enjoy negative thoughts, you are making your misfortune. You have to turn out to be increasingly mindful again and hear the words as you express them to yourself to sift through the pessimism. When you can perceive the negative words and thoughts, you can stop and counter them with positive or elective messages. By being certain and hopeful, you can transform antagonism into truth, not fear.

Because things haven't turned out in different connections or you have been frustrated in the past doesn't imply that they won't be diverse this time. Pessimism doesn't need to be something you are tormented with until the end of time. You are the ace of your destiny, and when you change pessimism to energy, all of you, your hopeful standpoint radiates through your relationship.

Another issue that stems from low confidence and nervousness is desire. Desire can assume control over your life if you don't take a few to get back some composure on it and it can overwhelm you, it can be a terrifying feeling to feel. It can frequently destroy connections and propagate a negative idea. At the point when you enable envy to overwhelm you or to shape how you think about yourself or your accomplice, you are conceivably disrupting your relationship. By attempting to comprehend where your envious sentiments are originating from, figuring out how to manage them, and discovering approaches to adjust to your feelings, you are allowing your relationship to thrive. The individuals who experience the ill effects of uneasiness know about these dangerous musings experiencing your psyche, yet envy starts to frame when these thoughts begin to get fanatical.

The main problem comes in when those with uneasiness will, in general, retreat trying to shield themselves from the envisioned risk or torment that they believe is happening. Be that as it may, the more you retreat, the more removed your accomplice will become, and the more envious you will turn. By effectively chipping away at your nervousness and your jealous sentiments, you are making your relationship a need and deciding to love and close with your accomplice rather than desirous and unreliable. At the point when you choose to battle desire, you are intentionally telling your accomplice that you have a sense of security and are secure enough in yourself and them to place your trust in your relationship.

The most well-known indications of a relationship in a difficult situation are how the accomplices differ or battle with one another and how they settle the contention between them. Their goals, whether negative or positive, can influence the tone of the relationship and how clashes are taken care of later on. Contradictions that form into petty squabbling or on edge consistent clashes, as a rule, end up in a more uncertain possibility of the relationship enduring. Fortunately, there are arrangements, and settling strife can be moderately simple with the assistance of a specialist. If that you and your accomplice are not yet capable and the purpose of seeing a therapist, rehearsing sympathy without judgment will go far in settling strife. Sympathetic tuning in and proclamations should be possible by telling your accomplice that you are tuning in. Since as individuals, they experience the ill effects of tension that are commonly centered on themselves, they will, in general, contend such that it makes them like themselves. At the point when individuals practice compassionate tuning in and correspondence, they guarantee that their accomplice realizes that they are being tuned in to. Fortunately, it gets considerably more straightforward.

While building a compassionate proclamation, one should utilize, "So you feel that...." This maintains the emphasis on your accomplice and away from your sentiments of uneasiness. At the point when the two accomplices utilize this system to listen cautiously to the passionate needs of their life partner, it stays away from strife and addresses the more profound issues close by.

A specific degree of anxiety is something to be thankful for and inquire about and shows that great pressure can inspire and energize an individual in their lives. Nervousness can be only the admonition sign. You have to carry attention to your present circumstance and roll out some important improvements throughout your life. Consistent stress and anxiety can be a sign that a few parts of your life are off track and need altering. Even though your nervousness indications can be hard to oversee, by setting aside some effort to investigate and taking a shot at adapting to your uneasiness, it very well may be a genuine open door for self-development. Whenever tension strikes, think about what message it has for you and the potential changes you may need to make in your life. As opposed to continually being viewed as an obstruction, tension may assist you with feeling progressively inspired and arranged when looked at with difficulties.

Anxiety doesn't have to control your life or wreck your relationship. It very well may be utilized to fabricate a solid character and help with building up an impressive, regarded character. A solid character doesn't mean you should be boisterous, scary, or over the top to show your character. It is conceivable to have a solid character in calm certainty too. Uneasiness has its favorable circumstances. It sends a sign to the body that something is significant or could represent a peril to you. Having uneasiness about your accomplice shoes that you care for them on a more profound level, if you didn't encounter nervousness, you would most likely, at some point or another, find that you couldn't care less for your accomplice.

Intense tension should be abolished, however, particularly if you will probably push ahead into an important association with your accomplice. Although nervousness can't be relieved, it unquestionably can be controlled, and you as the sufferer of tension have a decision in whether you decide to participate in your very own negative conduct. Nervousness builds inspiration, reason, and satisfaction to a certain degree. Truly, we concur that it can feel dreadful, yet outfit effectively, nervousness can feature regions in our lives that we have to investigate. It urges us to roll out the improvements we have to make to carry on with a more joyful, increasingly happy life.

Take control of your anxiety today. Build a more grounded relationship and be a superior you!

JEALOUSY
IN RELATIONSHIP

THE BEST GUIDE TO OVERCOME JEALOUSY AND
USE IT TO STRENGTHEN THE RELATIONSHIP

MINDFULLY MANAGE YOUR FEELINGS TO GET
OVER YOUR TRUST ISSUES

PHILIP RELATION

Introduction

I n its basic sense, jealousy is an emotion that refers to feelings and thoughts of insecurity, concern, resentment, anger, or fear of something of personal value. It is often associated with and used interchangeably with envy. However, whilst being somewhat synonymous with one another, these two terms do have slightly different meanings.

Jealousy is commonly experienced in a myriad of situations, such as the workplace, between siblings, and within friendships, just to name a few. For this book, however, we will focus on the type of jealousy that is evident in romantic and intimate relationships. As this is the most predominant place you will encounter it. Let's be honest, this is where its debilitating hooks dig into us and do the most harm.

No one is completely immune to the green-eyed monster; it seems innate and natural within us all. It has been observed in babies as young as five months old! Researchers claim that jealousy is evident in all societies and cultures, regardless of environmental factors such as upbringing. In truth, jealousy is a complex emotion. It strikes both women and men alike, although is commonly thought to be a female trait. Again, it is usually aroused whenever an individual perceives a threat, real or not, to a valued personal or professional relationship from a third party.

Can Jealousy Be a Good Thing?

According to evolutionary psychologists, jealousy should not be suppressed entirely. It has to be considered as a wake-up call or signal. Anyone who experiences these feelings should be on high alert that a relationship may be in danger and that the necessary steps should be taken to assess the situation. In this sense, jealousy is a vital emotion since it maintains social bonds. Also, it motivates individuals to engage in behaviors that preserve important relationships. It's the canary in the coal mine, so to speak, which can signal that something might be amiss between you and your partner.

Dr. Helen Fisher, an anthropologist and author of the book Why We Love, states that a little jealousy can be healthy in relationships. It can serve as a reminder that your partner is attractive and that you are fortunate to have them. I'm not saying you should become submissive in any way, but a little gratitude for what you have can go a long way. But as per usual, it is the extremes in emotions that begin to hurt us most. It's when jealousy becomes chronic, overt, and debilitating.

Dr. Lauren Papp, a professor in human development and family studies at the University of Wisconsin, suggested that chronic jealousy is a huge red flag and that people should stop mistaking it for interest, care, or affection. Many people seem to believe that their partners are more interested or in love with them if they are possessive or jealous. The reality, however, is that jealousy is almost always a sign of insecurity.

What Causes A General Sense of Jealousy?

Many societies regard jealousy as a natural reaction to the sharing of something important or sacred with another person. However, this is a huge misconception. The real root of jealousy is not the sharing of special things. It's the feelings that these circumstances bring about. It's a sense that something has been lost or taken away from you. Jealous people do not want to share the things they perceive as valuable to them through fear of losing them. It's a protective mechanism that typically backfires on the person sooner rather than later.

In a romantic relationship, this "special thing" is typically the other party. For instance, a woman may become jealous when she sees her spouse giving another woman attention. Likewise, a man may become jealous when he hears his girlfriend profess positive things about another man. In these instances, the affected partner sees the other individual or the third party as a threat.

Below are some of the most common causes of jealousy:

1.   Fear

Indeed, jealousy is heavily rooted in fear. However, there are various forms of fear we must address. In romantic relationships, the constant worry of losing a new partner is frequently experienced. For example, a woman who has been cheated on by an ex-husband may become highly cautious with her new partner as she fears that the same incident might happen again. She displays jealous behavior because she does not want to lose her new partner.

2.   Insecurity or Lack of Self-Confidence

If you do not believe you are worthy of being loved in return, you may believe that your partner will always want to be with someone else. This can occur due to low levels of self-esteem and self-confidence, which are almost always developed in childhood. You may have grown to be insecure due to unsupportive, unloving, or a lack of caring parents when you were young. You may have also grown up in an environment wherein people often tried to mock or belittle you. Don't worry, we will explore the notion of raising the overall self-esteem later in the second part of this book, as it is critical for overcoming jealous behavior.

3.   Comparison

This concept also ties in very closely with a general sense of insecurity and lack of self-confidence. A person who constantly compares himself/herself with other people is likely to become jealous much easier. Likewise, a person who often feels that he/she is not good enough can grow to resent the people whom they believe are better than they are.

How to Deal with Jealousy

The latter part of this book will deal more thoroughly with the practical steps one must adequately deal with chronic jealously effectively. For now, let's just say that during these situations, you and your partner need to have a serious and frank conversation. You have to assure one another that loyalty and commitment must be front and center within the relationship. It is important to address any problems or misunderstandings from the outset.

Besides, you have to take note of any signs that may indicate an abusive relationship. If you notice these red flags, you must evaluate your situation very carefully and decide whether to solve the problem or perhaps move on. Sometimes, exiting the relationship is the best option. You have to get out of a potentially harmful situation before it gets out of hand.

Indeed, jealousy can sometimes be justified. For example, if you cheated on your spouse, then you can expect him/her to have a hard time trusting you again. Then again, even though infidelity has already played a role in your marriage, you should still refrain from being controlling. You should not display any jealous behavior, as this will just make your relationship worse.

You and your partner can either choose to save your marriage and start over or file for divorce. For many folks, ending the relationship is the easier option. They can find peace of mind as they no longer have to suffer trust issues with the same person. For others, having a mature conversation and saving the relationship remains the preferable option as they may have children and shared properties, for instance. You should never stay with someone for these reasons alone, but they can be deciding factors in whether to give things a second chance.

Even though the trust is gone, you can bring it back again with a little work. To do this, you need to evaluate the behavior of your partner and determine if this person is truly trustworthy and worth a second shot. You have to examine his/her history, such as incidents of cheating. You have to determine if your partner is the kind of person to always find an excuse for their behavior or does not show remorse. If they do these kinds of things, then they may not be worth the effort.

See to it that you evaluate your decisions very carefully in this respect. You have to determine whether to push through or just quit the relationship. Your state of mind is very important, and if you cannot trust your partner, then you will always feel insecure and jealous.

Refrain from playing mind games as they do nothing but further reduce the trust in the relationship. It will simply ensure that your partnership will worsen over time. Bear in mind that relationships need two people to function properly. If you are constantly playing mind games, you undermine the very nature of what you are trying to achieve. The whole must be greater than the sum of the parts. So don't self-sabotage the bond you are creating by continually second-guessing one another.

Refrain from letting your imagination run wild. For instance, if your spouse comes home late, don't immediately assume that he/she went out to see the "other" party. But rather give your partner the benefit of the doubt, afford them time to explain where they were. Do not assume the worst in every situation. Avoiding negative thinking spirals is imperative to healthy and functioning relationships.

A wild imagination can be highly damaging to your partnership. So try to remain grounded and realistic. If your significant other has always been loyal to you, then you should listen to their explanations.

In addition to this, you should refrain from becoming too possessive. Always be aware that your partner is still his/her own person. Even though you have a common bond, you still do not own the other person. He/she may live their life on their terms. Enough space is critical to maintaining affection and attraction between one another. Each body is connected in an everlasting orbital dance with one another, but with enough space to continually view the others' wonder.

With that said, you should not prevent your partner from doing the things they love to do, such as pursuing their hobbies and interests, as well as maintaining friends and associates outside of your shared social groups. Again, this aids in providing that slight but essential breathing space between the two of you, illustrating the fact that you are still indeed individual people. If you choose to share everything at the end of the day, that is up to you.

However, it is not acceptable to become upset over trivial things. If you become jilted over these instances, you simply become fearful, insecure, and jealous for no reason. You may start to exhibit unreasonable and controlling behaviors. You need to be very self-aware in this respect and notice your thinking patterns and actions. You also have to educate yourself on how to control your emotions.

CHAPTER 1:

Understanding Jealousy

J ealousy has its mind. When we're angry, thoughts and emotions sometimes hijack us, which makes us think we're unraveling, that our world is falling apart, and that something needs to be done right away. We think we need the answer right now because we believe that unless we get rid of them immediately, our feelings will intensify and our partner will betray us unless we control things right away. The alarms go off, blaring and making us confused. We are put off by the jealous mind's emotions and feelings.

To warn us about our needs and any risks to our wellbeing, all our emotions have developed. As mentioned earlier, jealousy is an established and nuanced emotion that has been preserved because it ties in with our need to protect our genetic property and to ensure that offspring have the best possible security and support. But when our thoughts and emotions are strong, we don't think about this, or even about the truth. We react to the primitive and strong alarm in our brain. We get abducted.

Our threat-detection mechanism is triggered when we are jealous. We're searching for some indication that our partner may be interested in someone else, or anyone else might be interested in him or her. We see others as imminent threats, and the ambiguous thoughts and emotions of our partners are potential signs of deception. Our minds are committed to seeking clues, no matter how tiny and subtle they can be.

Here, when we are in jealousy mode, we can discuss how our minds function, which is a mixture of emotions, feelings, actions, tactics, and interactions that sometimes work together. Our threat-detection program activates the *Envy Mode* when it decides that something may happen. When we're caught up in the *Jealousy Mode*, we're having a hard time getting away. Our feelings are growing up. When Jealousy Mode is triggered and the show going, it has dramatic consequences like taking things personally, reading things in mind, forecasting catastrophes, adding unrealistic expectations and laws to our relationship, triggering anxiety as a way to cope with the unpredictable, and focusing on all the negative things, imaginary or real that our mind can dredge. As a result, we get nervous, irritated, frustrated, and depressed.

The jealous mind has four parts: core values, rule-books, critical thought and concern, and rumination. Each part enhances the others, keeping us trapped in a framework that does the following: retains and elaborates the initial threat detection; magnifies the relevance of events; guides us to confirm our fears and keeps us stuck in wondering what could happen or what we think has happened. Let's look at each of these components in more detail.

Core Beliefs

We have the core beliefs that drive our selfish thought about ourselves and others. Core beliefs are generalities which explain the way we think things. They establish unconscious prejudices of which we are often unaware. This central conviction is the prism you see the world through, but you never know you're wearing a mirror. Imagine all the time wearing dark sunglasses, which make them look dimmer and darker than they are. When you don't know you've got those glasses on, you end up believing the world is just dark. That is what a basic belief does. It's a lens that biases the way things are seen. You should have put your mask of envy on. You can see anything via the prism, and very little light or positivity will get you through. You get your view blocked out.

When Beliefs Appear as Facts

Our opinions and feelings may be mistaken for reality. Sometimes it happens. Here's an example of how that's going. Say you're in a strange city and that's late at night. You are alone as you head back to your house. Nobody else is on the street. Then, behind you, you hear two people walking at a fast pace. You think, "These guys will mug me, they might even kill me." Your dangerous mindset causes you to become increasingly nervous and scared, you walk faster, and fear you might not make it.

The initial facts are the same in both cases; being on the highway, late at night, with two strangers walking faster behind you. What's important is the understanding of the truth, whether they are harmful or not. Our definitions may be either accurate or incorrect.

We sometimes view our feelings as though they were facts when we're nervous, frustrated, or sad. The thoughts surface in your mind and you then come to conclusions: your partner has to be involved in someone else, he or she is going to betray you and you are no longer cherished or special. But not all ideas are real, and you do not know until the details are checked out.

Is a Core Belief a Fact?

When we're angry or nervous, our feelings are sometimes viewed as though they were real. Our conviction that we are right becomes evidence. Yet believing anything to be true doesn't make it that way, and our faith isn't proof.

Identify the core values that float in your head, leading to envy. Then look at the evidence and reasoning for determining the truth. You may be right about whether your partner is intending to cheat, or you may be wrong.

Core beliefs that contribute to jealousy are negative thoughts that we treat as being real. Here are some which are that.

When you have a fundamental conviction that you are not lovable, then you might be afraid that your partner will find someone more desirable or fascinating than you.

You may think you cannot take care of yourself: you need someone else or you don't think you can be happy on your own. This core conviction will cause you to be deeply afraid of losing a person who cares about you or is a friend.

Many people have a fundamental conviction that they are unique and special, or superior to others. With this view, you see others as threats to your position and you think, "If my partner is involved in someone else, then that means I'm not unique and exceptional."

Core Beliefs about Other People

We should have other people's core values too. One main belief is the people are judgmental. This can lead to envy because you think the relationship would be undermined by any negative decision your partner may have. You keep the impossible quality your partner wants to like about you. Additionally, this emphasis can lead you to believe that your partner and others constantly think you're inferior. With a central belief in other people's harshness, your self-esteem is weak when you believe that if someone doesn't like something about you, then you have to be inferior or unwanted. Based on how you think other people are judging you at any given moment, your self-esteem goes up and down.

Looking for Confirmation Rather Than Facts

Confirmation bias is a result of core convictions. This is our unconscious propensity to pursue evidence that supports our pre-existing convictions. We're never aware of this bias, it's our minds on autopilot, looking for information in the world that shows we're correct.

Memory also targets knowledge that confirms our core beliefs. When people are depressed, they selectively recall disappointment, rejection, and deceit. Our memories are guided by current moods and negative beliefs. The same applies to our core convictions about ourselves; we selectively recall knowledge that is consistent with an assumption that we are not lovable or important, or capable of sustaining ties. It's not because we intend to suffer. This happens because our mind works in an automatic mode.

The same tendency to affirmation functions when we think about others. For example, if you believe others are untrustworthy, you can selectively note and remember information suggesting other people are lying, cheating, and manipulating. I've heard both men and women share fundamental views that "Men can't be trusted" and "Women can't be trusted." Of course, to support your negative opinion, you can find proof from both men and women, but you can also find a lot of proof against it.

Our minds have not developed to care about averages or baseline rates, that is, the number of people who are trustworthy and real. We put a much greater focus on information that has a story and image.

We also depend on biased, unforgettable information which is an anecdote and is important to us personally.

Where Do These Beliefs Come From?

Here are a few common ones that fuel jealousy.

When we are surrounded by untrustworthy, invalidating, and deceitful individuals, we're likely to build a core conviction that individuals can't be trusted.

If we are told that appearances are all, then we may develop a core belief that the only thing that keeps the relationship together is being attractive to our partner. It can lead to envy when we believe our partner considers someone else attractive because we have to be the most desirable person to him or her and, therefore, our partner will assume that we are the only attractive person.

Our parents' lack of attention may contribute to the core assumption that we aren't interested in. We may internalize the concept of not being desirable or lovable, which leads us to mistrust the people with whom we get involved.

Talk about your core values, about yourself and others. Are there any prominent patterns? Can you recall how your childhood memories or memories over your entire life span might have reinforced those beliefs about yourself and others?

CHAPTER 2:

Types of Jealousy

J ealousy is not a single emotion. It's a mixture of several strong, confounding emotions, such as rage, anxiety, fear, frustration, anticipation, helplessness, hopelessness, and regret. In reality, someone in a romantic relationship may feel jealous about perceived infidelity while feeling sexually aroused about the infidelity's fantasy too. We get baffled because we prefer to assume that we can only have one emotion at a time. Plus, passion is in the mix. The painful negative feelings will mingle with our positive love feelings. We want to feel only one way, positive or negative, but we have all kinds of emotions, sometimes coming in waves, which also overpower us.

There are three main categories that jealousy could be classified with: normal, delusional, and abnormal. There can be labels attached to these classifications as well, depending on the situation when it is felt.

Delusional Jealousy

Delusional jealousy is a kind of jealousy that has no basis and sometimes results from conjured images in the jealous person's imagination.

Abnormal Jealousy

Abnormal jealousy is then described more accurately as pathological or psychotic, depending on how severe the feeling is. This is manifested by actions such as excessive monitoring, stalking, repeatedly calling, and monitoring social media accounts. If not controlled, this can be a cause for a more severe problem.

Normal Jealousy

Normal jealousy is manifested by reacting to a real threat that can and should be resisted. Normal jealousy can further be broken down into different kinds. These are:

Family Jealousy

This is a type of jealousy that takes place within families. Most of the time, family members compare themselves to another member. Sibling rivalry is one significant example of family jealousy; for younger kids, it could be about two kids who want the same toy, and for older kids, this could be about the comparison of accomplishments made and achieved. It could also take place if a member of the family has special needs (i.e. disability), resulting in him/her to feel as if s/he is deprived of love and attention.

Romantic Jealousy

This type of jealousy is said to be the type that is most commonly felt by romantic couples. It has been said that jealousy is one of the reasons why couples fight for the first time. When two people enter a romantic relationship, they share a strong romantic bond, and they feel like nothing, or no one can come between them. Thus, when a perceived threat arises such as suspected infidelity and cheating, insecurities can occur, leading to jealousy issues.

Friendship Jealousy

This type occurs when a friend gets threatened by the presence of a new person entering their friendship. The jealous friend is afraid he will lose the bond in case the other person is valued more. The causes are similar to those of other relationships: feelings of competition, fear of being substituted by another, and feelings of comparison.

Work or Power Jealousy

This typically takes place in the workplace, wherein an employee feels jealous of a colleague about a work-related issue such as a promotion or a salary raise. Jealousy may take place if the employee thinks he has worked harder and feels that he deserves the promotion or raise more than his colleague.

Jealousy Gets Boosted by Social Media

Social media gives us all the ability to feel like we've been snubbed, ignored, or left to fend for ourselves, while others seem to enjoy the friendships and relationships we've always desired for ourselves. We are asking ourselves: "Why wasn't I invited to this party? Didn't I get tagged for a reason? If only I could afford to fly as he does." When Paul looked at Ron's Facebook posts, he found that Ron was on a boat trip with Larry, Ken, and Nancy, enjoying themselves without Paul. He burned with anger and felt publicly embarrassed, reminding him that he was left out again.

CHAPTER 3:

How Jealousy Becomes a Problem

Chronic Infidelity Persists

Is your relationship falling apart? Cajoling your partner around obstacles is easy if you both agree on the thing that is bothering you. It is simple to see that if a person is not true to his or her partner, meaning they have a liaison with someone else at the same time they are in a relationship with you, it is a difficult situation to resolve. For some people, living with double standards may be a routine thing. But, for most people, it is not the proper thing.

Take a Reasonable Stance

One doesn't eat from two tables or wear two pairs of pants at the same time. Infidelity gets encouraged in certain segments of society, such as among those who practice polygamy. If you belong to those segments, it is alright. But, for the common man, such occurrences cause pain. So, what would you do if you got into a relationship with an unfaithful woman? There is nothing you can do, and that is why you must have a deep discussion with anyone you wish to become friendly with.

Suppose the partner doesn't stop seeing the other person, then it is time to put a stop to it by breaking off your commitment. Sometimes it is not what you gain but what you lose that makes your life better. If you can find a way to lose that unwanted outsider, it will help you.

Cannot Hold Frank Conversations

One mustn't ignore the elephant in the room. When you are talking about a specific thing, your partner is busy doing something that is contradicting what you are saying. It may not be enmity that made him or her do that. Instead, it might be that they did not pay attention and may have misunderstood what you meant.

Your Partner Avoids Issues That Need Clarification

Discussing things with your partner becomes difficult sometimes. Your partner doesn't want to hear what you say. There are many issues that you do not wish to discuss with your partner and so you keep avoiding these topics. When you converse, you steer clear of these touchy subjects and so the conversation remains stilted. Your manner of speech becomes furtive and you often resort to calumny to show your disapproval of your partner and his or her actions.

Partner is a Narcissist

When one is always posting selfies and building their image, the person is a narcissist. Having a relationship with such a person is tough, you will need to bend over backward at times to accommodate him or her and their ego. These days anyone who is vain and selfish will get categorized as a narcissist. In normal cases, narcissistic relationships occur when a partner displays some sort of narcissistic behavior that troubles the other. They suffer from an inflated sense of their importance and cannot directly relate to ordinary things as other people do.

Dealing with NPD Relationships

About 1.5% of the population suffers from Narcissistic Personality Disorder (NPD). Many of them do not seek treatment, and so they do not come within the collected statistics. The challenge of those in this kind of relationship is that the person with NPD doesn't recognize the other person as a separate individual. So they are not able to relate to their needs and feelings.

You cannot do much to influence the relationship without curing the person of the malady. One will have to put up with a certain amount of abuse because they lack empathy for others. By turning the orientation of the person from self-esteem to self-compassion, it becomes possible to cure narcissism. Here the concept of shared humanity is the healing factor.

Lack of Appreciation

What is the best thing about two people in a relationship? Appreciation and tolerance are concomitant aspects of any relationship that helps it grow. We have seen how a lack of tolerance can stem from hatred and taking a shortsighted stance on the matter of dealing with your partner. If there is no contempt from either partner, it might still not work out. This might happen when the partners do not take the time to show each other their appreciation.

The Sound Of Music

One needn't be effusive in their show of allegiance to each other, but one must make the effort to vocalize their appreciation clearly. Isn't it a wonderful thing to hear good things about yourself? Say things like, "That is well done!" Or even things like, "How terrific you are to help me do that," and "I wouldn't know if I could ever manage here without you" as often as you can. This will help the partner realize their importance and value the work they do.

Keep the Relationship Strong

Lack of appreciation is one of the main reasons why couples break up. Consider this: your partner doesn't mention a word of appreciation when you do something, but all those around you compliment you on the work you do. This kind of behavior will tend to erode the respect one has for the other. Look for the answer to what a relationship is and work on it. Make it a point to say one nice thing about your partner once in an hour at least.

Sex Drives Remain Incompatible

Having a partner with low or incompatible sex is a sure-fire way to kill any relationship. If the libidos don't match, the women are the first to leave the relationship. And, at times, people with hormonal imbalances and hyperadrenalism might show high sex drive. When libidos mismatch, sex life goes haywire.

Sex Is Important In a Relationship

When you are into a relationship and find that you want more sex but are unable to get it, you can become very frustrated. Resuscitating the relationship would seem to be like rolling a boulder up a hill. If it is difficult to get out of this abysmal relationship, one must mend it. The way forward is to break up your sex times into two zones (morning and night) so you get your satisfaction and your partner is not stressed by the activity. The obvious solution is to avoid getting into such a bind in the first place. That is, get out when you see a huge incompatibility in your sexual activities. Discuss a wide-ranging list of sexual activities including light touching, kissing, and intense sex acts. If the other person is in your range, she (or he) will make the correct responses.

Dealing with Money

Money problems can become a huge conflagration that has the potential to burn down your entire marriage. The issue of mine, ours, and yours becomes blurred when money comes into the picture. You will have to spend money and being in a relationship is not going to change anything. The money will create more complications because now one person has to take responsibility.

Avoid the Mercenary Attitude

If one is in a relationship for the money alone, his or her cupidity is obvious to all who see them. When you don't work out the mechanism for payment properly, resentment over each thing they buy will grow over time until the relationship becomes inept in handling the emotional and psychological burden. Being demure about the issue will not solve them. This does not mean that one must go on and on about the problem with money. Rather, one must devolve an amicable solution and stick to this method throughout the relationship.

Boredom Kills the Relationship

Boredom inhibits creativity and the right way to deal with it is by showing initiative. When two people have done the same things over and over again, both of them get tired of it. You need some kind of heckler to upset this cycle of systemic boredom. You want the joker in the pack to give your romantic interaction the edge it deserves. Dull conversation, boring sex interludes, and both partners getting tired of each other - the stage when you need a diversion has arrived.

First Off, Stop Being Lazy

You know how it is, you don't do something because your partner can predict your move. Then you don't do it because you know what her reaction will be. There is nothing wrong with repetition, most couples thrive on it. They build up interesting side-acts that fit in with the main theme. Taking the time and effort to create these sideshows takes some doing. But one can do it. When you see how well it works, you become inspired to do more and more things with your partner. It is like making an omelet and adding breadcrumbs the first day, tomatoes, the second, and so on until you arrive at a whole new dish altogether, but you must try it sometime and the best time to start is now.

Condition Your Mind

Reorient your mind to accept that you two are inseparable. Each cannot live without the other, you are the moon to his sun, or she is the wave to your ocean. When you get bored, sing a song. It helps reactivate the brain that is going down the drain. Go for a movie, check what's on the television, and catch a show together. Move your mind from its present lethargic state and take the boat to the excitement waiting for you. It will happen only when you get ready for new things—when you accept the change. It will not happen if you sit and meditate on the past alone. Make up your mind to move on and to go towards better things. Life is tough for all couples, so take it in your stride.

Coping with Children

Children are in the formative stage of life, and they do not know how to behave in most scenarios. Decision-making takes up all their creative energy if you do not guide them. Now, you are also facing problems in your relationship and you must have the freedom to make choices at important junctures. Marriage doesn't take the romance out of the relationship when you have kids. Partners relish the idea of teaching their children, reaching out to them to mold them into becoming the right kind of citizen they would be proud of.

Stress on the Parents

Relationship woes might stop one (or both) of the partners from interacting properly with the children. About 92% of couples feel some sort of conflict while raising children. In about 13% of these cases, the couples filed for divorce or separation. Now, this needn't happen at all. All it takes is the right method of dealing with the crisis. The stress build-up is normal when you have an extra member of the team. Give this member the extra space they want and then take it from there.

Helping Children Survive

Children develop a secure and healthy attachment to happy parents. This promotes the linguistic, emotional, and mental well-being of the child. Most of the time, when the child needs help with some idea or word, they imitate their parents and try to form words that their parents use. When you spend more time with the kids, the development is better, and it helps make the relationship strong. Both the partners realize that the child and the relationship need both people.

CHAPTER 4:

Steps to Overcome Jealousy in a Relationship

The first step to overcoming jealousy is accepting that it exists in the first place. It isn't surprising that many people cannot even admit that they have jealous feelings. They can't even admit it to themselves, which is an issue. You know the signs you experience, the anger and unrest you get whenever you feel your relationship is threatened. You know that you have these seemingly exhausting jealous feelings, so you must confront these emotions.

Factors You Should Accept About Jealousy

Accepting that you are jealous is a fact. There are other facts that you need to accept as well before you can begin working on your jealousy.

Jealousy won't disappear overnight: Do not make the false assumption that your jealous feelings will suddenly dissipate into thin air. Recognize that the jealousy is present, and you need to learn how to deal with it without allowing it to take over your beautiful life and relationship. This is a feeling that has probably resulted from an underlying problem with your confidence or self-security. Realize that it might take some time for you to learn how to deal with this feeling. You might have to do a lot of work on yourself before you will finally begin to feel in control of your emotions again.

You have to confide in your partner about your jealousy: Remember that the object of your jealousy is your partner, and they are probably not comfortable with the signs of jealousy they see in you. They might have even tried to reassure you that you have them all to yourself. But it still doesn't diminish these jealous feelings. So, why not talk to them about your feelings instead of expressing anger or frustrations or blaming them for something that might be in your head? Remember that you love this person. So, have that talk with them where you refrain from putting any blame on them but try to be as open as possible. You can say something like "I have these jealous feelings whenever I see you chatting with ___(another person)___. I know I shouldn't feel this way, but I can't seem to help it. I will love for you to help me with dealing with these feelings." An understanding partner should be able to treat the issue as if it was another challenge the relationship was facing and not leave their partner to sort things out all by themselves. You and your partner now need to accept there is an issue of jealousy that needs to be resolved. Hopefully, with your partner's full support, you can begin to take positive steps towards working on jealousy.

Make room for jealousy: As hard as it may sound, we all need to make room for some jealousy in our lives, especially in love relationships. We need to realize life itself is complex, as are relationships. We wish only to experience good times but are forced to realize we face bad times. Your beloved partner will sometimes annoy you, frustrate you and even drive you nuts. No one gets rid of their partner because they made them angry. You probably could do that to someone else who means absolutely nothing to you, like a random stranger on a train who stole your seat. But when this deals with someone you love and are probably committed to, you must learn to deal with their emotions, which, unfortunately, might include some jealousy on occasion.

Now we understand the different reasons why jealousy can occur in a relationship, and acceptance is key to tackling jealousy and dealing with it in general. We will now look at more practical ways to overcome these feelings that have been invading your mind and relationship.

Step 1: First, Identify the Cause of Your Jealousy

Jealousy doesn't act on a person like that, and by now you should understand that your partner may be the object of your jealousy, not the reason. Something they do or say can indeed trigger your jealousy, but you can't blame them for these feelings if you genuinely want to overcome jealousy. The reason for your jealousy has to do with you fundamentally, and it is time to determine the cause. I have put together a few important questions you can answer. Hopefully, your honest answers will lead you to pinpoint the exact cause of your jealous feelings towards your partner. These questions have been divided into different categories according to what I have found out to be the leading causes of jealousy.

Step 2: Acknowledge Your Jealousy

If you have been able to identify what's causing your jealousy (i.e., insecurities, low self-esteem, fear, or doubt), then that's great! We can now move on to the next step of overcoming jealousy. If you are still unsure where the jealousy arises, then hopefully after this stage you should have got it right. Then you can properly learn to deal with these feelings. Here we will look at acknowledging your jealousy in an efficient and workable way; through writing.

Experts in psychology have over the years used this method of writing about feelings like anger, worry, pain, and unforgiveness to help individuals confront their thoughts and emotions so they can face them properly. It is also a way of positively motivating yourself and feeding your mind with the kind of feelings you want to have or the kind of person that you want to be. For example, a person that believes they are not good-looking can write down somewhere visible in a positive way they would instead look at themselves.

Writing down statements like "I am beautiful inside and out," "I am an attractive man/woman," and "I am a unique person" and reading them to yourself every day can help gradually build your low self-esteem and help you become more confident. This approach can also work for jealousy if you can honestly write about your feelings. It will reveal to you the extent to which your jealousy is affecting your relationship. So, get a writing pad and paper (or whatever works for you) and get started.

Step 3: Turn Your Jealousy to Pride

"Jealousy is not you, and you are not jealousy," says Robert Leahy of the book, "The Jealousy Cure." He also explains that you can view jealousy like a breath of air, which we inhale and exhale without even paying attention to it. This means that jealousy can be something that enters and leaves our minds. The problem arises when jealousy remains in our thoughts and starts to gain control. Jealousy should be viewed as an emotion, which can come and go like anger or hurt. You can't continue to feel angry all the time, can you? It goes away eventually, and so can jealousy.

Let us look at how to channel jealousy into a more positive feeling like pride. Pride in this sense means instead of feeling all the anger and resentment towards your partner, you begin to see the good about them and you are proud of them and your relationship. Pride here also means countering your jealous thoughts with more positive energy and feeling.

Here are some more pointers on how to turn jealousy into pride:

Step 1: Be Confident In Yourself All the Time

Enough can never be said of how the lack of, or low self-confidence, brings about jealousy. So, become confident. Believe that you are enough for your partner and that they understand. Remind yourself of the great features that you possess and why your partner is lucky to be with you. If you don't blow your trumpet, who will? So, tell yourself over and over again. "I am a handsome/beautiful, funny, hardworking, and a great partner." Simply put, love yourself! If it helps, then write these positive statements down to remind yourself and tell yourself every time you find that you are caught up in jealous thoughts. Invest in reading motivational books that can boost your confidence if you find this helpful. It is unlikely that jealousy can dwell in your mind for a long time if you are confident in yourself.

Step 2: Stop Comparing Yourself to Others

Remember that everyone is unique in their way, so please stop comparing yourself to that guy/lady your partner might be chatting with. No one can be you so believe in yourself. Comparisons can create envy and jealousy. No need to state this again; be proud of yourself. And when jealous thoughts begin and you think "It's because I don't drive the kind of car that he does," "I am not as pretty as she is." Counter those thoughts with "His car is great, and my car is good enough for me now, I worked hard to get it," "I am an intelligent and attractive woman."

Step 3: Believe In Your Partner

Have some faith in the partner you have chosen. Believe in them and decide to trust and be proud of them all the time. Let your partner know that you are pleased and confident in them even though you can see the threats all around. It helps them to respect and be proud of you as well because of the level of maturity and security you are showing instead of jealousy.

Step 4: Ignore the Competition

"They are not your competition if you don't even compete," says an anonymous writer. There is no open competition except that we create. A lot of jealousy is fundamentally derived from comparing ourselves or relationships with others. We think, "Why is that guy always trying to talk to my partner? Does he think he is better than me?" "He has a better job than me. Maybe that's what she sees in him," "Maybe if I were as slim as she was, he would pay me more attention." A lot of these thoughts go through our heads and create jealous feelings. But why the comparison?

There is indeed a fundamental part of our primitive nature that wants to compete. This is like the animals we see in the jungle that compete for almost everything, including food, territory, and mates. But we are not the animals in the jungle, and we have higher and more advanced capabilities to control some of these instincts. We are unique in ourselves and rather than comparing and letting jealousy take a better part of us. We can focus on our relationships and ourselves. We can continue to add value to ourselves and do what we want to do, not because of the influence of any competition.

Step 5: Handle Awkward Situations like A Pro

People wonder how to handle awkward situations with their partners without getting jealous. For example, how do you handle other men talking to your female partner when you are right there watching and probably waiting? How do you handle others dancing with your partner? Giving them hugs, kisses perhaps? Does that stir up jealousy in you? Some of these situations can be daunting, almost like a temptation calling out for you to get upset or fight with your partner. But there is always the right way to handle things without exploding in a rage of jealousy and doing any havoc to your relationship.

CHAPTER 5:

How to Create a Healthy Relationship

Tips for a Healthier and Happier Relationship

The following tips will help keep your relationship healthy for a long time.

Avoid Nagging

Any kind of criticism of your partner's idiosyncrasies either leads to quarrels or makes you feel annoyed. Psychologists believe that criticizing your partner in many cases is a projection of your shortcomings.

Rather than frustrating your partner with complaints, you might think about what makes you uncomfortable about their traits, and work on reframing your viewpoint.

Understand That Your Partner Is Their Personality

You must accept the fact that your partner is an individual with a unique personality. Nevertheless, we subconsciously and sometimes consciously treat our partners as if they are an extension of ourselves. Accept that your partner is a being with a character of their with appropriate feelings and perceptions, opinions, and experiences.

Accept Your Partner's Mistakes

To err is human. Your partner is not an angel, so they are bound to make mistakes. When that happens, learn to forgive and do not capitalize on the mistakes of your partner.

Above all, there are lots of things we cannot change about our partner, so rather than grumbling or nagging, why not learn to live with them?

Small mistakes are not a matter of life and death. If you find it difficult to cope with your partner's idiosyncrasies, call their attention to it, and politely explain yourself. Don't blame or accuse; simply discuss.

Do Not Tolerate Destructive Behavior

Learn to tolerate your partner as long as their behavior is not destructive or life-threatening. If you discover that your spouse or partner is very aggressive, don't paint over the situation and learn to "cope." Your safety is important. If you ever feel threatened, don't stick around to try to keep the peace. Get out.

Take Emotional Time Out

Our skin needs sunlight for the production of vitamin D. However, prolonged and frequent sunbathing can cause life-threatening skin cancer.

So the right dosage is important. This applies to relationships, as well.

Of course, we need each other to fill our lives with happiness. But, we also need emotional time-outs in which one does not think of the other person or is involved in the planning of joint activities.

Meet alone with friends or join a club alone to develop yourself as a person. If both partners experience something different from each other, there is also something to talk about at the dinner table.

Do Not Tie Conditions to Gifts

A gift is a gift. And favor is a favor. In a marriage or intimate relationship, you should never attach any condition to a gift or favor. If you want to do something good for your partner, then go ahead without any ulterior motive.

Do not make a game like "I'll give you a message if you give me one." The same applies to the prices of gifts. Just because you have given your partner a computer, that does not mean they have to express their affection with something equally expensive.

Accept favors and gifts for what they are: gestures and symbols of love. Incidentally, this also applies to compliments.

We often tend not to take the compliments and praise from our partners seriously. But just because your partner loves you, that does not make their opinion worthless. If your partner tells you that you're pretty, then accept the compliment and do not disappoint them by dismissing it with an "Oh, that's just what you say."

Be Honest

Honesty is the best policy. Not only is this concept over two centuries old, but it exactly hits the point where relationships can fail.

Half-truths and lies cannot be kept secret for long if you aim to live peacefully together with your partner. Also, do not hide any material facts that could have a direct impact on the growing relationship. For example, if you have children from a previous relationship, that's something that will have to come out, eventually.

Be Faithful and Sincere

Unless you have made other arrangements, share a duvet exclusively with your romantic partner and no one else. To be deceived and cheated on by a close person is one of the cruelest experiences that can happen to anyone.

If you love your partner, you will spare them that experience. Ultimately, faithfulness builds such deep trust that you can't replace or fix it once broken.

Address Problems

No partnership is in complete harmony. You are two different personalities with thoughts and feelings. A relationship, no matter how much love and dedication you feel for each other, is always the result of many compromises.

Instead of holding long-standing resentments, you should discuss issues openly with your partner and work together to find a solution without immediately interpreting them as signs of a nonfunctional relationship. Precisely because you can talk about difficult points, you have a strong partnership.

Bear in mind that nobody can read your mind. A certain amount of empathy is to be expected, but over-relying on it can lead to misunderstandings.

Therefore, face critical matters head-on rather than waiting for the other to address the problem. Couples therapists unanimously agree that communication is the key to a long, healthy, and fulfilling relationship.

Appreciate What You See In Your Partner

The first infatuation does not disappear forever. Most of the time it gives way only to another feeling, that of deep attachment and love.

You have found that you can rely on your partner. That they think of you, and in so many ways suit you perfectly. That you as a couple harmonize and like to be with one another.

These are all the things you have always dreamed of. Now that they have become reality, are you taking the time to appreciate them fully?

Consider your partner once from these points of view, and you will see how happy you are to have them. Show your partner some of that happiness and gratitude. Talk to them about your feelings, and you will see the old familiar infatuation soon building again.

Romantic Excursions

Enjoy your closeness and take out time for romantic excursions from everyday life. Take a nice walk in the fall, or have a special dinner together in the evening.

Everyday life can dull us to the magic that is being with another person. Get away from the routine to rediscover your partner.

For a relationship to work, you have to do a lot for it.

CHAPTER 6:

How to Identify Triggers of Jealousy

To this point, we have identified that jealous has to do with the mind of a person, especially how you interpret something or a situation that happens. Take, for instance, you are sitting with him in a park, and all is going fine, both of you are enjoying your time. Then out of nowhere, a certain girl appears. She is smartly dressed than you, and she looks more beautiful than you. Then she starts talking to him. You are fully and consciously focused on them, looking at how she looks at him and how he smiles at her. You become less confident, scared, and angry. This is what we have termed as "jealousy." The situation described above is a trigger to feeling jealous. The following are common situations that will help you identify triggers of jealousy.

1. You Worry That Your Partner's Family or Friends Are Encouraging Your Partner's Undesirable Behavior

There are situations where your partner has friends or family members who influence them to do things that can potentially end up causing tension in your relationship. It is something that you cannot ignore and hope to change with time. However, in some cases, you may be the one making up issues that cause tension to your relationship rather than the family or friends of your partner. You need to be sure that you are not making up issues. Ask yourself whether you approve of your partner's friends or family.

Do you try to manipulate your partner into believing that their family or friends are a bad influence? In a situation wherein you do not like your partner's friends or family for no valid reason, you probably have a controlling or possessive behavior, and it is advisable that you deal with it. In a situation wherein you both agree that some of your partner's friends or family members are a bad influence, then the two of you must talk about it.

2. Your Partner Puts Themselves in Situations with Intentions to Test Your Ability to Trust

There are numerous things that a person may do in this context, which include staying up late, going to a party, or hanging out with friends of the opposite gender. Also, your partner may be deliberately avoiding answering their phone when you are calling. Relationships are about becoming vulnerable, and trust can be a major trigger. It is a fact that without trust, one can feel extremely uneasy in a relationship. In a relationship, if you constantly feel worried, sad, or moody, then it qualifies as a trigger for jealousy. Others go to the point of crying their hearts out because their partners are out having fun without them. While your partner's actions and activities could be to test your faith in them, you fear that they might go too far. Also, you may fear that in the course of their trials, they may come across someone better than you are. Women and men tend to fall in love differently. Women tend to love with the help of oxytocin, which is the trust molecule. It will build as one learns how to trust someone, and the only way to trust someone is to be patient.

3. You Realize That Your Partner Is Lying About Small Things

It is one of the main triggers for jealousy, whereby upon realizing that your partner lied, you become angry and insecure. In certain cases, your partner may lie about having done something you do not like because telling the truth will make you angry. Lying is not good, but when there is the possibility that you will become angry, it becomes hard for them to tell the truth. The unfortunate thing with lying is that it tends to create suspicion and distrust in the relationship. It is common to think that if your partner is lying about small things, then they will be lying about major things, such as about being committed or about who and where they hang out. If it becomes a trend, then subconsciously one will become doubtful of everything their partner tells them. Indeed, a feeling of jealousy comes along whenever you see them with other people. This is because you will think that they are dating someone else.

4. You Worry When They Go Out Without Informing You and Without You Knowing What They Are Doing and Who They Are With

There are indeed people who do not worry about their partners' whereabouts as long as they are all right. Not worrying is not an indication that you do not love your partner well enough. There are situations where your worries are directed to certain mindsets, such as thinking that your partner is going to cheat on you. Surprisingly, some will go to the extent of unexpectedly showing up in an unexpected place or snooping around.

The danger in doing this is that it may slowly drive you into madness and cause tension in your relationship. It is important to note that prohibiting a person from doing things that they love will hurt them, create discomfort, and eventually lead to consequences that will ruin your relationship.

5. You Feel Insecure Because Your Partner Is In Contact With an Ex or Frequently Talks about Them

Betrayal is the most immediate feeling in such a situation. Exes are known to be triggers for fear and insecurity in most relationships, especially in a situation where you feel there still exists a spark between your partner and the ex.

Worrying about this will trigger abandonment, anxiety, and jealousy. In that situation, you feel that another person is taking away your partner's admiration or love, which belongs rightfully to you. There are situations where the feeling of betrayal is justified, but not all. Of course, the feeling of jealousy has to be triggered by something that happened that made you feel insecure or threatened. This is one of the most difficult triggers to deal with, and the best approach is to deal with the fear of being replaced, fear of loss, and insecurity.

6. You Always Worry Because Your Partner Has a History of Infidelity

Unfortunately, if at one time you caught your partner cheating, it is difficult to trust them again completely. Some people are quick to forgive and forget, but some keep the case of infidelity as a point of reference.

They are quick to relate to the issue of unfaithfulness when a similar situation comes up even when it may not be true. You might have been created in your relationship, and although you have given your partner another chance, you might still suspect that your partner is not being honest with you. It is easy to suspect that they are on dating apps or talking to other people.

7. You Worry That Your Partner Will Leave You for Someone Else

It is a fact that only a small percentage of people are completely happy and confident in themselves. It is common to find a person who feels that they are too short, too thin, and overweight. A lot of people feel that they do not have a sexy body figure, and some even doubt their sexual performance. At a young age, one of the major worries is whether you can satisfy your partner sexually. On such a basis among others, people tend to worry that their partners will look for a person they will be more satisfied with; someone who is more beautiful, funnier, or richer.

When you are jealous, you always assume the worst scenarios in the relationship. Truthfully, there will always be someone more interesting, more intelligent, more attractive, and richer out there. Remember, if your partner wants to leave you, there is nothing you can do since it is their decision. However, it is paramount that you take care of your spirit, heart, mind, and body because jealousy is harmful to a person's well-being.

8. You Fear That the Issues You Encountered In Past Relationships May Happen Again In the Current Relationship

It is noted that most triggers are about the past and develop fears of the future among most people. Traumatic events in the past are hard to escape even when a person starts a new relationship. Psychologists affirm that if someone experienced something traumatic at the beginning of their relationship, it would keep on recurring. For instance, if you found out that the person you were dating was married and you did not know, it could come up over and over again being a major fear of the future. Truthfully, the past events and encounters play a vital role in shaping one's present and the future. If you can manage to stay in the present and be at peace at the moment, then it will be easy to escape and realize that these triggers of jealousy are irrelevant.

9. You Start To Worry or Feel Insecure That Your Partner May Have an Emotional Withdrawal

In the case where your partner stops doing things that he used to do for you (for instance, calling or texting all the time), you may find yourself worrying that your partner is not giving you enough attention. If they are no longer complimenting you on small things, such as being smartly dressed, it can trigger your thoughts that they are having someone else. Such thoughts of them telling those things to other people will cause sadness and, in other cases, anger. If you find them with another person who may even be a family member, you will be quick to react negatively. You may find yourself distracted, crying, or even causing a drama even without having all the facts about the situation. The feeling of insecurity that may have developed at that time is directly tied to the element of jealousy. Communication in a relationship is important and plays a tremendous role in addressing most challenges and issues faced by couples. While you may think that your partner is having someone else because they are less available, it may turn out that their lack of emotional availability may be caused by other reasons.

10. You Are Disappointed Because Of Unmet Expectations

In most cases, while in a relationship, you expect and want to be treated specially by your partner. You expect them to remember your birthday or anniversary or even know things you like, such as your favorite meal or color. Also, over the years, there are various holidays, such as New Year's, Christmas, and Thanksgiving, not forgetting others such as Women's Day. You may be expecting a surprise from your partner on any of the holidays or special occasions. Thus, if your partner does not give you gifts or surprises, you may become anxious, and you may think that your relationship is not moving forward. Negative thoughts (such as the thought that your partner is no longer finding you special or they want to end your relationship for someone else) are common in such cases. However, you may find that none of that is true. That is why it is important to talk about holiday plans or what you would like to do with your partner.

CHAPTER 7:

How to Defuse Jealousy Triggers
When They Arise Within You

Raising your overall self-esteem is a great way to overcome almost all negative thinking. It allows you to rise above the pettiness and low-level emotions in such a way that these feelings hardly register when they do arise. However, nobody is 100% confident all the time. Everybody experiences peaks and troughs when developing positive thinking patterns. I have worked on myself tirelessly over the years but still suffer these momentary lapses in confidence from time to time. That's just part and parcel of being human.

Fortunately, there are a few tools we can call upon in such instances. One of which involves identifying and defusing jealousy triggers when they show up. To snuff them out before they develop into full-scale negative thinking spirals.

This method isn't exclusive to combating jealousy, but all destructive thought patterns. However, the following are some ways we can use this technique to appropriately deal with the feelings of envy when they do arise:

1. Be Open and Honest About Your Thoughts and Feelings

If you are feeling uncertain or insecure in your relationship, you have to have an honest conversation with your partner. Refrain from playing mind games or expecting your partner to read yours. If you want to convey a message, you have to be direct and to the point. It is all right to talk about your desires, concerns, and doubts.

However, you should talk in a way that will not make your partner feel accused. Refrain from making gestures that can provoke your partner to feel attacked, such as finger-pointing and the like. You can ease any tension by being open and understanding, as well as allowing your partner to explain his/her side.

2. Do Not Act On Your Feelings Right Away

Feelings tend to come and go throughout the day. Hence, you should not act upon your feelings immediately, especially at the extremes. Whenever you begin to feel a strong emotion, either good or bad, pause for a second and take a few deep breaths. Carefully evaluate what you are experiencing and find out why it has arisen within you. Think of the possible consequences of acting on this particular feeling. Chances are, you will later regret what you said or did if you chose to act without this momentary contemplation. Hence, the next time you feel jealous, simply assess the situation first. Do not do or say whatever comes to your mind in the first instance. Evaluate your thoughts carefully as we generally change the way we view these instances after just a few seconds of pondering on them. Be open to feasible reasons and explanations. For example, if you see your spouse talking to his ex-wife, you may feel jealous and tempted to confront them both. Don't jump to conclusions, there is almost always a benign explanation for such occurrences.

3. Appreciate Your Self

Before you met your partner, you were your person. You were likely happy and content with life. You did whatever you pleased for the most part. You had everything you needed. Whenever you feel jealous of someone else, such as a friend or co-worker of your partner, you have to remind yourself that your partner is not your whole life. You have family, friends, and a career. You have your goals and interests. You are perfectly whole. Your partner is just a very nice addition to your life. By realizing this, you can once again rebuild your self-esteem.

You have to know that you are a wonderful person. You possess great qualities that attracted your partner in the first place. Never forget that.

4. Allow Your Wounds To Heal

Many people experience extreme levels of jealousy due to negative experiences. They may have experienced abusive and dysfunctional relationships in which they were cheated on, abandoned, used, or psychologically abused. They may have been hurt so badly that they find it difficult to let go and trust another person again.

So, the next time you find yourself making unreasonable assumptions about your partner's whereabouts or activities, pause for a while and evaluate why you are feeling this way. Did your previous partner come home late each night because he was seeing another woman? If so, you should remember that you are no longer with that person. You have a new partner who might simply be doing overtime at work or is stuck in traffic. Again, the benefit of the doubt must be given for your sanity.

You have to move forward and let go of your past hurts, guilt, anger, and other such feelings. You need to understand the reasons, roots, and triggers of your jealousy to grow and be healthy. Whenever you start to feel jealous, you have to make a conscious decision to heal old wounds. You have to remind yourself that your past and present are not the same and that you can make your present relationship work.

5. Trust Your Partner and Yourself

When you enter a relationship, you have to accept that there are risks involved. No relationship is perfect. No person is perfect. There is also no way to see the future and find out exactly how things will play out. If you want to be happy, you need to be optimistic about your relationship. Refrain from thinking and expecting the worst. Act with faith instead of fear.

Remember that what is true for you, is ultimately true. So, if you believe that your relationship will eventually end, you will unconsciously do the things to sabotage it. You have already imprinted this outcome in your mind. It will just then become a self-fulfilling prophecy.

You have to trust your partner and yourself that both of you can make the relationship work. Accept the fact that you cannot control your partner. Remember that no matter how hard you try to keep him/her away from temptations, he/she is still their person and needs the freedom to express themselves too.

You have to trust in yourself that you will be all right no matter what happens in your relationship. Even if your partner is unfaithful or leaves you, you are still a wonderful person who is worthy of being loved. You can still find a new partner and be happy in a new relationship. By giving yourself this reassurance, your feelings of jealousy can take a backseat and your self-esteem receives a boost once more.

6. Tame Your Imagination

I have touched on this in previous chapters already. But if you have a wild imagination, you have to find a way to keep it in check. A reckless imagination can ensure that jealousy germinates and grows. Hence, you should recognize the times when you are engaging in negative self-talk and blowing things out of proportion. Refrain from playing events over and over in your head. Obsessing over perceived wrongful events does no good whatsoever.

Aim to tame wild mind chatter by practicing mindfulness meditation. You have to train yourself to focus on the present moment and simply acknowledge your jealous thoughts. Instead of holding on to them, let go. Mindfulness meditation can help clear your head and allow you to have more rational thoughts.

7. Take a Reality Check

Similar to the above, identify your jealousy triggers and evaluate them carefully. Are they truly realistic or are they simply by-products of your imagination? Assess your obsessive thoughts. Replace conspiracy theories with real facts. Be objective rather than subjective. Oftentimes, people get carried away with their jealousy, so they are no longer able to think clearly and rationally.

One such way to force a reality check is to write things down. When you write out your thoughts, you can evaluate them better. It's a cathartic and calming experience. Each time you begin to feel jealous, write down everything that comes to mind. What are the things or actions that you plan to do? Why do you feel jealous? What is the triggering factor causing you to feel this way? What is your observed reality of the situation?

For example, you and your partner made plans to go out of town this weekend. Suddenly, he cancels on you. Then tells you that he has to go on a business trip and meet with a client instead. This makes you upset and jealous. You begin to contemplate all the ways your partner could be acting to justify these feelings.

Again, it's simply about assessing things rationally. Don't let yourself feel the emotions of jealousy until your other half gives you a real reason for doing so. Don't hasten the demise of your current relationship for momentary insecurity. Remember to trust and communicate with your partner. This will defuse 99% of problems when they do arise. Communication is king, which leads us very nicely on to the next chapter.

CHAPTER 8:

Learning to Trust & Reconnect:
Communication Advice to Repair Relationships

A well-functioning romantic relationship is one of, if not the most rewarding thing in the world. It's heaven on earth if you can get it right, which is why it's so worthwhile striving to achieve. However, we live in the real world where sadly these unions can break down much more frequently than we'd like.

When this is the case, we need to do adequate work to repair the damage. If you are in a relationship, in essence, you need to do your share. Maintaining a relationship is not easy, it requires much to give and take. There have to be open lines of communication, honesty, loyalty, and commitment to give yourself a fighting chance.

According to statistics, 60% of second marriages and 41% of first marriages end up in divorce. According to author Dr. Sue Johnson, expectation mismatch and stress of living causes couples to have problems for the most part. Their previous attachment issues also bring problems into their current relationships far too frequently.

No relationship is perfect, but if you are willing to work on it, it is possible to make a union last for a lifetime. My parents are a shining example of this. High school sweethearts who are about to celebrate 55 years of marriage. Granted, we live at different times today, however, it's still possible to cultivate such a relationship with the right ingredients. This often requires a large degree of trust and communication skills. If you find yourself struggling with this, the following is some advice to help you reconnect and repair your relationship once more:

1. Hear Your Partner Out and Stay Present

Allow your partner to speak. Do not take over the conversation. When your partner begins to express themselves, listen intently to what they are saying, as opposed to simply waiting for your turn to talk. Stay present and refrain from thinking of other things or finding ways to undermine your partner. Bring down your defenses and be open to reconciliation. Keep in mind that it is not about defending yourself, but rather attempting to understand your partner in the sincerest way possible.

Do not allow your pride or ego to dictate your decisions. Since your goal is to repair your relationship, you have to be willing to forgive. You do not necessarily have to forget what has transpired. However, you should be willing to move forward and refrain from continually bringing up past mistakes. Let your partner know that you hear and accept their unmet needs and that you are willing to make the necessary changes.

2. Empathize With Your Partner

Along similar lines, you should not just listen to your partner. You have to put yourself in their shoes to fully understand what they are trying to say. When you empathize with your partner, you can fulfill their needs much better.

You have to understand their feelings as well as pay attention to yourself. When your partner opens up to you, you should listen but think twice before giving advice. Sometimes, people just want someone to listen to them. They are not seeking to have their problems solved. So, unless your partner asks for it, you should refrain from giving advice or proposing a solution too soon.

Besides, you have to watch your tone and choice of words. If you are not careful, your partner may view your advice as judgmental or overly critical. This will only make things worse. You have to stay emotionally engaged as well as express compassion to provide connection and comfort.

3. Address Concerns and Be Willing To Make Changes

You have to be willing to address the needs of your partner as well as make the necessary changes in your actions, not simply paying lip service to what is being said. For example, if your partner feels anxious, you may make an effort to call more often to let them know that you are thinking of them. You may also want to do things that make them feel more appreciated. It's the little things that make the biggest impact here.

Your partner will feel respected and valued if they see you taking their concerns seriously. This will result in a positive cycle in your relationship. Your partner will be more willing to do their part in mending the union as a result. So make the first gesture on this, I promise it will make a big difference.

4. Love As Unconditionally As You Can

If you love someone, your feelings for that person aren't jeopardized by momentary and menial negative thought patterns. If you are experiencing problems in the relationship, you can reconnect with your partner by recalling their good qualities and the good times you had together. Remember the things which attracted you in the first place. These should be plentiful, but you only need one reminder to rekindle the spark you once felt.

Forgive your partner and yourself for the things you did to damage your relationship. Do not hesitate to reach out or show positive gestures. Show your love and concern. When you love unconditionally, your expressions are not contingent on outside forces. Instead, they involve support, forgiveness, caring, and understanding. If you still have unresolved trust issues, you should think of ways to rebuild your trust.

Then again, remember that loving unconditionally is not the same as being a doormat. You should not allow anyone, including your partner, to disrespect you and walk all over you. If you love yourself and your partner, you will draw healthy boundaries. But once again, the whole is greater than the sum of the parts when this works!

5. Make Improving Your Communication Priority Number One

Communication is probably the most vital skill anybody can learn in life in general, and no more so when it comes to romantic relationships. A lack of communication almost always causes problems between couples, and often terminally too. When you communicate with your partner, you have to gain perspective on what matters to them. You should not just be mindful of your interests. You need to practice thoughtful transparency, which is crucial for trust-building. Create an environment in which your partner can feel safe and secure.

Do not forget to contribute to gratitude. Specific, personal, and sincere appreciation elevates communication and builds trust once more. You can give your partner gifts or tokens of appreciation regularly to make them feel loved. You do not have to wait for your anniversary or holidays for these shows of affection. Simply reminding your partner that you love them and that you are thankful for them being in your life, goes a long way.

Furthermore, you should align your words with your actions. If you say something, you have to act accordingly. In other words, you have to "walk your talk" to build trust. Do not say something and then do the opposite. Your behavioral integrity can have a significant impact on your relationship and the way your partner sees you. So make this open and honest communication a priority, and everything else will fall into place that much easier.

CHAPTER 9:

How to Stop the Spiral of Jealous Thoughts

P eople often use the feeble excuse: "I can't help it. It's just the way that I am." Here is some news for you. If you want to ruin your relationships, then continue being jealous. If, however, you want to have lasting and happy relationships, you need to make the effort to stop jealousy in its tracks. If it's something that you have made into a part of your life, you need to do something about it because until you do, you won't be a happy person, and you are likely to make your partner very unhappy, too.

Start To Understand the Good Things in Your Life

You certainly need to know how to count your blessings because jealousy stops you from seeing all the positive things about your relationship. Tell yourself all the good things you have in your life and your relationship, and see how much more important these are when compared with the negative things that jealousy brings about. For example, if you and your partner have a nice house, a nice car, or are lucky enough to have a couple of kids, you may just be a lot luckier than others. There are people in the world who are homeless. There are people without kids who desperately want them, and there are people who live alone and who have no one to love them.

It may sound obvious, but we put aside all the good things when we are jealous. The thing is that when you do introduce jealousy, you introduce something horrible into your lives. Instead of doing that, start to see the positive, and be happy that your partner comes home to you at night because many partners stop coming home when jealousy is all they are greeted with.

Jealousy over Possessions

We see people say, "I am so jealous!" on places like Facebook, and usually, it's very tongue in cheek, but the problem is that we let it infiltrate our personal lives outside the Internet, and some of us are jealous when others get more than we do. That's one of the unhealthiest things because you don't realize all the good things that you have.

If you haven't realized by now that happiness is what's inside us regardless of who we are, then you need to work on the happiness factor. The two things are fields apart. Try to look at things differently. Instead of feeling jealous because someone has something you would like, use that person as your inspiration to work towards getting the thing that is so important to you. Admire them for their ability to be whoever they are and start putting a positive spin on it. Accept that we all have different things, and be happy for those who have more than you. If having more means that much to you, figure out a way through which you can have just as much within your life. Jealousy won't help you get it. All that it will give you is unhappiness and a feeling of being unfulfilled.

Use People You Admire as an Inspiration

When you look at someone else and it makes you sick with jealousy, try looking at them differently. Look at them as your inspiration, and compliment them. Often, jealous people take it out on others for things that they are unaware of, and that's so negative. Being spiteful because someone is better than you in one respect is pointless and just reflects your bad character. If you admire someone for some attribute you would like, talk to him or her, and find out more because you may just amaze yourself in the process.

The girl who managed to lose weight in the weight loss class against those who struggle can be used as inspiration rather than being talked about negatively. Learn from your inspiration, and become a better person so that jealousy doesn't need to come into your life.

These solutions are real ones that help you build yourself up so that you don't feel like you have something to feel jealous about. If you can follow them, you will find that you make yourself much happier, and you don't take it out on people around you. That, in turn, makes you a much better person with better self-esteem.

If none of this works for you, then you have a real self-esteem problem and need to deal with it. Self-esteem isn't any more complex than being the way that you see yourself, but it is a powerful fuel for jealousy. If you look at areas of your life that you are unhappy with, there will be a reason for your unhappiness. You need to get to the root of the problem and stop working your way around it. See a psychologist if you need help, but make the focus of those sessions "Why do I feel so jealous?" That's the issue. That's what is holding you back. Don't go to the sessions hoping to get sympathy because that's where a lot of people go wrong. They tell their stories and expect to find the therapist nodding in all the right places, and sometimes, they do. What you need to do is visit a therapist and tell him or her that the root cause of your problem is your jealousy. Tell the therapist that this is ruining your relationships, and make sure that the sessions deal with this aspect rather than others.

There is a three-part process to getting rid of jealousy that you can work on by yourself if you wish to, but you need to be strong-willed and be able to recognize jealousy as and when it happens. Follow these three steps:

1. Learn to look at this from another perspective.

2. Be aware of the way that triggers work with you.

3. Change the triggers to something positive.

So how does that work in practice? The fact is that when we feel jealous, we know we are feeling jealous. Let's say you are jealous of your sister because she has more than you. Look at it from her perspective. Is she gloating? Is she rubbing it in? If you can look at things from her perspective, you may see what a negative person that makes her. Be sorry for her instead of letting her rile you. Be sorry that she has to display so much material stuff to validate who she is. You don't. You've never had to. You are a person whose needs are not material. Thus, who's the weak link? You need to see things from a different perspective to step away from jealousy.

If you are aware of the triggers of jealousy, you can recognize them when they happen. Stop taking the bait. Look what happens when you step away and ignore them. The world doesn't come tumbling down. There isn't such a difference in your life that you can't live with it. The lack of jealousy means that the triggers don't work anymore. That makes them less powerful, which gives you a lot more personal power than you have now. It's funny because when you change your viewpoint, you begin to see jealousy for the petty thing that it is. Although it's petty, it's also extremely destructive.

If you have experienced being on the receiving end of jealousy, you will already have a fair idea about what jealousy can do to you. Your jealous partner may make you feel that you have nothing to offer anyone. You may have seen it in movies where a husband tells his abused wife that she is worthless to anyone else and that she won't leave because no one else will have her. The fact is that jealousy can erode self-confidence and even put people who had confidence in a state in which they lose self-sufficiency. That's why it's so important to have that set in stone before you step into a long-term relationship.

This will also help you to be able to establish relationships, such as friendships, on an equal basis, which is great because you will surround yourself with people who do not use jealousy as a means to get what they want.

CHAPTER 10:

Earn Security

Boost your Self Esteem

You can do all or some of the following depending on your assessment of current personal self-esteem level:

- Control the "inner voice" or critic that you have within your mind. Yes, that voice is still you and you can replace the way that it talks. If you are finding this voice saying things that can put your belief in yourself off balance, simply tell it to stop. Prepare a sequence of constructive (positive) thoughts that you can use to flood the negative ones already in your mind. When it is telling you that something is your fault, you are lazy, you don't deserve something, or other similar things, just scream the word "STOP." Of course, this screaming should be done on your mind only. Follow it up with a flood of positive thoughts.

- Properly motivate yourself. Doing the inner voice control as stated above is not that easy. For this matter, you can motivate yourself by listing down the benefits you are getting from it daily. Put this list in a place where you can always see it. Learning to like what you are doing will also lead to the development of a positive habit towards the changes you are trying to incorporate into your life.

- Give time for self-appreciation. When you take a break, pause for a while and think about 3 things that you can appreciate about yourself for the day. Have you helped someone? Did you listen to a friend who is in the process of grieving for something? Even little things that you did for a day would count. List it and make a compilation of lists. You'll feel your self-esteem growing as the pile gets thicker.

- Be on the righteous path. This means doing those things that you feel and believe to be right. Did you reduce the volume of your TV because you know that your neighbor is putting her baby to sleep? Did you fight off the temptation to smoke your cigar in a public place because you saw that there are kids around? By doing the right thing, you feel good and this leads to an increased level of self-esteem.

- Don't compare your life with that of other people. You are setting yourself up for disappointment if you will see some things in their life that you want but don't have. Instead of doing this, examine your life and focus on the achievements that you have made.

- Know your purpose in building your self-esteem. By doing this, you will have the drive to continue what you are doing based on the tips mentioned above.

Yes, the steps mentioned above might seem very simple to do. However, each of those steps is guaranteed to produce positive results that you might see soon enough if used or applied. Carry on with the task and reap the benefits of building your self-esteem.

Get Rid Of Negative Thinking

If the glass is half empty, it is almost difficult in each encounter to see the positive potential, or silver linings and life lessons. In a partnership, it is extremely difficult for you or your partner to be content with this mindset. If your partner feels he or she cannot please you and maximize your satisfaction, for example, he or she can feel less, weak, inadequate, etc.

How to Suppress Negative Thinking?

Rewire your brain. Recognize and transform a negative thought or belief into one of the most positive thoughts you have developed.

This is an unbelievably important change in your mind, so it takes time, energy, and persistence to get the idea you want in a safer, new way. However, once you constantly correct it, you will see that your negative thoughts dissipate, and healthier ones arise.

This is how you take down the negative lens and look at the world more honestly and with more hope.

A few other tips to make your dating and relationship life more satisfying as you change your mind to achieve the love you wish for are:

- Always remember that taking care of your expectations is important to your relationship's success. Discrepancies and conflicts are inevitable in the world of relations, so remember that it is natural and all right. The most important thing is how you and your partner manage and develop in difficult times.

- Remember, your partner is also a person. Not all your partner does is "right" or "good," but you resist the urge to change your critical lens when you are frustrated. Communicate your desires and do not try to generalize the entire relationship for a moment when you feel hurt.

- Consider the partner deliberately in a positive light. Thank you for the little things and compassion that your partner shows. Say, thank you. It perpetuates a cycle of optimistic and caring relationships.

- Do not take things personally. There will be poor dates, difficult conversations, and times that can be frustrating at the time. Do not add these experiences to your negative pile; take life lessons instead and imagine yourself moving towards your goals. Engage yourself to be happy on your journey to marriage.

How to Overcome It

There are all kinds of things that can ruin an entirely good relationship. Cheating and incompatibility, for example, are two major issues. According to experts, there is one thing that can ruin a relationship more than anything else.

"The truth is that we are making our reality," says Joann Cohen, matchmaker and dating coach, to Bustle. "If we believe we have a good relationship, we work through things that believe that things are always ok. But when you come to relationships with a negative thought, you always expect the worst not only for your partner but also for the outcome of your relationship." You need to find ways to make them positive to prevent negative thoughts. Listed below are some things you can do according to experts to stop forming toxic ideas and sabotaging your relationship.

1. Think about the First Time You Have Fallen In Love with Your Spouse

When you pass a rough patch, it is easy to let that cloud judge you. Talk about the "real" feelings of your partner when you start invading your mind, the first time you fell in love with them, and talk about how you felt. "Shutting your eyes and seeing the bright eye person with whom you fell in love will make things look much more positive and doable," says Cohen. At times, we need only a little reminder of the good times to resolve the poor.

2. Letting Go of the Past

To be honest, letting go of the past is easier said than done. To be fair, "We all have a piece of our history with us to shield us against getting hurt again," says Cohen. And if you continue to bring your old relations and harm to your new relationship, then you sabotage and create the truth that things just do not or will not work. If you can separate your relationship from your new one, being more involved is much easier for you.

3. Find Other Ways to Channel Your Energy

Toxic thinking will cause you to do unreasonable, relationship-sabotage stuff, like hack into your partner's phone or sabotage it. To counter this phenomenon, Dr. Issa says that he knows what your thoughts are doing. For instance, why do you feel you need to just "check-in" your partner 20 times in a row? You would also want some affirmation or confirmation that your partner cares. "Once you know that you can do (these) stuff, take some time to practice those skills to help you, like to count to ten and relax," she says. Find ways to reduce the intense feelings you have so that you will not act in ways that you will regret.

4. Do Not Assume You Know What Your Partner Is Thinking

Negative thoughts are often based on perceptions that do not always exist. "If we put our negative feelings on somebody else or direct them toward our significant other, the anger of the other person is what you are reading," Cohen says. The important thing here is never to presume. Do not jump to conclusions. Jump to conclusions. Do not cook it yourself if you cannot help it. Get to the edge and chat with your friend. "Try or ask for clarification, take the words on face value," she says. "You never believe you know how they feel."

5. Have That One Person You Go To, To Vent Your Anger

If you are mad about your partner, it is not uncommon to put all your problems to anyone who is listening. If you are mad about your partner. But, according to Cohen, "When you do that, you create a gap between your meaningful other person and your world, creating more negativity than you know." If you must lower yourself down, choose one person, and stay with them. "Saying to everyone is not helpful to your ugly business and will only encourage more negative feelings," she says.

6. Create a List of Your Toxic Thoughts and Come Up with Positive Ones

Preventing toxic thoughts from destruction takes some self-reflection with constructive alternatives. Take it a step further and write down hard proofs for or against any thought. After that, come up with a more concise and adaptive alternative thinking. For instance, if you think your partner is no longer interested in you because they did not reply to your text, please list all other things they could do. "Think about other occasions they have taken a while to answer or to show that they are still involved," says Dr. Issa. Here the alternative thought may be as simple as "Just as I have not heard of them, yet it does not mean they do not care." Then, the more detailed you are, the more effective it will be.

7. Take Breaking-Up Totally Off the Table

Whatever the toxic thoughts are, usually, they are from the same location; fear. In particular, the fear that your partner will leave. "I use the analogy, *You burn the ship when you comment,*" Cohen says. There is no way to get out of the island when you burn the ship, so work together to survive. If there is no solution, you start seeing what is good in a situation. When you take the chance to break the equation (that is 'burning the ship'), you can support your relationship from a place of love and not fear. If your words and actions come from a place of affection, it is much easier for you to remain positive.

Thinking is only a thought at the end of the day. It is not necessarily the truth. If you do not let your relationship consume you, it will improve your relationship.

CHAPTER 11:

Taking Inventory of Your Emotional State

One of the most important things you can do when initially starting on your emotional intelligence enhancing journey is to take stock of what you are currently feeling. There are no right or wrong answers here in terms of what comes up. As our limbic legacy shows us, humans are inherently emotional creatures, and suppressing them is almost impossible to do entirely.

However, you do have control over the way you react to these tendencies, thoughts, and behaviors after the fact. The following factors should help you take a closer look into how to identify and deal with these feelings when they do arise to ultimately move you to the next level in your E.Q. journey.

Acknowledge Your Emotions

The first thing to do when attempting to increase your E.Q. levels is to get good at acknowledging and perceiving the emotions that you are feeling. This is the starting point for every model and framework of E.Q.

Whenever I feel an emotion arise within me, I always take a pause and acknowledge its presence. I take a moment and feel it so I can understand and label it in my mind. This isn't the same as reacting or acting upon the emotion just yet, but I want to know why it may have arisen and if it could be useful to me. If it's a feeling of anger, fear, or frustration I do not deny or try to hide it, but instead acknowledge its presence and dismiss it as not being productive and move on.

If you start to dwell on emotions such as these you will quickly fall into a negative spiral thought process that will have you framing everything in a pessimistic light before you know it. I used to play out entire imaginary scenarios in my head of something going badly and the knock-on effects that I 'knew' it would have, only to realize that it NEVER worked out that badly and that I'd fabricated it all in my mind. Sounds familiar?

If on the other hand, it is an emotion of excitement, joy, or anticipation, I also pause for a moment, acknowledge and label what it is that I'm feeling, and try to cultivate and utilize it if I think it will benefit the situation such as situational empathy (which we will get onto later).

It is also important to take responsibility for these emotions that you are feeling either way, good or bad. Know that it is something inside of you that is eliciting such a response and that you have to deal with it and not sweep it under the carpet so to speak. This is usually the most challenging step for people, but it is also the most rewarding. Yes, it may be some outside influence or stimulus that sparked the response in the first place but remember that the emotions you are feeling are coming from within you and that it's your responsibility to deal with them.

Understand That You Are Not Your Emotions

So following on from that, you also need to constantly remind yourself that the emotions which arise within you and the conscious entity which interprets them are two very different things. Most people walk around in somewhat of waking sleep, for the most part completely at the mercy of any feeling, thought, or emotion that pops into their head. You have to understand that many thoughts and emotions will pass through you almost on a second-by-second basis, but again it's entirely your choice how you perceive and choose to react to them. There is also a very large egotistic element to this process as well. Thoughts and feelings of jealously for another person or fear of performing a task is just your ego trying to keep your preconceived notions about the world intact and keep you operating within your comfort zone. This is a topic for much greater discussion i.e. regarding the tactics to counteract such self-sabotaging behavior, but needless to say that detaching yourself from your overall emotional state is very a beneficial thing to do.

Learn to Forgive Yourself & Others

"Life becomes easier when you learn to accept an apology you never got."

(Robert Brault)

Again, along the same lines as letting go of a negative emotion that arises within you, people have a great tendency to hold on to what they perceive to be negative acts that they have either committed themselves or others against them. Holding onto this ill-feeling again serves absolutely no purpose to you in the immediate future and certainly not in the long run. "Holding onto anger is like drinking poison and expecting the other person to die," as the Buddha so aptly put it.

If there was one thing that got me ahead in my business life so quickly it was this concept. Once I stopped getting caught up with what I thought I deserved from a situation or others around me and started pushing ahead regardless, I made so much more progress. You can't stop and throw stones at every dog that barks, and that includes yourself when you mess up.

This isn't just applicable to adult and business life either, it's related to everyone young or old. If I had taken heed of this advice when I was growing up, I know I would have had better overall relationships with school/college friends and family alike. That's not to say things were necessarily that bad, but they could have been better, or at least I could have saved myself a great deal of heartache and stress along the way.

Don't Get Involved in Negative Self-Talk

As I mentioned above, letting negative self-talk get out of hand is a very bad habit to take up. I would say that it is the one thing that plagues humanity more than anything. We often talk ourselves out of things before we've had a chance to start them. Again this comes down to letting negative thoughts and emotions cloud our thinking to a point of almost no escape. You have to stop this in its tracks as quickly as possible if you want to build high overall levels of emotional intelligence.

This also includes negative self-talk and 'gossip' regarding other people. In danger of sounding like one of your parents or school teachers here, you don't need me to tell you this is a worthless exercise and one that will ultimately bring your E.Q. level down with it. No one is perfect; just make a point of catching yourself when you start to talk in this way.

Also along the same lines as the above, you must try to do your best not to judge others where ever possible. This freed me greatly in a psychological sense when I managed to stop doing it a few years ago. I never thought of myself as an overly judgmental person, but I still realized I would do it from time to time. But stopping myself altogether from judging anyone I came across in even the smallest way saves me so much mental energy and almost certainly daily misjudgment.

Nowadays I simply let others go about their day in their way without even the slightest judgmental thought about their behavior. That is not to say that I tolerate bad behavior or that I do not try to empathize with people and attempt to understand their situation better, which is critical to building fruitful relationships. But I don't judge them on how they got to where they are, I never walked in their shoes or went through the struggles they did so I let them do the talking on this one.

Again this isn't some 'holier than thou' situation, I'm not perfect and do very occasionally catch myself automatically judging someone. I just now catch it very early and stop myself in my tracks straight away. It's so much more liberating when you do.

CHAPTER 12:

How to Recreate Love and Admiration towards Your Partner

Love is developed during the monotonous routine. It's the little, apparently good-for-nothing snapshots of association that are the most critical of all. At the point when we go to our partner, we assemble certainty, enthusiastic association, and an energetic sexual coexistence.

As loopy as it would sound, the grocery store's adoration for sentiment is elevated. In the inconsequential inquiry concerning connections like "do we need milk?," the appropriate response is "I can't recall that. I'll simply get a couple on the off chance that." This has a great deal of effect as opposed to shrugging your shoulders impassively.

The number one explanation behind a couple quarreling isn't over cash, parents-in-law, or sex. The greater part of the grumblings seeing someone is about the powerlessness to impart inwardly.

The Emotional Bank Account

Each connected second in your relationship develops an adoration sparing that can be utilized in extreme occasions.

At the point when a few have more positive than negative stores, they are more averse to doubt each other during intense occasions. Be that as it may, on the off chance that their record with the emotional bank is underwater of separation, at that point trust and closeness blur away.

Comprehend the Love Maps of Each Other

Numerous couples accept that their partner feels saw and comprehended. The way to realizing your partner doesn't originate from guessing what you might be thinking, but instead from the difficult work of placing your partner in a spot that they can uninhibitedly and genuinely convey.

Do you know the feelings of trepidation and weights your partner is encountering? What are its desires and expectations? What are its needs this year? Is it accurate to say that they are not quite the same as the earlier year?

The key to realizing each other is: Ask questions; mind the appropriate responses; and keep posing inquiries. It is a deep-rooted procedure to become acquainted with your partner better and to communicate your internal identity. A fantasy film for your partner probably won't be equivalent to what it was five years prior.

The better the inquiries that you both make, the more noteworthy the enthusiastic venture. In case you're searching for proposals to answer relationship issues, go here.

Build up a Route of Mutual Respect and Gratitude

Recollect when the man intruded on his significant other and asked her story? Do you imagine that the relationship based on friendship and regard?

We as a whole have character inadequacies. Rather than focusing on the deficiencies of your partner, figure out how to acknowledge them.

What's more, when you can, your partner's express what you appreciate. The thought is to get your partner to do it right and say, "Thank you for doing it. I found that you exhausted the dishwasher, and I truly welcome it." Your significant other feels a passionate bond each time you do such. Accordingly, you are placing your passionate additions to the emotional bank record of your relationship.

Love isn't centered on significant occasions or extravagant presents. Presumably the most significant of these are the unimportant snapshots of correspondence.

When Would You Be Able To Get The Energy In A Relationship?

It's confusing and a long hard street without convenient solutions, however, there are some slam dunks you can do to recoup a partner's consideration, regardless of whether it's a drawn-out beau or another one. It happens to potentially anyone. It is a specific moment that something appears to break, and you suddenly or gradually realize that the relationship has become exhausting, and the profound love that you had has now become only a kinship with each other. You're glad to be together, yet you're not enthusiastic about it.

Everything is fresh out of the plastic new when we start a relationship, so the sentiments that you experience are captivated and fill you with happiness. In any case, it's ordinary that those sentiments begin to scatter after a specific timeframe. Despite everything feel something in your life towards the fundamental crush, love no longer envelops everything. So when a coupling arrives at that stage, how would you recapture love?

Stage One: To Go Ahead, Take a Step Backward

Attempt to recollect what the initial, not many days, weeks, or even years resembled (in case you're fortunate). Mention to yourself what you have done any other way, and how you have rewarded each other. So then attempt to remember those occasions, with the assistance of your sweetheart or spouse. Go to a pleasant extravagant eatery again on a first date, and perhaps request similar dinners you'd eat in those days. Recuperate love and passion! Disregard calories and children for 60 minutes, and spare the week! In attempting to trigger your psyche in recollecting how you felt about somebody and why you felt how you once felt, these seemingly insignificant details can be significant.

Stage Two: Compromise, Bargain, Bargain, And A Bargain!

Bargain: Compromise! You presumably know when your loved one will respond to anything now in your relationship, or when he'll need to participate in an action that you don't have any enthusiasm for. You will make a quick reaction framework to battle these things: "No, I would prefer not to do this" or "We're heading off to the evening gathering, in any case." These sorts of stock reactions are not helpful for a decent, upbeat relationship and can prevent your relationship from recovering adoration. Rather, ponder your response to one of the solicitations from your partner, pause for a minute to consider and consider what he is asking, and offer a straightforward, determined reaction. Ideally, you will figure out how to concede to specific issues after some time, and if he needs the relationship to go on and your affection to return to him, at that point he will understand that and answer. Regardless of whether you differ on something, or state no, before reacting, the way that you considered an answer will do you a lot of good. Furthermore, better believe it, you may appreciate a portion of the things that you'd never done!

Stage Three: Make New Destinies and Get Even More Real Existence Outside

You need to augment your points of view first to recover love because the man in your life begins to hunger for consideration. You'll partake in your time together, significantly more, when you're investing the energy separated! Such outer interests could be something you find intriguing (except an undertaking) or you've for a long while been itching to look at it. If you have children, become more acquainted with and invest some energy with different guardians. If you prefer to get fit, enter a fitness center and begin practicing your body for yourself, not him.

You may have likewise longed for investing energy in drawing, or some other masterful leisure activity. This is your opportunity to complete it! Such acts, all share something for all intents and purpose; your man in these undertakings will go along with you. On the off chance that he does, at that point, you may locate a mutual love for a side interest or expertise, just as investing some additional quality energy with one another. On the off chance that he doesn't at any rate, you'll begin to be more joyful with your new life, and it's simpler to recapture love all around when an individual's more joyful.

Stage Four: Don't Have Games to Watch

You may feel supported in what you state or do in one of these verbal battles, yet after some time they destroy you as well as pulverize the longing of your partner to be with you. Begin to be straightforward with one another as opposed to shrinking away from the real issue and offering scornful comments. Brain games can be pleasant, and in specific cases, innocuous, such as prodding in the room or playing battle. In actuality, these can help construct an effective relationship, and be solid updates on why you love each other. The frivolous contentions that can begin crawling into a relationship sooner or later, be that as it may, do little to assist you with beginning recovering adoration as you did when you initially met. Getting things done or saying "to get back" at someone will consistently prompt lament.

Stage Five: Be Forthcoming

Trustworthiness, a basic term, however maybe the most significant component of a relationship, and a necessary piece of reestablishing love that may have fallen away. It is certain that at some phase in your relationship, when nothing had all the earmarks of being a no-no, you were candid and could advise your partner everything there was to think about yourself. Things change as we advance, and two things do occur.

As a matter of first importance, you will feel increasingly loose with your life partner, and you would have the option to discuss stuff that would have embarrassed you in advance. The second thing that occurs, however, is that you start to feel awkward revealing to him certain data, for example, about a collaborator who hits you or you've been feeling sexual restraint.

You deliberately disregard things since you would prefer not to. It probably won't be large; however, all these little lies and deceptive nature can wind up costing your coexistence. Attempt to be 100 percent open with your partner. You will locate each other opening up together, and just as developing an adoration for one another, it will likewise enable you to visit, and interface.

Stage Six: Just Trust One Another

Following on from the last advance and working connected at the hip with it, the way into an enduring power of profound devotion is a certainty. If you're not confiding in your partner, at that point love isn't self-evident. Doubtful musings overwhelm us if we permit it to. It will be a daunting struggle to reestablish love without first recovering trust, thus begin working through your on-edge sentiments at the earliest opportunity. Wonder why you lost your once-held confidence in your man, and what you or he could do to recover that, and make things right once more.

Stage Seven: Contact Is Fundamental

Correspondence, alongside genuineness and certainty, is one of those fundamental components in recapturing love and is vital for any drive to revive an association. Truly and genuinely address each other about the climate, the new American Idol, and the film you'd prefer to see. Ask him how his day went at work, and mention to him what yours resembled. Although it might appear glaringly evident, the number of couples declining to simply plunk down and address one another is stunning. Little changes will assist you in making the ways for the principal subjects you have to consider.

CHAPTER 13:

Overcoming Obstacles in a Relationship

All connections will have boundaries; issues that should be cleared out (settled) for a connection to run significantly more easily. This can shift contingently upon the situation of your organization. These boundaries can be something that two people can get over, making them an all the more impressive couple, or they can be seriously satisfactory to harm a couple, perhaps.

A great many people that deal with one other desire to manage issues that surface as opposed to overlooking them with the expectation that they disappear. By overhauling these obstructions with one another just as defeating them, you are building up the structure that hinders a solid structure for your association.

At the point when somebody is open and wishes to examine a worry (or a few) with you, that generally recommends that they are endeavoring to rescue the relationship, not end things. Except if clearly, they have attempted to talk with you on different occasions just as have seen no results; from that point onwards, indeed, people will without a doubt have an impediment to exactly the amount they will endure. In case you're avoiding doing your part, would you be able to reprimand your significant other for wishing to call it surrenders?

Moving beyond challenge(s) takes a great deal of work from the two people. If you're not open and just as glad to do your segment, at that point these difficulties will continue reemerging until dissatisfaction (and feeling like the other individual couldn't care less) can (and presumably will) cut off the association.

Correspondence

Association is a two-technique road. It's when two individuals can sincerely survey fundamental and difficult issues, being able to look at one another without flinching while at the same time staying away from crossed arms. Correspondence isn't the point at which one individual talks and the other different individual restrains their feelings and just uses gestures. At the point when this happens, it tends to be anything but difficult to charge the communicator of "irksome" or "talking at you."

Here are the basic things concerning conveying, you may not generally have reactions or arrangements directly after that and there. It's okay to amenably tell your significant other that you expect time to reach back, two or three hours, or maybe a day or two is incredible, as long as you let your partner comprehend that you are as yet meaning on discussing focuses. Saying nothing just shows that you weren't tuning in and couldn't have cared less. No one needs their sentiments and stresses cleared under a carpet.

If finding the suitable words to connect effectively is a worry, talk with a confidante or an individual from the family to help you in finding the words, use sources on the web, or if this is an issue for you, at that point search for an incredible specialist.

Trust Support

Many of us have relied upon issues from our past connections that we regularly convey subliminally into our next associations. If you walk directly into a business with doubt, and you are unequipped for letting this marvel about going, by what means will your association have the option to continue?

By not depending on that, your partner is starting from a mindful area when he/she brings their concerns or issues they have about you and the relationship you share. Chiefly you won't be as open to focusing. Keep in mind, your current association isn't your past organization.

At the point when difficulties are created, just as your partner is available to interfacing these worries with you, believing them proposes that you don't assume that they accept you're an awful individual or that they need to partition with you except if they illuminate you. Rather than pulling ceaselessly, leaving, or getting defensive since you dread a separation, completely open your heart and brain to hear your friend guarantee that you can effectively survive and migrate past boundaries.

Tuning In To Your Friend

Frequently sports vehicles won't proactively hear each out other. Subsequently, if anything goes horrible; you very well may become scatter-brained, shut down mentally, or snap. It's awful when your partner just hears and takes out all the negative stuff from the discussion that was guaranteed. By dismissing mostly (and a lot of times all) the good focuses that are being stated, you will miss the discussion. This will in general occur (and we as a whole have been liable for doing this) since we need to hold up until it's our chance to ensure that we can vent back and put out our grievances.

At the point when you shut down and quit hearing your friend, at that point you are accidentally letting them perceive that you couldn't care less. Numerous individuals voice an issue since they want their partner to hear them out and pay attention to what they are asserting. Nobody likes to share something and feel as though they weren't heard a while later; it's terrible and very inconsiderate.

Give Productive Input

We all need criticism and such information that is given without a doubt will be wonderful, warm, and even fluffy. In any case, when you care about somebody, be aware of leaving verbally abusive and over effectively available swearing out of your remarks, alongside hurling focuses. It's intense for anyone to focus if you stay in a crazy attack mode.

If by chance, you have stood by to give these remarks or you have discussed this issue previously, and you haven't seen any alterations about the situation, there will potentially be a ton of dissatisfaction as well as harshness in your voice, just as you convey your dissatisfaction. In any case, that may imply that you choose your words extra cautiously, which is also sensible.

Be Available To Remarks

At the point when you are shut to input, that point can get directions to distinguish yourself as the 'victim.' When you endeavor to chat with somebody, seeing worries as their first reaction shows that they can "do nothing right," which is an unmitigated cop-out.

Here are the things most individuals don't get a kick out of, expecting to give reactions. We would unquestionably appreciate accepting that our relationship is secure, going just as lighthearted; in any case, that is simply a crazy dream talk. All associations take work.

Catch Up With Solidness

Having an issue discussed and accepting that you are on the same wavelength as your significant other because they educated you that you were, is an incredible inclination. Isn't that so? Indeed, it doesn't feel that great when you think you are on the same page once more, because your life partner has implied this. However, from that point onward, you learn you are most certainly not.

Connections incorporate their portion of hindrances, just as while some are close to nothing, likewise minor, others are sufficiently critical to break what you've created with one another. Yet, regardless of whether you're experiencing what feels like a difficult obstacle, it's as yet conceivable to overcome organizational boundaries just as being more impressive than any time in recent memory, as indicated by adoration specialists and couples that have done it without anyone's help. Indeed, that incorporates the enormous ones: extramarital relations, financial trouble, significant distance, and an inconsistent harmony in the coordinated effort, generally given that you can move past if the two individuals need to put the work in.

In this way, if you and your significant other have included a relationship blockade, stay tuned. Moving ahead, pros share the huge difficulties that customers survived through while giving their proposals on how you can do it, too. From relying on balancing your obligations to managing separation to bouncing in the same spot concerning money-related assets, you'll look at recommendations from the masters just as two females that have existed, themselves. What's more, notwithstanding disposing of these hindrances, you may likewise come out on the opposite side more impressive than any time in recent memory.

Inconsistent Collaboration

Trouble can emerge when one partner feels like they're done while the different other's drives are dreary. "I see this worry regularly in exactly how couples share the housework and habitation upkeep needs," examines Toni Coleman, LCSW, CMC, a specialist, association mentor, and separation referee. She characterizes an 'ordinary circumstance' in which a division of obligations is checked on. Nonetheless, when a single individual has finished, he gets a move on. After some time, this empowerment brings about ill will and the passing of notoriety between the couple.

For issues like this, the advisor says her technique is 'antiquated' just as holding each other liable is fundamental. "I exhort turning work outlines, planning for time for obligations, costs paying, and discussions about the money related assets and joint duties, just as devices that give proposals, just as a help to help ensure development," she asserts.

Essentially recall: The factor isn't to dispatch a blow for blow trade. "This has to do with support, valuing the sensations and needs of their partner, just as looking for a successful win, since it's never a success except if the two individuals win," she finishes up.

Monetary Hardships

An extra example of inconsistent joint effort concerns you assuming it to be money. "A second, just as a normal situation, is the point at which one friend pays all the expenses, attempts to work within a spending plan, does considerably more saving, and doesn't bring credit card costs," states Coleman. Trouble can likewise rise when an occasion like an invasion of clinical costs, work misfortune, or flippancy undermines monetary insurance.

In either circumstance, the starting point issue is the energy it creates.

CHAPTER 14:

Jealousy and Fear of Abandonment

The fear of abandonment is a complex phenomenon in psychology that is believed to originate from childhood loss or injury. This worry has been examined from a variety of perspectives. Concepts behind why anxiety of abandonment occurs to consist of disturbances in the regular advancement of the little ones' social and mental capacities, past connections and life experiences, and direct exposure to certain norms and also concepts. Although it is not the main phobia, the fear of desertion is probably among the most common and most damaging worries of all. Individuals with the fear of abandonment might tend to display necessary actions and also thought patterns that affect their connections, inevitably leading to the abandonment they dread becoming a reality. This anxiety can be ravaging. Recognizing this worry is the very first step toward solving it.

The worry of abandonment is the frustrating worry that individuals close to you will undoubtedly leave. Anyone can create anxiety of abandonment. It can be deeply rooted in a stressful experience you had as a youngster or a stressful relationship in the adult years. If you fear desertion, it can be virtually difficult to keep healthy and balanced relationships. This incapacitating concern can lead you to wall surface yourself off to prevent getting hurt. Or you may be unintentionally undermining partnerships. The first step in dealing with your anxiety is to recognize why you feel in this manner. You should be able to resolve your issues and problems on your or with treatment. But the fears of desertion may additionally be part of a personality disorder that requires treatment. Continue analysis to explore the reasons and also long-lasting effects of a worry of abandonment and even when you ought to seek assistance.

Signs of a Fear of Abandonment

Numerous people have a problem with anxiety. Nearly 10% of individuals in the U.S. have some type of phobia. When it involves connections, its resulting habits consist of:

- You are fast to attach, also not to available partners or relationships.

- You are reluctant to commit fully, as well as have had very few long-lasting partnerships.

- You might be quick to move on just to guarantee that you do not get attached quickly.

- You aim to please. For some ladies, a study has also located an increase in the desire to have undesirable sex.

- As soon as in a partnership, you stay, despite how undesirable the relationship is.

- You are often hard to please as well as nitpicky.

- Emotional affection is hard for you.

- You feel insecure and unworthy of love.

- You locate it tough to rely on individuals.

- Being jealous of everybody you satisfy is not an odd sensation to you.

- Feelings of separation anxiousness are extreme.

- Feelings of underlying stress and anxiety and also clinical depression are very common to you.

- You often tend to overthink points and also work hard to identify the concealed significance in everything.

- You are hypersensitive to objections.

- You have quenched anger and also control issues.

- Self-blame prevails for you.

Sorts of Concern of Abandonment

You may be afraid that someone you like is going to leave and not come back physically. You may fear that a person will undoubtedly desert your psychological requirements, either can hold you in relationships with moms and dad, a partner, or a good friend.

Fear of Psychological Desertion

It may be less apparent than physical truancy. However, it's not less stressful. We all have psychological needs. When those demands aren't fulfilled, you may feel unappreciated, hated, as well as separated. You can feel quite alone, even when you remain in connection with somebody existing. If you've experienced psychological desertion in the past, primarily as a youngster, you may reside in continuous fear that it will certainly take place once more.

Desertion Anxiousness in Partnerships

You may be frightened to let yourself be susceptible to a company. You may have depended on issues as well as stress excessively regarding your relationship. That can make you suspicious. In time, your anxiousness can cause various other people to drawback, bolstering the cycle.

Signs and Symptoms of Fear of Abandonment

If you fear desertion, you may recognize a few of these signs and also indications:

- Overly conscious criticism

- Problem trusting in others

- Trouble making friends unless you can be confident they like you

- Taking severe procedures to avoid being rejected, or separation

- A pattern of unhealthy connections

- Getting affixed to individuals also swiftly, after that going on equally as promptly

- Problem dedicating to a relationship

- Functioning hard as well to please the other individual

- Blaming yourself when things do not exercise

- Remaining in a connection even if it's not healthy and balanced for you

Abandonment Problems in Relationships

If you fear desertion in your present partnership, it might result from having been physically or emotionally abandoned in the past. For example:

- As a teen, you may have experienced the fatality or desertion of a parent or a caretaker.

- You might have experienced parental abandonment.

- You might have been turned down by your peers.

- You experienced a prolonged health problem of an enjoyed one.

- A charming partner might have left you instantly or behaved in an undependable fashion.

Such occasions can result in fear of desertion.

CHAPTER 15:

Dealing With Unhealthy Jealousy; What Couples Need to Know

A bit of jealousy makes a relationship a little spicy, yet an excessive amount of jealousy might be dangerous in any intimate relationship. Jealousy happens when a life partner feels undermined by a third individual whom the individual accepts as an opponent and a risk to their relationship. Jealousy can be healthy, or unhealthy.

Unhealthy jealousy which is pointless and absurd can destroy a marriage.

When Jealousy Becomes Unhealthy?

Jealousy is healthy when it makes couples more committed, more loving, and more sensitive because they love their partner an excessive amount that they would prefer not to lose each other. Unhealthy jealousy makes the relationship difficult. Unhealthy jealousy or superfluous allegations of unfaithfulness makes the jealous partner act and think illogically. Outrageous jealousy can push a life partner to have silly thoughts and show unsuitable behavior. These unsatisfactory behaviors may incorporate: following the blamed partner, checking and observing the accused partner's things like mobile phones, clothes, notebooks, social media accounts, bags, and so on, for confirmations of sexual unfaithfulness, blocking partner's relationships with friends, unforeseen visits to their working environment, meeting or examining them and the most exceedingly terrible is acting violent to cause the blamed lover to admit.

How to manage unhealthy jealousy? There are approaches to manage unreasonable jealousy. The following are useful hints;

- Recognize that your unreasonable jealousy is the issue and not your partner.

A jealous partner usually perceives that their jealousy is irrational and dependent on unwarranted bits of proof but finds it difficult to have charge of the doubts or the feelings of jealousy which makes the person in question hopeless. The jealous person trusts that if their doubts can be legitimized, at that point the person in question will feel much better. Sadly, this isn't possible because irrational contemplations or doubts can't be disproved by rationality. For this situation, you need to confide more in your lover and understand that your silly jealousy is the issue.

- Understand the hidden reasons behind your illogical jealousy.

There's a reason a jealous partner continually accuses and believes their lover isn't loyal. One of the reasons could be that a jealous lover may have seen their parent not being loyal when they were young. Fearing abandonment is a second reason if a jealous lover had experienced being left by a loved one. Feeling inadequacy or deficiency might be another reason why you uniformly compare yourself to other people. For example, a lover of older age with smaller sexual capacity might feel he's not enough to satisfy a younger wife sexually and endangered or jealous of young men. Addictions might also influence one's reasoning to be more distrustful and jealous. Finding out why you are irrationally jealous might help you get to know the causes of your unhealthy jealousy and find the cure for it.

- Deny engaging in unreasonable thinking and attempt to prevent your senseless demeanor.

At whatever point you have those contemplations of jealousy and you're blaming your spouse once more, stop promptly and divert yourself. Instruct yourself to prevent this superfluous jealousy again and advise yourself of how this undesirable jealousy is harming your relationship. Record the brilliant things your lover accomplished for you to remember how much they love and adore you. Talk to someone close to you. Keep yourself caught up with the things you enjoy. Take the necessary steps to avoid those silly contemplations and keep yourself from doing unacceptable things. You can't succeed each time since you can't change how you think and act in one night, however, you need to continue attempting till you eventually prevail regarding developing your foolish thoughts and conduct. Compensate yourself every time you prevail regarding overcoming your silly jealousy.

- Get professional help.

It can be difficult to deal with foolish and unhealthy jealousy without seeking professional help. Some people are professional and can help you get rid of it. The less you wait with seeking help, the faster you'll get it out of your relationship. If you wish to save your relationships, get help now, before it's too late.

Jealousy in a Relationship; Things You Should Know

What's the meaning of jealousy? Jealousy is an auxiliary feeling, and it refers to the pessimistic thoughts and feelings of anxiety, fear, and insecurity over a loss that the individual values, particularly regarding a human connection.

The Source of Jealousy

Jealousy is mostly caused by two things:

1. Past experience

If someone has ever cheated on you, it'll encourage you to be more selfish, so it doesn't happen again. You'll strive to prevent and deter the potencies that cause your partner to turn away from you.

2. Own issues with self-confidence and lack of self-esteem

These factors are the main cause of jealousy. You feel that you're not good enough and someone else looks better than you, so you feel threatened by it. Watching your significant other interacts with other people, makes you feel worried that they may be "stolen" from you. If you've only been with your lover for a short time, the close bond they have with their friends whom they've known for a long time may even bother you.

Is Jealousy Dangerous?

Jealousy is divided into 3 phases:

1. **Natural Jealousy:** For example: not enjoying the sight when your partner is taking a walk and photo with another person, or feeling disappointed when it turns out they like someone. Such jealousy is still common, and nobody has a problem with it.

2. **Healthy Jealousy:** You feel anxious and suspicious of your partner. However, if this jealousy isn't settled quickly, this jealousy will probably grow to the final stage.

3. **Obsessive Jealousy:** You question the loyalty of your partner and soon this jealousy will lead you to anger, aggression, and a rude attitude. Even a friendly conversation between your partner and the other person will be considered as flirting. This is a form of defense mechanism against the potencies that threaten your relationship.

Jealousy would threaten a relationship when it reaches the 3rd stage because it will eat up the sense of trust one with another and you will often spend your time together fighting.

Furthermore, you'll focus on what could happen rather than what is happening. If jealousy is a problem in your relationship, I suggest trying to consider your behavior and what's underneath it, and then you can try to make it better.

Dealing with Jealousy

In any relationship, one can't refrain from feeling this strong feeling at one point or even more sometimes. Jealousy genuinely is a strong and revolting feeling that can destroy a relationship. Soon as it shows up in a relationship, couples should try on managing jealousy because once left unattended, it can develop into distaste and power battles. Even healthy and happy relationships can be crushed by jealousy that had gone more terrible.

Anyway, what truly is the base of all jealousy? For what reason do we need to deal with this feeling of jealousy if, in our conscious mind, we know or think we love and cherish our partner? On a cognizant level, jealousy truly originates from fear and mistrust. Individuals who fear being abandoned and being left by their partners feel jealous more often. This dread of being abandoned causes one partner to lose trust in the other. Furthermore, if you recall, trust is probably the most meaningful establishment of a relationship. Trust is an extraordinary healing device. Trust is crushed when jealousy sets in. Battles would result because jealousy is a relative term, one partner may feel that it's just an overreaction while different feels that their jealousy is advocated. These false impressions bring about silly discussions and contentions when the topic is about jealousy. This is the reason individuals can't carry out when managing jealousy.

On a deeper level, the subconscious level, when dealing with jealousy, Jeff Allen, a great relationship therapist in 'Psychology of Vision' once said that the extent you're jealous is the extent that you aren't committed to the relationship. The jealous party has placed their pain or heartbreak above their partner. When this happens, trouble follows. Jealousy or truly stems from two experiences when we were very young. From our parents. We might not have remembered the exact details of the incident, but it might have been that maybe our parents choose our siblings over us, and even very simply, you saw your parent of the opposite sex getting intimate with the parent of the same sex. Hence, a sense of loss and envy evolved in our heart, the pain of the loss will lead us to only one feeling: jealousy. Dealing with jealousy is a skill, and also it's a great heartbreak that has surfaced in our intimate relationship for us to be healed.

Couples must learn abilities at managing jealousy with their partner and their very issues by going up against their internal identity and by thinking rationally as possible. Are there any legitimate reasons not to confide in your partner? Addressing your needs and calming one's feelings of worries and fears in a relationship truly prompts problems and issues. Figuring out how to trust is a key component in managing jealousy. Fundamentally, trust becomes deeper as your relationship progresses to another level. Relationships will remain stuck in limbo when trust is absent and jealousy festers. Sometimes, the relationship will disintegrate and prompt breakups except if you truly try managing jealousy.

In dealing with jealousy, you need to learn to untie the knots in your heart when it comes to relationship issues. Consciously, commit, and commit to your partner, repeatedly. It's tough but is the only way that couples can open up a new realm of possibilities and the next beautiful honeymoon. Open yourself despite the risk of making yourself more vulnerable to being hurt. Walking towards your partner always beats walking away from them. Realize that being able to trust, and the knowledge about dealing with jealousy makes you mature enough for serious relationships. Be ready to trust your partner to keep jealousy away from your relationship. Trust, like what Jeff Allen said, is a great healing tool.

Learn abilities in managing jealousy and spare you and your partner all those feelings of grief, damages, and agonies that accompany it and have a blissful and lasting relationship. It saves time and above all, vitality. Imagine how you will feel if you are on a honeymoon every day? Life would be a stroll in the park! Success in love and winning against issues such as jealousy should be a common effort of you and your lover. Be brave and take steps, make your move, and show your lover that you want to make it work.

CHAPTER 16:

How to Manage Your Thoughts and Negative Emotions

Jealousy is an involuntary feeling that occurs to us when we feel insecure or concerned about something with our partner. We mainly feel jealous when we see someone else with something that we don't have. This is especially worse when that thing is a natural endowment, such as the physical appearance of another person.

In human nature, no one has it all. We all lack something that other people have. At times, you will have money and no time to spend it. Other times, you will be broke but have all the time. In another case, however, you will have a lot of possessions but lack peace of mind. When we lack what someone else has at a certain moment, that is the point we begin to become envious, and if we have no control over this feeling, it becomes jealousy. This is not exceptional in relationships. You will be envious of a third party (a perceived rival) for something they have and that you lack in. You might also be jealous of your partner because you think that they are better than you and more privileged. After all, it seems like they have no remorse when they hurt you like they intentionally do things to hurt you.

While it is normal to feel envious, preventing the feeling of envy from turning you into a jealous animal determines the success of your relationship. It determines how you process and handle information about your partner, how well you hold a conversation, and how well the two of you relate. Therefore, it is paramount to track and control your emotions at all times to avoid coming off as an unfriendly and irrational partner.

The first thing you should know is that feelings are not facts. What may be true for you may not be true for another person. It is all about the perspective from which you look at things. Sometimes, we tend to forget to separate our feelings from facts. We fail to ascertain that whatever we are feeling is true, and we base our decisions and actions on flawed feelings and assumptions.

Being able to separate feelings from facts is entirely useful in managing jealousy. There is a fine line between acknowledging the truth of our feelings and not projecting them onto our surroundings. Being entitled to your feelings is the same as being self-righteous, and it is entirely destructive to a relationship.

We are all bound to face moments of frustration and desperation in life, but giving in to these feelings is the worst thing we can do. Fortunately, there is a way in which we can be aware of this monster within us and overpower its demoralizing power. You can learn to silence your worst fear and appear as the most courageous and confident person. You can always calm your insecurities and negative feelings toward your partner.

The following is a guide on how you can do this:

Stop Being a Perfectionist

The truth is that perfectionists tend to get jealous. It may sound good to say that you are a perfectionist in a job interview, but this is detrimental to the greater part of your life, especially in managing relationships and failure. If you are a perfectionist, you do not expect your romantic partner to make mistakes. You are easily offended by mistakes, and you have fed your mind with all the attributes of perfectionism that you think is appropriate. You have extremely high standards and overly evaluate and criticize yourself.

As a perfectionist, you will always expect that your partner judges you harshly and that you have to display perfection to secure ultimate approval. Some mental problems associated with perfectionism are stress, anxiety, and depression. Perfectionism has been largely linked to young people. We are overly fed by social networking sites with things that are perfect. They always show us how an ideal life should be. However, we do not get to see the real side of the people we interact with online. Do not expect your partner to be perfect, and do not think that your partner will love you only if you are perfect.

Learn to understand that nothing is perfect. No one is perfect, and neither can anyone be perfect. Embrace your flaws and understand that your partner has their flaws as well. Then learn how to utilize your strengths to address these weaknesses. In this way, you can always avoid being jealous of things you probably cannot change.

Perform a Personality Test to Understand Yourself Better

It is natural for humans to want to know who they are. Try to take a personality test. The results will uncover your real traits, and you will probably find out what aspect of your life and relationship you need to work on. Personality tests help you connect with others cordially by making you more aware of yourself. You might discover things about yourself that you might otherwise be unaware of. You will realize what drains your energy and what fills up your spirit, and this can be used to understand why you react the way you do to envious triggers. You can learn to cope with these emotions and control them and not the other way around, and you can create happiness for yourself.

Personality quizzes are all over the internet today. It is almost impossible to check social media sites or go through websites without being prompted to take one. You should leverage this availability to perform one. Most people perform them for fun, and they end up revealing nuggets of wisdom that help shed light on various aspects of their lives.

It might seem trivial, but the results of a personality test can go a long way in making your dating and relationship phase successful. It can help you determine who you can best be compatible with. You may be feeling jealous, insecure, and all other negativities toward your partner because you are not compatible with each other.

Results of a personality test help you understand other people better, and you will know how to handle their reactions. You can understand their perception of the various aspects of life. The most common mistake people commit in relationships is assuming that other people have the same views and opinions as them.

Essentially, a personality test is among the major ways through which you can understand how best you function. It is a major step in making your life and your relationship better.

Keep a Journal to Track Your Emotions

Most successful people in history have kept journals that detail most aspects of their lives. Even though you do not see the need for one, a journal is among the most powerful tools through which you can succeed in any journey of life. While you may think that journals are best for investments, studies, and other major projects, journals are crucial for tracking your moods and emotions on a day-to-day basis. Keeping a mood-tracking journal has great benefits that you can begin to enjoy instantly.

Assuming that you have already made a decision to stop treating your feelings as facts and that you are willing to work on yourself, a journal should become your best friend. First, writing releases your daily stresses because it helps you relive the moments you experienced in an environment. It can also boost your esteem and make you feel happier.

Overall, journaling helps to calm your fears and prioritize problems in daily life. Through the journal, you can easily track down your triggers of jealousy and establish proper ways of handling them. It gives you a window into identifying when negative thoughts seem to cross your mind and have positive self-talk. When you feel too much of the negative feelings caused by jealousy, including insecurity, stress, and fear of loss, you can easily turn to your journal to try identifying what is causing these feelings.

However, it is not just the writing but also the thinking and feeling what you are writing about that matter in journaling. You do not just state your feelings plainly, but you tell your personal story of what you were thinking at the moment you had a certain mood.

The journal serves as a good reminder of the mistakes you have done in the past, and it also helps you to decipher the most probable reason you did so. This helps you in your retrospection to guide you on the best behavior to assume going forward. Furthermore, there are various ways to journal your moods, including keeping a notebook or using one of the various journal apps.

The best tip for maintaining a helpful journal is to keep it easy. Do not write fiction stories. Write every day if you can and let your words flow freely. You can be assured that it will help bring order to your life and your relationship even when it feels like it is full of chaos. Most importantly, find some moments to revisit the journal, especially whenever something makes you uncomfortable.

Improve Your Emotional Intelligence

We cannot deny that emotions are powerful. Whenever you are happy, for instance, you have the confidence to take on the world without anything stopping you. On the flip side, when you are sad or anxious, you experience the opposite attitude. Every emotion influences us in different ways. The problem comes when we allow emotions to get a hold of us in a bad way because the excess of any emotion leads to disastrous decisions and actions if not controlled.

Also referred to as EQ, the concept of emotional intelligence has become increasingly relevant as the demands from people's lives exert so much pressure on them and reduce their ability to form meaningful relationships with others. Understanding this concept helps you to recognize emotions, understand the powerful effect these emotions can have, and be able to apply this knowledge in your behavior and thinking. Learning how you react to various situations can help you to improve your relations with other people. This comes in handy in your relationship as well since you can identify when you feel jealous and how to address this feeling.

Even after performing personality tests and adapting a journal as your tool to track your emotions, it all boils down to how good you are at recognizing and dissecting these emotions to know what they mean for your relationship. People with low EQ tend to hold grudges. They get stressed easily, thus making assumptions and defending them vehemently. They often feel misunderstood. These are the major ways in which you react to your partner whenever jealousy strikes you.

To improve your EQ, try to be aware of your emotions and understand how they affect your functioning. Do you wish they could change or improve? Pause whenever you are experiencing strong emotions to avoid saying or doing something that you might regret later.

CHAPTER 17:

Managing Your Jealousy in Relationships

J ealousy can unfortunately ruin even the best relationships. It can be a powerful signal that it is time for you to change, or risk losing an otherwise fulfilling relationship. Jealousy can be a good checklist to better understand your underlying feelings, taking immediate action, and protect your relationship from experiencing the disastrous fallout of your jealous thoughts or behavior. Here are some of the most foolproof techniques to help you tackle jealousy and insecurity in relationships with ease.

Question Yourself Each Time

Each time you find yourself feeling even remotely jealous, question the underlying feeling behind the complex emotion of jealousy. Is jealousy a consequence of my anger, anxiety, or fear?

What is it about this situation that makes me jealous? When you question your jealously critically, you are a few steps away from taking constructive steps to convert a cloud of negativity into a bundle of positivity.

Be Open About Your Insecurities

Discussing your insecurities with your partner will help you create a frank and open communication channel. Rather than doing and saying crazy things to your partner, be upfront, and share your feelings. Say something similar to "I apologize for bothering you regarding your friendship with ABC, but it is not my lack of trust in you. I simply feel insecure about it."

Admitting it is you and not the other person goes a long way in resolving your relationship issues rather than hurling accusations at your partner. Together, you can work better on your insecurities if you both acknowledge it and take active steps to eliminate it.

Learn to Trust People

Learn to consciously get into the habit of trusting people more. Choose a trusting disposition over a distrustful attitude. Unless you have concrete evidence about someone, take their word for it. Going around snooping, stalking your partner, and behaving like a suspicious maniac only harms your relationship further. Rather, if there is no reason to be suspicious other than a feeling of insecurity or jealously, let it go.

Get to the Root of Your Feelings

It can be hard to objectively assess why you feel pangs of jealously each time someone compliments your partner, or he/she speaks warmly with his/her colleagues. It can be highly tempting to blame another person for your emotions. However, getting to the root of your jealousy by being more self-aware is the foundation to free yourself from its shackles. Take a more compassionate and objective look at the origination of your jealousy. Think about the potential causes of feelings of insecurity.

For instance, if you find yourself being increasingly jealous of your partner; know why you feel it. Is it because you don't want to lose him/her? Is it because your previous relationship ended due to a similar reason? Do you suffer from a false sense of self-entitlement that your partner's time belongs only to you? Do you feel what you feel because of a sense of inadequacy that constantly makes you think "You aren't good enough?" Once you identify the underlying reasons causing feelings of jealousy and insecurity, it becomes easier to deal with your behavior.

Write Down Your Deepest Thoughts

Journaling is known to be one of the most effective techniques for bringing forth your deepest feelings and emotions. It helps you discover multiple layers of your personality to achieve greater self-awareness. For instance, you may constantly harbor feelings of insecurity because you were raised by neglectful parents or you may never feel you are "good enough" because you were raised by parents who had extremely high and unreasonable expectations of you.

People who have been neglected in their childhood often feel they aren't worthy enough to be loved. This, in turn, causes them to think that their partner is seeking someone more worthy or deserving of love than them, which creates feelings of insecurity. Writing down may help you discover certain events, circumstances, and facets which may directly be responsible for your irrational behavior. Once you've nailed down underlying feelings behind the jealousy, it's way simpler to manage it.

Learn From Your Jealousy

Jealousy can be converted into learning or inspiration if you channelize it productively. For instance, if your partner plays the guitar well and finds himself/herself the cynosure of all eyes at a party, you can up your skills, too, by learning from him/her or signing up for guitar lessons. Instead of wallowing in defeatist self-pity, you have transformed your negative feelings into something positive.

Jealousy Doesn't Mean Something Will Happen

We need to understand that our jealous hunches do not necessarily mean the act is occurring. Just because we fear something is going to happen doesn't mean it will happen. A majority of the time, our fears are unfounded and not even remotely close to coming true. Just because your partner is somewhere else, and you fear he/she is with someone else, doesn't mean he/she is proposing marriage on a date. Understand the difference between thoughts and actual events. The make-believe imaginations of our destructive minds are often far from reality.

Paranoia or replaying a worst-case scenario is common among people suffering from jealousy or insecurity. They imagine things that have no basis in reality. For instance, your partner may call or visit an ex to express his/her condolences when the ex's mother passes away. This doesn't in any way imply that your partner is still hooked to the ex. However, you may find yourself imagining terrible things that may be the result of sheer jealousy and paranoia.

Rather than imagining negative things, try shifting the focus of how wonderful your partner is to be considerate and pleasant with an ex. This might be the very reason that made you fall in love with him/her. See what you did there? You shifted your feelings from insecurity to pride, from untrue suspicions to a positive reality.

Get Rid of Past Relationship Garbage

A strong reason why you are always paranoid about your current partner cheating on you can be traced back to an earlier relationship. You may have had an ex-partner cheat on you with your best friend. The betrayal may have had such a severe impact that you view every relationship in a similar distrustful light. However, understand that your current partner has nothing to do with your previous relationship. He/she should not have to bear the brunt of what someone else did. Painting everyone with the same brush can be a disastrous mistake in any relationship. There is a solid reason your earlier relationship did not last, and you should leave the garbage of your earlier relationship where it belongs–in the trash can.

Surround Yourself with Meaningful Relationships

People are often so wrapped up in their romantic relationship that there is a tendency to distance ourselves from all other relationships. We believe in spending every waking minute of our lives with our partners.

This only leads to a greater feeling of fear and insecurity because we realize that once this relationship ceases to exist, we have no other meaningful relationship as our safety net. We tend to develop greater feelings of insecurity and jealousy when we have no one to fall back on.

It helps to not make a single relationship the center of your universe and to develop several meaningful friendships. Do no distance from your close friends after getting into a relationship. Talk to them, spend time with them, do fun things together (that you probably did in school or college), have lunch dates, travel with them, and more. This will give you a life outside of your and your partner's time together. Once you have a momentous life outside your relationship, you will be less likely to wallow in self-pity and self-induced sulks. You will always have someone to talk to if you are surrounded by family or friends who understand and love you unconditionally.

Mindfulness for Managing Your Emotions

Mindfulness is a great way to calm your nerves and manage runaway emotions. Tune into your physical and mental self by identifying your feelings, thoughts, and emotions by taking deep breaths. Try to detach yourself from overpowering negative emotions such as jealousy and insecurity. Every time you find yourself overcome with thoughts of jealousy or insecurity, practice mindful meditation.

Find a quiet corner that is free from distraction, sit in a comfortable position, and clear your mind by eliminating all thoughts and take deep breaths. Focus only on the present and your deep breathing without allowing your mind to wander. If you find your mind drifting, gently bring it back to the present by concentrating on your bodily sensations. Daily meditation sessions can help you break free from ugly thoughts and behavior patterns.

Do Not Judge Others Based on Your Past Actions

Ever notice how suspicious people are always suspicious of others? Or how liars think everyone around them is lying? Our perceptions of people and their motives are often a reflection of who we are. Stop using your past or present behavior as a yardstick for perceiving your partner's actions. For instance, if you have a history of being involved with married men/women, do not assume that no married man/woman can ever be trusted and start mistrusting your spouse. Just because you did or are doing something does not mean he/she is indulging in it, too.

People who often have loyalty issues themselves constantly attack their partners for being unfaithful or immoral. There is a greater need to shift the blame from their inability to cope with issues related to unfaithfulness. Acknowledge that there is a problem, talk to a therapist about it and try to treat it rather than making your partner bear the brunt of your follies. Sometimes people fail to understand why despite giving their partner no reason to feel insecure or ever being unfaithful to them they are still made to feel like lying scums. The problem often lies with the person suspecting them and not the person at the receiving end of these unfortunate suspicions.

Avoid Being a Victim of Relationship Games

People often try to feel great about themselves by purportedly getting their partner to feel jealous. Do not fall into the trap. Displaying any signs of jealousy will only encourage your partner's behavior. Tell your partner firmly that indulging in a jealousy/insecurity inducing behavior only demeans him/her and won't make him/her feel any better about himself/herself. Even if you feel jealous, try to keep a stoic and unaffected demeanor, which should eventually stop these excruciatingly uncomfortable, attention-drawing tactics.

Do Not Imprison People

Start relaxing a bit by letting go of your desire to imprison your partner. The harder you try to imprison someone against his/her will, the more forcefully they'll try to escape your domineering behavior. Let your partner have the freedom to spend time with his/her friends, talk to their attractive colleague, or do other things that otherwise make you feel threatened. Once they realize how secure and confident you are about the relationship, they will automatically be drawn to you. A secure and self-assured partner can be extremely irresistible. Tips to Resolve Disputes and Reconnect

Usually, after years of marriage, the emotional and physical bond that partners share tends to fade away slowly. To avoid this, you must work on putting in the necessary effort required to keep the relationship going; not just going, the relationship must thrive. When you are in a happy marriage, you will be happier in general.

At times, perhaps the best thing you can do is not to say anything. Give your partner a hug or maybe even gently pat them on the back to allow them to know you are there for them. Leaving a couple of things unsaid is a good idea. Whenever you are wrong, you must admit it. However, there might have been times when you were right, but by merely holding your tongue and by not saying anything, you can save yourself an unnecessary fight. Once your partner is calm, test the waters before you restart the conversation.

Even the darkest cloud has a silver lining. Make it a point to look for any positive aspect of the relationship and stop concentrating solely on the negative ones. Couples who share positive communication are usually more satisfied with their relationships. It takes about five positive communications to undo the impact of one negative communication. Keep this ratio in mind whenever you are communicating with your partner.

If the bond you share with your partner is strong enough, then your relationship can withstand pretty much anything that happens to you. To do this, you must concentrate on the positive aspects of your relationship. Always look for something good you can say. If you want, feel free to use any positive affirmations you feel like. If you both are in trouble, by telling your partner everything will be okay, and you will be there to support them along the way, this works as a positive affirmation. During a fight, stop for a moment, and tell your partner how grateful you are to have them in your life. I'm sure this will certainly put an end to the argument you are having.

Whenever in a conflict, you must never lose perspective. When in a foul mood, even the slightest thing can make you angry. In such times, everything may seem dull and gloomy to you. A lot of couples tend to talk about taking time away from each other or even calling it quits the minute they run into any obstacles. Well, obstacles are part of life. You cannot go through life unscathed. Your success depends on how well you handle those obstacles. There are some things you can avoid, and some you cannot. Learning to deal with obstacles will certainly save your relationship. Remember, whenever you hit a rough patch, all you must do is adapt and overcome the problem you're facing. If the issue at hand is rather petty and you know it, then merely ignore it. Some issues are just not worth losing your peace of mind over or hurting your relationship.

If you know your partner's emotional state of mind was your fault, then you must apologize. The bigger the mistake you committed; the bigger the apology you need to offer. It's not merely about saying sorry, but you must mean it as well. If you say you're sorry, and then keep making the same mistake over and over again, your apology will be worthless. You can always fix any mistakes you make in life. Don't allow your ego to prevent you from doing the right thing. If you make a mistake, up. It is okay to make mistakes, provided you learn from them. Don't try to lie or try to talk your way out of it. If you did something wrong, then the least you can do for your partner in such a situation is to be truthful and honest.

It is not unusual for couples that are passionate to find themselves riding an emotional roller coaster from time to time. It would be better to let the past stay in the past; this will give the couple a fresh start to begin things. Letting resentments build isn't good, and even the smallest of altercations can create a big fight. There is no point in holding onto unnecessary fights and arguments; all it does is build resentment toward your partner. Keep short accounts of any fights you had. For the sake of your mental wellbeing and the health of your relationship, learn to let go. You don't have to hold everything and learning to let go of petty issues will be quite helpful. However, I am not suggesting that you must repress your emotions. If you have an issue with something, talk it out, and express yourself. That said, it will not do you any good if you hold on to the fight you and your partner had over three years ago because your partner forgot to load the dishwasher! You cannot control much in life, but the two things you can always control are the way you think and feel.

If things start getting tense and a plan that you or your partner has made isn't working out, then it would be good if you could offer alternative suggestions instead of just saying you knew the plan wouldn't work out. Give your partner some time to calm down, and then you can probably suggest that it would be good if you two can brainstorm together to come up with a solution. Make sure that in a tough situation, at least one of you is calm because this will help resolve any issues. You can regroup and think things through before proceeding with a particular idea.

If you notice that any argument you're having with your partner is getting quite heated, then it is time to take a break from the conversation. At times, merely putting some physical distance between the two of you can help. Give your partner some space and take some space for yourself.

Maybe you can draw a nice path between you and your partner and even play some soft music to calm things down. Or you can go for a walk or jog if you want. Apart from this, even engaging in a sport together can help diffuse the tension in the situation.

CHAPTER 18:

Communication: How to Start a Conversation with the Insecure and Jealous Partner

ood communication is an essential aspect of all relationships and is a necessary part of a good relationship. Every relationship has ups and downs, but a positive form of communication will make it easier to cope with tension and create a deeper and happier relationship. We always learn how important communication is, but not what it is and how effective communication should be included in our relationships.

What is Communication?

Communication is, by nature, the transferring of information from one area to another. Throughout relationships, communication helps you to convey to someone else what you're feeling and what your desires are. Not only does that, the act of communication help to satisfy your desires, but it also allows you to feel linked in your relationship.

A communication model typically includes a sender, a recipient, and a (verbal or non-verbal) message that is interpreted by the sender and decoded by the receiver. It also requires feedback, the receiver's reaction to the message, as well as noise, which is something that may interrupt communication.

Encoding relates to the sender's translation of feelings into communicable texts. The recipient interprets what they get as a letter, both verbal and non-verbal. Although this seems practically straightforward, as you might guess, a lot is going on in between, so no message is ever decoded without discrimination.

How we interpret a word is rarely an objective reality. We also have our filters and expressive types that build a view of the universe as we see it.

That makes the communication cycle much more complicated as the reality is that the sender's response is not ever simply truthful information.

"We talk not only to remind us what we think but to remind ourselves what we think. Speech is a function of feeling." Oliver Sacks in his four-sided communication model, Friedemann Schulz von Thun (1981) points out that a word has four dimensions to it:

1. **Fact:** How I report (data, information, statements);

2. **Self-revealing:** What I have learned about myself (information regarding the sender);

3. **Relationship:** What I think of you (information on how we're going to get along);

4. **Appeal:** What I expect you to do (an effort to manipulate the receiver).

Communicating Clearly In a Relationship

Please talk to each other. No matter how much you learn and love each other, you can't understand your partner's mind. We need to interact effectively to prevent any misunderstandings that can trigger hurt, frustration, dissatisfaction, or uncertainty.

It requires two people to create a relationship, and each has specific communication requirements and types. Couples ought to find a way to connect that fits their relationship. Healthy forms of communication include preparation and diligent work. Communication is never going to be perfect all the time.

Be transparent as you interact with your spouse so that the word can be heard and understood. Double test your comprehension of what your partner has to suggest.

When you talk to your partner, try to:

- Set aside a room to talk without interference from certain people or disruptions, such as mobile, laptops, or television.

- Think of what you're trying to say.

- Be specific about what you're trying to communicate.

- Keep the point explicit enough that the partner can hear it precisely and appreciate what you're thinking about.

- Speak directly about what's going on and how it's influencing you.

- Talk about what you like, need, and know using 'I' phrases like 'I need,' 'I want,' and 'I feel.'

- Accept accountability for your emotions.

- Yeah, listen to your friend. Set aside your emotions for the time being and seek to consider their motives, fears, wishes, and expectations (this is called empathy).

- Share optimistic thoughts with your partner, such as what you enjoy and respect, and how valuable they are to you.

- Stay mindful of your speech tone.

- Negotiate and say, you don't have to be perfect all the way. If the problem you're concerned with isn't that relevant, decide and let the problem go, or consent and disagree.

Non-Verbal Communication

If we communicate, we can tell a lot without speaking. The position of our body, the sound of our voice, and the expression on our faces all reflect a meaning. These non-verbal forms of communication will say the other person how we feel about them.

If our emotions don't suit our expressions, it is mostly non-verbal communication that 'hears' and believes. For, e.g., saying 'I love you' to your partner in a flat, bored tone of voice brings you two completely different signals. Note that the body's vocabulary represents what you're doing.

Listening and Communication

Listening is an essential aspect of good communication. Effective listeners may inspire their partner to speak freely and frankly. The guidelines for listening well include the following:

- Keep eye contact relaxed (where culturally appropriate).

- Lean-to the other person and give movements to display affection and concern.

- Face the other person, don't sit or stand horizontally.

- Sit or stand on the same point to stop staring up or down on the other person.

- Avoid disruptive motions, such as holding a pad, staring at documents, or rubbing the legs or feet.

- Be mindful that physical obstacles, noise, or interruptions can render contact difficult. Mute mobile or other contact tools to make sure you're still attentive.

- Enable the other individual to talk without interruption.

- Show real concern and value.

- Using assertive phrases like 'I thought about ...' or 'What I need is ....' Be mindful of your language.

- Be willing to take some time off if you are particularly angry over it. It could be easier to calm down before you get to grips with the problem.

- Ask the other person for suggestions about your listening.

Improving Communication in a Relationship

Free and direct communication may be taught. Most people find it challenging to communicate, so they can require patience and support to share their opinions. We may be strong listeners, or they may be individuals whose actions talk louder than their voices.

You can help to improve your communication by:

1. Creating Companionship: Expressing the partner's views, desires, and worries, and showing affection and gratitude.

2. Sharing Affection: Love is not just a physical relation. Intimacy is generated by providing periods of closeness and commitment to your mate. It implies being able to relax and ease, and to be accessible and truthful. An act of intimacy may be as easy as taking a cup of tea to your partner, so you can tell them they're tired.

3. Having one or two main things that you may decide about, such as how resources are allocated, the objective you have, or the parenting styles or techniques.

To improve the way you communicate, start by asking questions such as:

- What creates a dispute between you and your partner? Are they saying you're not talking to each other?
- What sort of stuff offer you joy and feelings of connection?
- Which sort of issues is causing you frustration and pain?

- What stuff don't you think about, and what's preventing you from talking there?
- How would you want your relationship with your partner to be different?

When necessary, ask your partner about these questions and exchange your responses. Dream of, and seek, ways to connect differently. See if the findings would boost communication.

Once you learn something about how you interact, you'll be able to get better control of what's going on between you. Although opening up different avenues of conversation may not be simple at first, it will contribute to a more satisfying relationship.

Some Things Are Difficult To Communicate

Most of us consider it daunting to think about any of the experiences or issues. It may be unpleasant, or it may make one feel awkward. For example, certain people find it challenging to convey their feelings. It's always the things you can't think about that hurt worst.

When you have trouble explaining yourself or communicating with your partner about it, you may consider it convenient to speak to a counselor for tips on how to manage conflict with communication. Some are:

- Avoid using silent treatment.
- Don't leap to your assumptions. Find out more of all the truth than guessing at the reasons.
- Discuss what happened. Don't rule either.
- Study to grasp each other, not to fight one another.
- Think of the future in the current tense, not the past tense.
- Concentrate on the big issue and don't get confused by certain small problems.
- Chat over things that damage your partner's emotions. Moving on to conflicts of opinion matters.
- Using the 'I thought' argument, not the 'You are' expression.

How to Communicate If You Are Angry

It's normal to get upset in a relationship—everybody does at some stage! What's crucial is that you safely settle disputes. If you get upset with your partner, here are a few moves to take:

- **Avoid It**

If you're very angry about someone, relax, take a step back and breathe. Tell your spouse that you'd like to take a brief break until the discussion begins. Give yourself time to relax by watching TV, talking to a colleague, playing a video game, taking a stroll, listening to music, or anything you need to relax. Taking a break will prevent it from going worse.

- **Think About It**

When you're no longer angry, talk about the case, about why you're so mad. Is it because your companion is communicating or whatever they were thinking about? Figure out the true issue and talk about how to clarify the feelings.

- **Speak To Someone**

Eventually, speak to your partner, and if you do, obey the tips above.

- **Listen To Them**

When you tell your partner how you felt, try to stop speaking and listen to what they've got to suggest. Both of you have the right to communicate how you feel in a comfortable and secure climate.

Communicating is not always convenient. At first, some of these tips can sound uncomfortable or awkward, but they can help you properly connect and develop a healthier relationship.

CHAPTER 19:

Why Do Relationships Fail?

I s your partnership descending? It is not easy to maintain a partnership. Many couples face many bumps along the way to a healthy relationship. Until previously understood, these bumps may cause couples to step in the wrong direction leading to breakdowns or divorce. To avoid further harm, it is important to understand many such relationship psychos beforehand.

Loss in Contact or Lack of Coordination

One way to connect is to have good, regular communication between couples. Couples continue to fall away because of inadequate contact or loss of touch. Many issues with relationships begin with the lack of contact. Assuming you care what your husband or wife feels, your partnership is dangerous. Misunderstandings and disagreements are often the product of your wife or girlfriend, not talking. If this occurs in your relationship, you will realize that this is one of the reasons that relationships fail and that you have to do something to improve communication.

Not respectful of the aspirations, interests, and careers of each other. One of the reasons why marriages are collapsing is the difficulties between couples with jobs and aspirations. If two parties have conflicting interests and goals in a relationship and cannot agree or accept each other, the relationship will eventually fail. That is that two people have different goals and professions to seek, of course, so it is better to respect one another's desire or occupation to prevent pressure on the relationship. It is safer for a husband or wife who trusts and respects the career of his or her wife or girlfriend to work with. Where it is not possible to achieve 100 percent appreciation, approval, and support, a friend or a girlfriend would at least be able to adapt and find a role with both their jobs and families. Sacrifices are inevitable. They all will learn how to navigate their love-life careers. It's better to say than to do but not unlikely. There are couples who both excel in their careers while keeping a stable and healthy friendship. Don't get along with friends and families of your girlfriend. The friction with those nearest to the family or friends is one of the reasons why marriages collapse. Let's face it. You and your friend don't revolve around the world alone. You and your family can not exist without people like friends and relatives around you. Your friendship can not be compromised by not being close to your friend. If you and your partner's mother or best friend can't tolerate each other or live in a single room, the friendship can be difficult. Holiday meals and family gatherings will be unpleasant if the families and friends of your wife are not on good terms. It is best to get together with people important to your partner because you wish to build a healthy friendship with your partner.

Things of Life and Luggage

Life baggage occurs, and as a relationship is formed complications may cause harm. A residual ex can spark envy, distrust, and resentment that will weaken your relationship today, so it's best to be sure that this is now in the past, and you are adamant about your relationship today. This is, therefore, inappropriate and damaging to equate your current relationship with your past relationships. Children and past marital complications can be daunting and can also influence your relationship, and you need to learn how to cope with these issues to make the present relationship succeed. Another cause of relationship loss is the inability to manage issues and baggage in your life.

Issues of Capital

One explanation of why marriages collapse is financial problems. If not properly handled, money issues will ruin your relationship. Economic instability and hardship will eventually destroy a relationship. People or people who are overwhelmed by financial difficulties may become irritable, angry, violent, and cold towards their wives or friends, and they can eventually ruin a relationship. It is best to be frank about your financial situation from the outset, be open to discussing each other's investment patterns, money-sharing, and expenditures. With good and honest conversations, plans, and financial concessions, a tough couple can iron out problems and save their marriage.

Infidelity

Infidelity. It is difficult to sustain a relationship between two men, but involving a third person or abusing a girlfriend is a grenade that can ruin a relationship immediately. Infidelity is the greatest killer of marriages, and certain marriages cannot survive. Betraying your partner's trust is one of the key reasons why marriages collapse. There is no simple feeling to be replaced or cheated, which means that the cheated spouse or friend also leaves the relationship. Though there are people who can endure and make the relationship work again, it's best not to be infidel if you want a long-term partnership.

Disgusting Behaviors

While it is true that loving someone requires embracing all their flaws, some behaviors can get irritating over time and may cause your partner one day to wake up and decide he or she needs to end the engagement. Only small issues like not putting the toothpaste cap on, not cleaning the bed, not putting the washing in the laundry, or getting the shoes and boots filthy in the house will be picked up because issues do not go well and your wife will break the relationship. Nagging, being a battle, arguing openly, insulting your wife or husband, calling or shouting disputes, hanging on to rancor, punching your spouse or partner when you're angry, tossing away too much or unfair anger, ignoring conversations about issues in your partnership, deception or dishonesty to your spouse or partner is a bad thing! Being in a relationship should help partners to be happier people and not get worse because it is easier to improve and create a good relationship than to have negative habits that will ruin the relationship in the end.

Things Are a Ritual in Your Relationship

The fire and the passion in the relationship could die because you were too relaxed or content to have a routine rather than an act of love. You're looking more like family or friends than like lovers. Very relaxed with one another extracts suspense and passion from the relationship and makes it predictable and repetitive. When couples do the same thing over and again, as people and as friends, they stop through. Shake your routine and spice you up. You can do different things and have different desires to evolve as an individual, and there are things that you can do to bind together. It is important to encourage your husband or companion to do his thing or to enjoy the company of his or her mates, but it is also important to spend time alone with each other on frequent occasions or holidays to interact and build new enjoyable memories.

Intimacy and Sex Are Absent

Life can be too chaotic and difficult for partners to end up being too distracted or depressed for love or sex that is not appropriate in a relationship. Couples have to interact closely mentally and physically, and sex is the perfect way to do that. During a long-term relationship, sex will dry up, and partners appear to have less sex over the years. Couples are meant to discourage this. One of the reasons why marriages fail is a lack of affection or sexual dissatisfaction. When people avoid having sex, they appear to be isolated and withdrawn and are vulnerable to unfaithfulness.

Couples should lead a healthy sex life to keep the relationship alive and exciting. Although having your partner closely with you through daily sex is vital, couples should be aware of the pressure on your wife or girlfriend not to participate in frequent intercourse. Some studies suggest that having daily intercourse once a week is acceptable and enough to sustain the romantic relationship between partners. There are many barriers to doing this, such as job pressures, pressures of your daily life, caring for children, and the situation in which you are not in a sexual mood yet. Like all other problems in your relationship, the amount and scheduling of sex should be addressed and prepared. Intimate sexual connections are important in any marital interaction, and if partners do not have enough sex links, they have to do something to address this issue to save the relationship.

CHAPTER 20:

Coping With Your Jealous Partner

J ealousy can be so very annoying, and no one wants to be stuck with a jealous partner. At first, you might want to ignore your partner; you might even find it a bit sexy that your partner is getting jealous at the sight of someone making a pass at you. But what happens when your partner's jealous feelings begin to get more intense, and you don't seem to find it funny anymore. There might have even been some arguments and outbursts arising from their jealousy. You might have felt some embarrassment a time or two because of these same feelings, and it is becoming a real issue in your relationship.

So true. Jealousy can affect the love and intimacy in a relationship and, if left unchecked, can lead to the end of the relationship. So, you love your partner, and you feel that their jealousy is something you are willing to help them overcome, that you are not ready to give up on them.

The Jealousy Baggage

Everyone has baggage, whether they admit it or not. There is simply no perfect person, and no one is born an angel or a saint. Some people seem to think that they tick all the right boxes and are the ideal partners in a relationship. They, therefore, argue that they do not want to inherit another person's baggage. They are also quick to break things up with a jealous partner.

The truth is, your life might be less complicated than someone else, but that doesn't mean you are perfect and wouldn't encounter challenges. When these issues arise, we definitely would want the support of our partner to help us during a trying time; after all, you can't foresee you wouldn't encounter some form of baggage in your life. How can you tell your job or business wouldn't suffer challenges? What about challenges with your health, family, or finances? Some couples have worked through the most daunting situations like sickness, bankruptcy, and even betrayals, and some have endured stronger challenges. Jealousy should be viewed as another challenge your relationship is facing, and with the right support; you and your partner can also pull through this one stronger.

Simply put, relationships require a lot of hard work, and a relationship without problems is non-existent. Jealousy is another problem your relationship is facing even though it is coming from your partner. You probably might have had some issues where your partner was there for you as well, and you came through. Now you can argue that yours was not as intense as your partners, but that shouldn't be your mindset if you are going to make your relationship work. Genuine relationships involve carrying one another's baggage and bearing the weight as a couple; the jealousy baggage is no different.

Understanding Your Partner's Jealousy

Going on this journey to helping your partner through their jealousy has to begin with first understanding your partner's jealousy. Hopefully, if you have read this book to this point, you might have already started to get insights into where your partner's jealousy is developing. Even if you are unsure, you can still work with them on this journey.

So why is your partner jealous? This question can be answered by considering these pointers:

- **You Are Not The Cause:** You need to understand that no matter what it may seem like you have done, it's not your fault that your partner has a jealousy problem. The issue is coming mainly from your partner, although your actions might have awakened these feelings [30]. So, get this straight as you begin to help your partner through overcoming jealousy–you are not the cause of your partner's jealousy.

- **When Did The Jealousy Start:** Can you pinpoint exactly when these jealous feelings began showing up in your partner? Is that how your partner has been for a long time? You can search within to find out if there was something you did or have been doing that might have triggered your partner's jealousy. Has something changed recently with your partner? Perhaps some financial problems, a failed promotion, or a recent trauma? Only your partner can tell you what is going on, but if you have a clue, then it helps you when you want to discuss the issue with your partner.

- **Is The Jealousy Related to Low Self-Esteem, Insecurities, Fear, and Or Doubt:** Have you considered the main reasons for jealousy? Perhaps your partner has some insecurity issues or a self-esteem problem. Have they had trust issues with you or a previous partner? Have they been betrayed in the past, or are they afraid of losing the relationship? If you have seen any of those signs, it might be the cause of their jealousy. If it becomes obvious that any of the factors mentioned is affecting your partner, then, knowing where the problem originates, you can face the underlying issue and not your partner's jealousy.

Working Hand-In-Hand

Now that you are very close to understanding your partner's jealousy, you are ready to start working as a team to overcome this challenge in your relationship. Hopefully, you will get past this phase and tell stories about it later. Be ready to give your partner all the support they need from you at this sensitive period of your relationship. The journey might not be as easy as you imagined, as dealing with jealousy requires a lot of patience, so be prepared for some of the bumps on the way. Your love and commitment to your partner together with their cooperation should keep you motivated as you go through this phase.

Here again, are some tips that can help:

- **Invite Your Partner To Talk:** Let your partner know that they can open up to you about this jealousy issue. Invite them to talk about it, choosing an appropriate time for the conversation. Let them know you want to hear them out and that you wish to support them through overcoming these jealous feelings that are now affecting your relationship. Be warm and friendly about the conversation because they might be a bit embarrassed about their jealousy or not ready to open up to you. Let them know that you are here for them when they want to talk. Remember, this jealousy is affecting you as well. Let your partner know that you wish you could work on the issue so you can move past it quickly.

- **Let Your Partner Know How You Feel About Their Jealousy:** Tell your partner exactly how their jealousy is making you feel. Hurt, unloved, angry, disrespected, embarrassed, unhappy? Let them know that it is affecting you as well.

- **Don't Try To Be The Hero:** This is not the time to feel like the hero and make your partner feel like you want to rescue them from a pit. Remember, there are no winners or losers here. Even if you have been through a similar situation, now is not the time to act as though you weathered the situation like a pro. It's an issue for both of you, and it affects you as well as it affects your partner, so take their hand and let them know that you are in this together.

- **Don't Raise The Accusing Finger:** Even if your partner's recent actions have offended or hurt you, don't begin to lay blame. You will only end up arguing, and the purpose of the discussion will be defeated. Your enemy is jealousy and not your partner. You should see it that way, and this mentality can help you work effectively with your partner in driving away from this unwanted emotion.

- **Show A Lot Of Compassion And Love During This Period:** You want to let your partner know that you are there with them through this journey of recovery. So, try showing them a lot of love and attention in this period. Extra hugs, touches, and kisses can reassure them that you are there for them. You know what makes your partner feel loved. Deliberately decide to shower them with a lot of love and hopefully this can reassure them that you are not going anywhere.

- **Be Present For Your Partner:** Your partner may need a lot of quality time together as they overcome jealousy, so be present for them. Do things together and more often like date nights and vacations. Talk even if you have to listen to them sometimes. This will improve your bond and intimacy and can help rid your partner's jealousy.

- **Be Patient:** This journey may take some time, and your partner may show some signs of jealousy. Once in a while, when you think you have made some reasonable progress, be patient with them. A partner who is determined to overcome jealousy, and with your support, will achieve this goal eventually.

Knowing When to Seek Help

The effects of jealousy can become very dangerous to a relationship in its irrational form and can make people revert to violence and abuse of their partners. Jealousy, in its standard way, can be turned into a good course and doesn't linger for too long. Irrational jealousy is of primary concern because of what this emotion can do to a person when not managed correctly and in time. So, when do you draw the line on your partner's jealousy and resort to external help?

- **When Your Jealous Partner Turns To Abuse And Violence:** A relationship should be the safest place on the planet for you. Even though everyone encounters challenges in relationships, confiding in each other, and working through challenges as a team makes the relationship always worthwhile. But when you have to go through physical or emotional abuse, then the purpose of the relationship is not being achieved, and you should consider ending the relationship for your sake. A jealous partner who harms you as a result of their jealousy needs more help than you can offer. Their jealousy has now produced more emotional issues like extreme anger and lack of control. If you are going through abuse because of a jealous partner, or for any other reason, you should report to the relevant authorities. Please seek help and don't remain silent if jealousy has grown into such a stage. You can't help that partner anymore, and you should consider leaving them at least until they have recovered completely.

- **You Can Also Seek Help From An Experienced Counselor:** You and your partner can agree to see an expert counselor for advice and therapeutic remedies on jealousy. Many professionals can work with you and your partner. This will cost some money but consider it as an investment in your relationship, one that will "pay off" in the future. Your partner should be comfortable with this decision before you take the step. Don't threaten or coax them into agreeing to see a therapist because they might end up doing so to please you. Instead, try to convince them and wait for them to be happy with the decision before beginning any therapy. Again, you should seek this sort of remedy when things are still under control, and you are not in any danger from your partner's jealousy.

CHAPTER 21:

How to Help Your Partner Overcome Jealousy

Jealousy most of the time drives to a disagreement because the other partner doesn't feel it's justified. For them, it's just 'overreaction.'

Disagreements activated from jealousy often become absurd and emotional and it's tough to deal with the negative feelings that appear from it. Nevertheless, we should take them and use them to better our relationship. Here are tips for dealing with jealousy in your marriage:

1. Get a vision of your inner self.

Ask yourself what situation made you feel jealous. Did your lover do something to make you stop trusting them? Or your imagination made you think that it'll happen soon? Fear is usually what's generating jealousy. Trust is jealousy's enemy. If both sides trust the other person jealousy won't ever try to get into this relationship.

2. Is allowing those negative feelings to get a hold of your life worth it?

Our natural desire to keep safe what we have and keep our things and people close to us makes jealousy appear. Jealousy in specific portions can add some flavor to your marriage and keep the pressure living.

3. However, after some time jealousy becomes destructive.

Lovers will want to protect what's theirs and so a person we're married to is ours. It's just how human beings are and we can't do anything about it.

Remind yourself this you'll be able to improve your marriage by using those feelings.

4. **You have to detect the root of these feelings. Most of the time, your jealousy will be caused by the fear you're experiencing.**

Maybe this fear is caused by a situation or experience you've had with another partner long ago.

There may be also some other causes but usually, there's been one unique situation in the past that made you lose trust and replace it with distrust and fear.

If you can find the center of those feelings inside yourself, you'll be able to cope with jealousy better than before.

Jealousy can also have other forms.

Maybe you think your lover is misleading you. If yes, you have to find out if there was any proof, or was it just your own distrust.

You can only focus on your feelings if you can detect the center of the issue.

1. Fight foolish jealousy with a better understanding of yourself.

2. Think about how jealousy makes your partner feel.

Almost always, jealousy ends with a divorce or breakup if the couple can't find a way to take control of their negative feelings.

Did you ever think about how does it feel for your partner to always be jealous? Put yourself in their shoes and think about how you would feel if you were them.

If you realize that the reason for their jealousy is low self-esteem, change your attitude. It's easier said than done but many couples have successfully controlled jealousy by getting a better self-understanding first.

3. Accept risks.

Disappointment often causes jealousy.

However, there's no way you'll ever be able to exclude being disappointed. There are many difficulties in life and there's no way to avoid all of them. This is why you have to learn how to take a risk in your life and love.

Learning how to cope with these feelings might help you fix your relationship and make it happier.

Any marriage will be tough at times, but if you have an insecure spouse, the prospect of facing a stormy relationship increases exponentially. Unjustified jealousy can spring from one partner having trust or self-image issues. Left to run rampant, jealousy might cause irreparable damage to the relationship.

The Bitter Truth of Jealousy

Jealousy is both a characteristic and a ground-breaking feeling. Many people experience it eventually in their relationship; however, jealousy turns into an increasingly critical issue when it spirals out of crazy.

Jealous partners can be truly unreasonable and demanding. They most likely won't see that their jealousy is unwarranted (ensure it's unfounded) or even destructive to their partner. Your spouse may even get suspicious, if not inside, and out distrustful of the other life partner. They can't believe the individual they love is being straightforward.

Facing Jealousy

Sometimes jealousy rears its ugly head because of past problems in previous relationships. Prior infidelity or dishonesty can leave lasting emotional scars. The partner who was hurt may always worry that history will repeat itself.

On the other hand, jealousy can spring from a person's insecurities. If a partner has poor self-esteem, they may be afraid of being left behind for someone "better." Any word or innocent action can potentially feed this fear, causing an unreasonable reaction.

Adjusting to Jealousy

No matter how much a partner tries, he or she can't understand their jealousy. Regardless of whether it is established or not, the two partners need to hammer through the issue. This isn't simple, however, necessary if both plan to keep the marriage solid.

The spouse who's experiencing the jealousy needs to clarify why and when the jealousy has come about. Identifying trigger points will help in finding a workable solution. Honesty is critical about how they felt and why the prior incident stirred the jealous feelings.

The accused partner needs to calmly sit back and listen, temporarily setting aside their feelings, which is hard to do if you're feeling falsely accused. Simply put, the jealous individual may find it difficult to be honest about their insecure feelings need strong support to talk through it.

Grab Control of Jealousy

If the two life partners comprehend the basis of jealousy, they can cooperate as a team to battle it. The jealous partner can learn not to blow up and rather believe that their partner isn't purposefully attempting to cause harm. The other partner can figure out how to be increasingly delicate to triggers leading to a jealousy scene.

Although jealousy is normal, its effect can be devastating to a marriage. Both mates need to face it honestly, along with the insecurities that go with it.

CHAPTER 22:

Reasons to Let Go of Jealousy

When you drop jealousy, you find that your relationship gets a lot stronger. Your partner knows that you have trust, and that's a huge part of keeping a relationship alive. He or she will be happy that you have a relationship based on something other than comparison. When I spoke to a young lady who had come out of the other side of a very jealous relationship, she said that for the first time in years, she found that she no longer had to doubt herself or second guess her actions. She had been in an abusive relationship, and the abuse was caused by her partner's jealousy. Had he not been jealous, the relationship could have worked because she loved him, but she had acknowledged a long time ago that being married to him meant taking jealousy along for the ride, and it made the marriage a very uncomfortable place to be.

He accused her. He stopped her from seeing friends. He asked questions after every phone call that she made, and there was absolutely no trust whatsoever within the relationship. In fact, for a very long time, she believed that perhaps it was her who was sending out all the wrong messages. Abusers are very good at making their spouses think that they are in the wrong. The jealousy in this situation got so out of hand that the man became violent. When I asked her about that, she believed that her ex couldn't help the violent nature that he had, but she also believed that it was his jealousy that sparked off the violence. Thus, without the relationship, she began to see her values in life differently and started to find the happiness that jealousy had stolen from her.

He didn't. He went on to another relationship and yet another. He took the jealousy along with him because it was built into his nature. He blamed his ex for her seemingly unthoughtful treatment of him and gained sympathy from his new women–but the sympathy never lasted. The reason for this was that they soon found out the price of being in a relationship with this guy. It meant all or nothing, and all was too big a price to pay.

You Learn How to Measure Your Value

When you are jealous, you have little confidence in your ability to keep your partner. Every time that you display this jealousy, you make yourself even more vulnerable to hurt because the side of your character that you are showing to your partner proves that you are not as good as others. You are showing the dark side of your character. Stop trying to measure yourself up to others because it's a pointless exercise. You are a unique human being, and that's what you should be measuring rather than your partner's response to others. The trouble is that society encourages us to measure ourselves against the models we see in magazines, against the prettier girls or the more handsome men, and we forget that we are unique and lose confidence. Self-esteem issues are made even worse by jealousy because your lover or partner's response to jealousy will be defensive. You need to stop doing this to yourself because instead of looking more valuable to your partner, you become less attractive and more of a burden.

You will find that one trait among abusive partners is that they insult the person they are supposed to be in love with. The abused partners expect to be called names. They expect to be beaten; expect to have all of their privileges taken from them if they insist on exiting that relationship because a jealous person will not settle for less. They expect to be owned because that ownership is the only thing that will make him or her happy. Yes, you read that correctly. This applies to both sexes. A man in an abusive relationship is every bit as vulnerable as a woman is. Some women have been known to be violent and abusive, but because his partner loves him, he will put up with all of this bad behavior toward him until he can no longer take it.

If you want your partner to value you, value yourself. Learning a little self-love will go a very long way. When you are saying to your partner "I don't trust you," what you are saying is "I don't have any confidence in myself and fear you will leave me." That's quite a different message, and it's no wonder that people who demonstrate jealousy are usually those who come off the worst in relationships because it makes them very negative people to be with.

Learning the Wonders of Empathy

You may not know it now, but there is a lot of value to enjoying other people's victories. When you feel empathy, you feel good about the good things that are happening to others. That means that you are less likely to use jealousy as a tool to get what you want out of relationships. You value people too much to do that to them. You also enjoy celebrating their successes, and that's why you are so popular and loved by everyone. If you get jealous, you show yourself up to be weak and to have no empathy and will see that you are not that good at keeping any relationship alive. That's because jealousy is like grabbing sweets from a baby. After all, you want them. It's like looking better than the bride on her wedding day. It's just not done, and people who do this don't win any brownie points in the friendship stakes.

Learning to Share Success

When you are not jealous of others, you can share what they celebrate and not feel bad about it, but that also teaches you something very valuable. By looking at the example of others in a very positive way, you can use those experiences to try to improve your lot. Successful people are quite often good partners because neither one is jealous of the other. They merely use each other as a sounding board or even as a mentor to improve who they are because they want to stay successful and happy.

Imagine the wife who is jealous of her husband's success. She doesn't make him feel good about his promotion. She makes him feel like he is showing her up as a failure. Thus, he doesn't get to enjoy all the good things that he should be enjoying. People who love each other don't do that to each other. They celebrate the successes in life, and they use each other as examples to aim for the things that they need to achieve. There's nothing worse than coming home and telling your wife about your promotion and ending up being ridiculed for "trying to go one better all the time." Jealousy distorts everything. It exaggerates things and makes people bitter and angry. It's far better than you can be on the same page as your loved one, and be there when your loved one needs you to be, even in good times.

Accepting That Change Happens

When you display jealousy, you show your inability to cope with change. He worked late. You make a drama of it. He has a female client. You make a drama of it. You have to work with your partner, not against him or her. The point is that during a marriage, everything changes. It doesn't stay the same, and that's because you are growing together. You are learning new things, such as being a married person or being a parent, and change is part of that process. If you feel resentment because you are left holding the baby, talk about it, but don't be jealous just because your partner is still out there socializing on the business front. Share responsibility. Share hopes and aspirations, but embrace change. Don't use jealousy as an excuse to make it a very uncomfortable thing to accept.

Jealousy is one of the most negative things that you can have in your life. It will change your character. It will make people back away from you, and above all, it will make you unhappy. When you start to demonstrate jealousy, you show people around you that you are:

- Inadequate
- You have self-esteem issues
- You begrudge other people their happiness
- You are not a nice person to know

If these are the kinds of things that you want to be associated with who you are, then carry on. If you want to become a better person, then you need to assess why you are becoming jealous and deal with it because, unless you do, your relationship is ended, whether your partner is still present or not.

If you refuse to accept responsibility for jealousy by using such statements as those shown below, you are lost to jealousy. You will always feel it because you haven't yet realized that jealousy is something that happens because of what YOU feel, rather than how someone else acts.

- It's his fault.
- The marriage broke up because she wouldn't do as she was told.
- The relationship failed because she didn't want to be a good wife.
- It was her fault that I hit her.

Wake up! It's not anyone else's fault. Jealousy is your fault. Jealousy is what you have in your head, and you need to work out a way to stem it. Otherwise, regardless of your current circumstances, you will step from this relationship straight into another where jealousy will become an issue. Why? The reason is quite clear. If you carry jealousy in your suitcase with you, it's going to go wherever you go and that means even a new relationship.

Thus, you need to stem jealousy at its root and work out why it is that you let this negative trait become part and parcel of who you are. Until you do resolve it, you leave yourself open to hurt, not because others don't care, but because you don't let them breathe in the relationship and drive them away.

Would you want to love someone if you knew these facts about the way they see things?

- She won't let you have female friends anymore.
- She won't be happy if you stay late at the office.
- He won't let you go and see relatives when you want to.
- He won't let you go on vacation on your own.
- She won't let you dress up nice to go out without her.
- She won't let you keep your phone messages to yourself.
- He won't let you write emails without checking what you are saying and who they are to.

You are adults. None of these statements is reasonable. You should be able to keep your friendships and keep in touch with people without feeling that you are led by another human being.

CHAPTER 23:

Changing Jealousy to a
More Acceptable Response

The word "jealousy" is grossly overused. We hear people on social networking sites using the expression "I am so jealous!" over and over again. What they mean is that they wish something would happen in their lives, something that was equally as satisfying and rewarding. It's not as deep-rooted as real jealousy and may have even been said in jest, but this chapter touches upon more suitable responses that will make your life a happier place to be.

Your neighbor has a new car. He didn't know it, but it's your dream car. You have always wanted one like that, and he even chose the color you would have chosen. How do you respond? Some people accept the good fortune of others, while the jealous person does not. Have you ever seen expensive cars with scratches down the side? Well, this demonstrates the worst kind of jealousy and is usually done by someone who could not even dream of having that car. Such is their resentment that they want to spoil the experience for those who can afford it. Think about that. It's a criminal act. However, jealousy can make people act in very inappropriate ways.

Now, look at a more appropriate way of dealing with your neighbor's good fortune. If you congratulate your neighbor for his exceptionally good taste and tell him what a coincidence it is that he has your dream car, you can share a joke about it in a very good-humored way. You can also tell him what exceptionally good taste he has since he has chosen the exact model you always had in your mind as a dream car. It makes him feel good and validated. It makes you feel better because you haven't been snide about it, and it also does something else. It gives you a role model to follow. You don't have to go out and buy the same model, but if your neighbor was able to do it, you can use his example to aim toward the things that you want in life. Visualization works as well. If you want that car that badly, the only thing that is stopping you from getting it is YOU. You can make all the excuses under the sun:

- I don't have that kind of money.
- I have to put family needs first, and he's single.
- I could never justify having something as expensive as that.

Now, ask yourself realistically how important it is to you that you have that car, bearing in mind that the moment you put a new car onto the road, it becomes less valuable. Realistically, would you buy a brand-new car like that if you had the money? If you answer that you would buy one, then you need to discuss with your partner the way that you feel and work out a way through which you can afford one. Perhaps your neighbor can give you a few pointers. Perhaps if you go without something else, you can save enough for a down-payment. If it's that important to you, then it's part of who you are, and you should always strive to make your dreams come true rather than stand back and blame circumstance for your misfortune. That's when jealousy starts to eat away at you, and it's not a healthy way forward. You may have the means to buy a car like that, but until you investigate it, you will never know.

Your best friend buys a dress that is a designer style and looks fantastic in it. You are jealous and wish in your heart that you could afford to buy something like it, perhaps not in the same style, but with the same amount of prestige. You can deal with this in several ways:

- Avoid going out with her when she wears it because you feel it makes you look shabby.
- Enthuse with her about the purchase.

The second option is the only acceptable option. If you choose either of the other options, YOU have a problem that needs tackling head-on.

The idea is material things are worth less than relationships are. They are things. They are decorations in your life. When you die, you don't take them with you, but if you exercise jealousy all of your life, that's all you will be remembered for. You need to tackle jealous feelings because they are not attractive. They show you up for who you are. Not only are you someone who cannot afford a designer dress, but you are also someone who begrudges a friend a little happiness.

You guessed it. You are beginning to sound like a young girl who has been told by my mom that she cannot have something and who is having a tantrum. It's not only impolite, but it's also rude to your friend. You show a disregard for your friends because you are making the possessions or achievements of others more important than friendship is. People who go through their lives with jealousy as their guide will end up being lonely and very unhappy unless they tackle their jealous feelings head-on.

A more appropriate response when you see something that makes you wish you had what someone else has is to use that person as a mentor and to find out how he or she achieved it and follow suit. We all have role models. We all wish that we were as good as those role models, but we learn absolutely nothing by feeling jealous of them. It's a negative feeling that serves no purpose but to alienate you from them, thus taking away any chance you ever had of achieving the same level of success.

I Want That Doll!

A sensible parent will take note of what the child is saying but will assure the child that although she doesn't have it now, she could always ask Father Christmas for it. A parent who gives in and gives a child exactly what she wants right then and there is setting that child up to believe that jealousy and expressing it pays off. It doesn't. It is unrealistic and insensitive in adults and should never be carried from childhood into adulthood.

You Are Being Unfaithful!

You have convinced yourself that your man is seeing another woman. No matter how much reassurance he gives you, your jealousy makes you accuse him of the worst crime he could commit against your relationship. Beware. It may not be that your partner is being unfaithful. It may be that your jealous reaction to his actions is alienating him to the extent that he soon will be. Put your suspicions away, unless you have facts to go on and are ready to discuss what is happening in your partner's life.

I once had a client who came to me convinced that her husband was cheating. Nothing he did was going to convince her otherwise. What we found was that she was so accustomed to losing everything she loved in life that she saw this as a normal course of events. Her life had been a series of negative events, and she expected that to continue. Confronted with the fact that her husband had never been unfaithful for six months of marriage guidance, she knew that all of her insecurities were caused by past events in her life and her expectation of failure.

Luckily, she had a partner who was willing to stand by and take the abuse that she was giving him because he loved her, but jealousy can wear down a relationship to a point that a loved one will walk away. Their thought process can be something like this:

No Matter What I Do For Her, She Still Has No Trust In Me.

Often, the trust is in destiny rather than in the individual, but if you subject someone you love to constant harassment and accusations, it won't be long until he or she realizes that the trust he or she expects out of the relationship isn't there. That makes the relationship less tenable and more likely to fail.

A more appropriate response in these circumstances would have been for a wife to talk to her husband:

I Love You, But I Have Insecurity Issues Because Of My Past. Can You Help Me Through This Rough Patch, Please?

If you want your relationship to survive, you have to first admit that you have a problem. It's a little like alcoholics who won't admit to being alcoholics and thus, never confront their issues. These are your issues, not your partner's, but your partner has to live with the consequences of your issues. Thus, you need to be able to address these issues and move forward with a much more positive attitude if you want your relationship to survive. It's YOUR issue, not his or hers. If your partner is already privy to the fact that you have problems, he or she may offer to take you for help, and at this juncture, you would be wise to go along with the idea, no matter how scary it may sound, because by turning your back on the problem, you are making your partner feel that the relationship is no longer worth pursuing. A relationship without trust isn't worth it because you are showing no trust in your partner.

In many abusive relationships, the abuser takes control. He stops her from going out with friends, or she stops him from working late or even turns up in the workplace to check on him. This is not the way to conduct a relationship. If you are tempted to get a private detective to check out your story, then you don't deserve to have that relationship in the first place, and you need a reality check.

CHAPTER 24:

Is Jealousy Good or Bad?

J ealousy can be healthy and great in a marriage. If it's positive and makes couples progressively delicate with one another's emotions, makes them communicate more and show more love and it helps them remember their affection and promise to one another, then it's safe to say that jealousy is great. A little jealousy is an attestation that couples value and love each other so much that they would prefer not to lose one another.

If jealousy gets extraordinary, silly, and steps to pulverize a marriage, at that point, it's safe to say jealousy is terrible. If one companion nonsensically accepts that their life partner is unfaithful and erroneously feels compromised by a rival who doesn't exist, at that point the issue in the marriage comes in.

Extraordinary jealousy in a union happens when one partner looks at oneself to other people or to somebody she or he sees as an adversary and in the end makes a feeling of mediocrity, inadequacy, and insecurity. The jealous partner may likewise have a background marked by being relinquished or left behind by friends and family.

How Extreme Jealousy In A Relationship Affects A Marriage?

Extreme jealousy in a relationship can bring about a disturbed marriage. Many endeavors are squandered on superfluous jealousy. Unreasonable jealousy in a relationship prompts irrational considerations and feelings bringing about unsatisfactory behavior. Extreme jealousy in a relationship delivers a wide scope of results from humiliation to violence. The jealous life partner may take part in unsuitable stalking behavior to research their doubts which may incorporate looking through the life partner's garments and individual belongings like telephones and social media accounts, surprise visit to work, question spouse, irrational telephone calls to work and some go to outrageous lengths by using a private agent or engage in violence to make their spouse confess.

Healthy people become jealous if there are real dangers and their behavior is commanded by actual evidence. They aren't close-minded and they can adjust their behavior from new proofs. While undesirable individuals experiencing outrageous jealousy accepts that their partners are unfaithful, dependent on unwarranted proof. They won't change their convictions or their mind even despite clashing information showing their partners aren't guilty. This sort of jealousy can demolish a marriage.

The spouse of the jealous partner can likewise create uneasiness and sorrow from being denounced continually or from having a disturbed marriage. This extraordinary jealousy can be extremely damaging to a relationship or a marriage. Extraordinary jealousy in a marriage can influence it and the couple's kids. The jealous life partner can go to extraordinary lengths of requesting that their kids keep an eye on the blamed parent to fulfill their doubts. The couple's youngsters may be sincerely and physically mishandled on the off chance that they continually witness contentions and brutality in their family. It's imperative to figure out how to manage extraordinary jealousy in a relationship and couples should look for proficient help if their marriage is defaced by silly jealousy before it turns out to be past the point of no return.

Attitudes That Suggest Your Relationship Jealousy Is Unhealthy

Jealousy in relationships is misunderstood since we'll hold extreme positions on the jealousy scale. We either feel that outrageous jealousy is defended so we go through our days in doubt and question or we feel regretful being jealous when our partner is behaving inappropriately.

Therefore, there is healthy and unhealthy jealousy in relationships. So what are the attitudes central to unhealthy jealousy in relationships?

1. **It's A Basis:** What's in the center of your jealousy? It's part of your baggage from previous relationships or has your partner done something that warrants it? This question can be very hard to answer honestly because you 'view' your partner through the lenses of your hurts and past experiences and thus, what you 'see' tends to be distorted. To work out what the root of your jealousy is looking at your past and present relationships; do you see a trend? If you see a trend, then your jealousy is there because of you and is unhealthy.

2. **Self-Value:** In your heart of hearts do you feel that your partner is your equal or do you think they are too good for you? If you have a sneaky feeling that you aren't worthy of your partner then unfounded jealousy will plague you every time you see someone 'more' worthy anywhere near your partner. This is an unhealthy kind of jealousy that just sours your relationship. You have to discover a way of accepting your lover truly cares for you and not the other 'more' attractive people or discover a way to get rid of your unfounded jealousy otherwise you'll keep sabotaging your relationship.

3. **Partner's Attitude:** Do you think your partner values you above all else or do you think they don't give you enough of their attention? If you're constantly fighting for your partner's attention then you'll be jealous of all the other things that your partner prioritizes over you. This is healthy jealousy, but it tends to be misplaced because the problem is your partner and not the other things in their life. You need to get through to your partner that you're unwilling to be last on their priorities. If they're unwilling to change, then you may need to break-up the relationship, but if you're unwilling to leave, then you have to find out how to exist with the constant jealousy that'll be your way to live now.

4. **Self-Blame:** Does your partner behave badly and you feel guilty for being jealous, or do they downplay their bad behavior and make you think that your jealousy is irrational? If this is you, then your jealousy is unhealthy in the sense that you're burying your healthy jealousy. Jealousy is an emotion that helps you protect yourself and your relationships and burying it doesn't make it go away. If you genuinely think your partner's behavior is unacceptable; then listen to your heart. You have a right to them and nobody should tell you differently.

Jealousy in relationships can be healthy or unhealthy based upon what's driving the jealousy. Healthy jealousy encourages you to keep limits around your relationship and everything else while unhealthy jealousy just keeps you stewing in antagonism without taking any kind of action to improve or fortify your relationship limits. Truth be told, unhealthy relationship jealousy just reduces your self-esteem and gives pessimism a fortress in your relationship.

CHAPTER 25:

Back to the Roots of Jealousy

Attachment Style and How to Discover Yours

Numerous studies defend the influence of attachment in childhood in the subsequent establishment of love relationships. Depending on the type of attachment that has been experienced, there will be a greater or lesser tendency to achieve a healthy, toxic, obsessive, or distrustful partner.

Although many elements can influence the consolidation of a relationship, there is a component that according to studies intervenes very clearly: attachment. There are different attachment styles, experienced during childhood, that can condition, never determine the type of relationships we have later. Therefore, several theories that discuss the relationship between attachment and couple relationships are presented below. Before introducing the psychosocial theories of attachment and relationships, it is necessary to understand the role it has in human experience. Attachment does not exist by chance.

From evolutionary theory, it is argued that emotion is one of the main strategies to adapt to the environment. Emotions help us to survive, as they are alarm signals that the organism receives and that allow it to respond quickly and effectively to the demands of the environment. The same thing happens with attachment, which is defined as a kind of useful emotion to ensure the bond and help of adults towards the offspring. Through attachment, a union or association is created between the adult and the newborn that is postulated as necessary, especially in situations of threat or danger. Therefore, from this theory, attachment is considered as an emotional system.

The Objective of Relationships: Survive

On the other hand, it has been studied that in the consolidation of romantic relationships, one tries to ensure not only their survival but also the continuation of their genotype. There are similar motivations in both relationships, between the adult and the offspring and in the couple. It does not seem far-fetched to think that attachment can also play a fundamental role in couple relationships.

On the other hand, parallels are found between the behaviors that occur in both types of relationships, such as:

- High activation levels in the first stages of the relationship

- The security and happiness felt within the relationship, which is between an adult and the young but also in the couple

- The fear of abandonment

- Apathetic reactions to other members' separations

Attachment Theory: Why There Are Types of Partners

From the theory of attachment, it is argued that during the first years of life, the child will gradually develop an interpersonal relationship model. This means that you will learn to relate to the beliefs or expectations you have about how others will respond to your care calls.

Depending on how those care calls in childhood have been answered, this is how the person will relate and establish different types of relationships.

Types of Attachment and Types of Relationships

There are three types of attachment, depending on the help, care, and understanding they provide. From this attachment, types of relationships will develop.

Safe Style, Safe Couple

The secure attachment is characterized in that that the child can explore the world, but it feels safer when your caregiver or attachment figure is close. When you have needed it, you have been given such care.

People with a secure attachment style are more likely to develop relationships that identify feelings and emotions of worry and anxiety, in the couple and oneself, and know how to respond to needs. They are people who seek others without fear or fear.

Avoidant Style Does Not Rely on Anyone

The avoidant attachment arises when the attachment figure for the child does not respond to their demands practically; never care. Therefore, and since they have not become accustomed to that, these children do not seek their caregivers when exploring the world; they don't seem to exist.

Relationships that arise as a result of an avoidant attachment are elusive. The signs of anxiety and fear of the couple are not attended to, and neither is their help sought when one feels that fear or needs care. Such care is not requested and does not seek social support to solve problems.

Ambivalent, Compulsive Style

In ambivalent attachment, attachment figures sometimes provide care behaviors, and sometimes they do not. It is this insecurity that causes children to not want to explore the world since they do not know if when they ask for help, their demands will be answered or not.

This type of ambivalent attachment gives rise to people who, in relationships, do not know how to deal with their problems autonomously. Besides, they are people who direct their attention to anxiety and fear, and compulsively seek that attention and help.

Attachment as a Predictor of Relationships

Attachment and relationships are not only linked to the establishment of the relationship itself. Some authors find the attachment as a predictor of a good or toxic relationship.

Hazan and Shaver (1992) understand that the pattern of security often leads to happy, love relationships dotted with positive emotions and feelings of trust. The avoidance attachment would lead to an over-concern about ruptures and a very striking lack of trust. Finally, the ambivalent attachment would lead to exciting and painful experiences, much more intense but also more unstable.

Attachment and Opinion about the Couple

Other authors, Collins and Read, find that a safe style results in people who trust others, are much more emotionally expressive, and who usually have a positive opinion of their partner.

Regarding those who develop an ambivalent attachment, they are usually people with low levels of self-confidence and assertiveness, with very obsessive love relationships and high levels of emotional dependence.

Experiments On Attachment: Does It Influence When It Comes To Relating?

Many and heterogeneous investigations focused on the analysis of the association between the style of attachment and relationships. Simpson, Rholes, and Nelligan (1992) studied the type of responses that a group of women had when they were supposed to go to an interview with a job. Those who reported a secure attachment during their childhood preferred to seek their partners' support to calm anxiety. Those with an evasive relationship used not to rely on their partners and control their distress on their own.

Similarly, in a study of a particular group's daily interactions, Tidwell, Reis, and Shaver (1996) found that people with an evasive attachment reported greater negative emotions, particularly with people who might raise their love interests. The association between unhealthy attachment and depression, isolation, and anxiety were explored after these inquiries.

Furthermore, Fraley and Shaver (1997) also found that the relationship is related to the type of behavior that the individual would experience before the couple is separated. Results were found quite close to those mentioned above.

CHAPTER 26:

Behaviors That Can Kill Your Relationship

Take a moment to step back and think carefully about your relationship.

Perhaps you know exactly what is causing the friction between you and your partner. Maybe there is an issue in your lives on which you cannot agree. Or perhaps your marriage seems to just be one argument after another, with no evident underlying cause.

If your relationship is facing difficulties, there are likely to be several behaviors that contribute to the conflict. Some of these might be major disagreements, while others are everyday actions, we may not even be aware are causing conflict.

Let's take a look at some of the most common habits that can damage, or even kill our relationships.

Constantly Criticizing Ourselves and Pointing Out Our Flaws

When we suffer from low self-esteem, we often fall into a pattern of self-criticism that is so second nature, we barely realize we are doing it. But the truth is, more often than not, the only person who notices these flaws is yourself. Remember, your partner chose to be with you for your good traits, and he or she sees these features, even if you can't see them yourself.

But when you focus on your flaws—constantly pointing out your inability to say the right thing, or the fact that you keep burning dinner, or those few extra pounds you've put on—it can do damage to your relationship. When you constantly criticize yourself this way, you are sending a message to your partner that you are not happy, and it can become easy for your loved ones to blame themselves for this.

Conversely, when you constantly point out your flaws, they can begin to override the good traits that your partner had once focused on, and you might eventually convince your partner to see you in the same negative way that you see yourself.

Trying To Be the Perfect Partner

None of us are perfect, and we are only deluding ourselves if we try to be. Sure, it may be that you love your partner so much that you want to do everything for them; clean the house, make dinner, do the laundry, earn enough to support you both; the list can be endless. But as well-meaning as this habit may seem, trying to be the perfect partner can lead to resentment as you realize you cannot possibly maintain this image of perfection. Similarly, when you try to do everything for your partner, you are denying them the chance to be self-sufficient and independent, which is an important element when it comes to building a secure relationship.

Being Judgmental and Negative

It doesn't matter how much affection and love you lavish on your partner; when you are bitter and judgmental towards the rest of the world, it can have a damaging effect on your relationship. When you view the world through a negative lens and make a habit of sharing these thoughts, you infuse your space with negative energy, dragging down those around you; in this case, your partner. Such negative energy can cause your partner to also see the worst; both in the relationship, and the world around you.

Not Valuing Your Partner's Opinion

This can be a challenge for those of us who are particularly strong-minded or who have been single for a long time. In such situations, it can be easy to convince ourselves that we are always right and that it is not important to listen to the opinions of our partner. But of course, such behavior can be very damaging in a relationship. For a relationship to grow and prosper, it must be based on mutual respect and understanding; and a big part of this is listening to what your partner has to say. Even if your partner's opinion differs from your own, take time to listen to what he has to say without passing judgment or getting frustrated or angry. See any disagreements as an opportunity to learn more about each other and strengthen your relationship through compromise and understanding.

Overspending

In many cases, conflict within a relationship is caused by disagreements over money. Overspending habits can put particular strain on relationships, as can a reluctance to talk openly about the issue or over-tightening the purse strings. Understanding your partner's money-handling habits, beliefs, fears, and goals is crucial to avoiding conflict in this area.

Comparing Your Partner to Others

Comparing your partner to a former lover can be a natural thing to do, but when comparisons take place regularly, they can cause damage to a relationship. Of course, when you negatively compare your partner to others, it can be very destructive to their self-esteem, but it is important to note that favorably comparing your partner to past relationships can be similarly damaging. Each time you refer back to a prior relationship, you send your partner a message that you are living in the past, and that your ex is still in your mind. Instead of focusing on things that no longer are, embrace the present with your loved one.

Drawing comparisons can also go further than assessing your partner against former lovers. Learn to become aware of any throwaway lines you use that compare your spouse to others in your life. These could be seemingly innocuous comments such as "When Mom used to make this dish, she put more cheese on top" or "My best friend has a better taste in movies than you." Such comments can be damaging to your partner's self-esteem if they build up over time, causing cracks to appear in your relationship.

Dwelling on Past Mistakes

Similarly, another damaging behavior is dwelling on past mistakes. If you keep count and linger on your partner's errors and faults, it is likely to lead to fresh conflict. Also, when you dwell on a mistake instead of confronting and solving it, you run the risk of bottling up your negative emotions which can lead to bigger problems in the future.

Giving Subtle Hints Instead of Being Direct

Likely, we've all been here at one point or another. Your partner has upset you, and when they ask what's wrong, you simply murmur "Nothing," then sigh and walk away. We do this in the hope that our partner will realize their mistake and come to their senses. But the reality is, dropping hints like this, rather than openly expressing your feelings, rarely gets the message across. Sure, your partner might pick up that you are upset, but will probably struggle to determine exactly why you are making it impossible for them to fix any mistakes they may have made. Even in the most trusting and loving relationships, we cannot expect our partners to read our minds.

Dropping hints rather than openly expressing disappointment or anger sends a signal to your partner that you are not able to be honest and upfront with them, or are unwilling to take responsibility for your words.

Trying To Make Your Partner Jealous

We often do this when we feel we are not getting enough attention from our partner or are feeling underappreciated. But when we try to punish our partner by making them feel jealous, we are undermining the security of our relationship.

Forcing Your Partner to Say I Love You

Hearing "I love you" from the right person can bring us endless amounts of joy. But the phrase loses its meaning when we goad someone into saying it. Expressions of love should be given spontaneously, without prompting, or else they run the risk of feeling forced, insincere, or routine. If you find yourself constantly asking your partner if they love you, take a moment to consider why you are engaging in this behavior. Likely, it is a sign that you feel insecure in the relationship, which is a concern you should raise with your partner.

Spending Too Much Time on Your Phone

In today's day and age, it is all too easy to get caught up in social media, the news, or the latest sporting results. We find ourselves constantly checking our phones, often instinctively, without truly feeling the need. But when you and your partner spend your time "together" glued to your phone screens, it causes a disconnect in the relationship. Particularly if you have children, and/or a busy work schedule, alone time can be precious and rare. Ensure you put your phones away and give each other your full attention.

Constantly Threatening To Leave

For some of us, our instinctive reaction to troubles in a relationship can be to make threats to leave. We may use this as ammunition when we are losing a fight or facing a seemingly insurmountable issue. And yes, there may well be times when leaving is the right response (particularly if any kind of abuse is present.) But if you are truly invested in a relationship, and are simply using this threat as a bargaining tool, it can cause endless damage to your relationship. By threatening to leave, you are sending a signal to your partner that you do not necessarily value your relationship, and that it is easier to walk away than to invest time in fixing what you have built.

Needing To Know Everything about Where Your Partner Has Been

One of the traits of healthy relationships is that each partner has their life outside of the coupling. To allow your relationship to grow and strengthen, you must allow your partner to have his or her interests and friends. Refrain from asking your loved one for every detail of time spent apart. When you do this, you are suggesting that you do not trust them and may come across as controlling and paranoid. By all means, show an active interest in your loved one's life, but do so when they offer information on their accord, rather than hounding it out of them.

CHAPTER 27:

Types of Relationships That Last Longer

I s there a way to know if your relationship will last? Do you know if it was meant to be? If you are still dating, is there a way to know whether if it is "The one?"

Well, all these are questions that we have all asked ourselves at one point in life. Some people are still in a dilemma today about their relationships. They are wondering whether it will stand the test of time. It would be lovely if there was a definite way to predict with accuracy that your relationship will be strong, healthy, happy, and long-lasting. But the truth is, there is no one way to tell for sure.

Look around you, family, coworkers, and friends; there are so many of them that are cynical about love. No one can blame them for being cynical because all the statistics out there concerning relationships are very grim. Everyone is getting into a relationship, wondering whether it is the one. Our commitments are not fully from the heart. We choose to put in one foot and the other outside in case things don't work out for the both of you. One thing you need to realize is that your relationship cannot be successful if you get in with doubts. Realize that the success of your relationship depends on the choices that you make today. You have to believe that yours will beat the odds. Contrary to what most people have made you think in the past, your relationship can last more than you give it credit for.

The truth is every relationship we get in is a risk. We are not sure whether it will last, but we allow our hearts and minds to guide us to the one we want to spend the rest of our lives with. The good news is that there are various types of relationships and signs that each type carries that indicate success and long-lasting unions. These types are;

Relationships That Are Shared Around Forgiveness

As we have already mentioned, conflicts are bound to happen in a relationship one time or the other. How you deal with them will determine whether yours will stand the test of time or not. When you fight with your spouse, how can you tell if you will be able to address the issues at hand in an amicable manner?

Well, the truth is that a strong relationship will not seek to reduce conflict. This is mainly because there will always be conflict in any relationship, and there is nothing you can do to prevent that from ever happening. When you choose a partner, the fact is that you chose a certain set of problems. They come as a package!

If you are looking for a partner that you will never have to fight with, get mad at, or even complain about, then you will never find one, at least not in this world. While it is often difficult to believe, fighting in a relationship is good. According to research, it is evident that a couple that does not fight at least three years into the relationship is indicative of an unhealthy marriage.

A healthy relationship is one that is stable but also has a healthy conflict. Arguing with your spouse is not a sign that you are destined for doom. Understand that this is all healthy and normal. The trick is for you to focus on addressing the problem instead of attacking each other. Once you resolve the issue, you choose to forget each other for the parts you contributed and move on.

But What Do You Do If There Are Poor Conflicts In Your Relationship?

The truth is, this is a sign that your relationship is unhealthy. That said, you must make a choice not to stay angry with your spouse after fighting. One mistake I have seen couples make is hold a grudge even long after the disagreements have been infused. Others choose to sweep issues under the carpet instead of addressing them head-on. What is worse is that other couples freeze their emotions and completely shut down as though the rest of the world does not exist.

You must work with your spouse to rebuild the emotional connection that you once had together. Make it a commitment to restore security into your relationship. You can do this by first ensuring that you override your hurt feelings. Choose to be happy rather than being right. When you hold a grudge against your partner, you are simply choosing to breed resentment that will eventually destroy your marriage.

Understand that it is not about what you are fighting about; it is how you choose to fight!

Relationships Based On Adventure

If there is anything that often stands in the way of lasting relationships is boredom. We have all seen couples get married with all the fire in their bellies. They cannot keep their hands off each other. However, a couple of years down the line, they can't stand the sight of each other. They get into these grey areas where everything seems to be predictable, uninteresting, repetitive, and boring to death!

Why Is That?

So many things come and distract them from paying attention to each other. We have careers, children, and side hustles that make life a real tough nut to crack, and we get so busy chasing goals that we forget to stay connected with our spouses.

But How Can You Stop This From Happening?

According to research, there is evidence that couples who enjoy an intense love and a strong bond with each other are those who enjoy taking part in challenging activities together. They love going on an adventure with each other. It is these new adventures that often are arousing and stimulate the brown into interpreting it as an attraction for your spouse. This is what reignites that spark that you had when you first fell in love.

If you want to shake things up, going on new adventures is the best place to start. The truth is that with new experiences, you activate the reward system in the brain, and you have a release of feel-good hormones, dopamine, and norepinephrine.

Stay open to new activities!

A Relationship Built On Trust

As we have already mentioned, if there is anything important in a relationship is trust. It takes time to build trust, and when you have this, you know that you are up for a long-lasting relationship. If you lack trust in your relationship, then it becomes difficult to maintain a strong bond between the two of you.

Take a look at yourself in the relationship, do you think that your partner can rely on you? Do you think that they can count on you on anything? Are you trustworthy? Do you hide stuff from your spouse? Do you cheat on your spouse behind their back? Do you have feelings that you are trying to hide from your partner?

Realize That Strong Relationships Take Trust, and That Is Not Achieved By Keeping Secrets

Rather than choosing to focus on small things and nitpicking mistakes that your partner has made, choose to look at the big things. If you have anything that you are keeping from your spouse, it's time you start letting the cat out of the basket.

If you don't trust your spouse, then you will never believe in a strong union together.

Relationships Built Around a Shared Future Together

A long-lasting relationship, in most cases, is about sharing dreams and goals with your partner. It is about seeing your future as a place where you both are the major players. It is about both of you sharing values and goals before you can even get into a relationship with each other.

A survey interviewed couples who had been married for over 40 years. What this survey revealed is that sharing core interests, values, and a general outlook of life with your partner will often go a long way in stacking the odds in your favor. Research conducted in 2009 showed that couples who are happy in their marriage often share similar personalities.

But What If You Are Not Certain Of What Your Relationship Goals Are?

Well, one thing you need to understand is that common goals often work together and make your lives work together harmoniously. You can start working on this with your part. Start by finding out what you both consider as your couple goals, whether you would like to start a family together, if you plan to a house, how many children you would consider ideal for the both of you, among others. It is these common goals that go a long way in strengthening your relationship.

However, if by any chance it ever crosses your mind that you wouldn't want to start a life with your partner, then probably it is time for you to start moving on.

Relationships Based On Shared Vulnerabilities

At one point in your life, you must have heard someone that was scared of falling in love, or maybe you did. There are so many reasons for this, and one of the most common ones is the fear of commitment. In other words, you feel vulnerable.

The thing is, several people, wish to be in a relationship, but then they don't know how to open up to their partner when they are hurt. They feel vulnerable often because they fear that if they opened up, they would be rejected. We often feel that if our partner finds out that we are anything less than perfect, strong, or intelligent, they will walk away. They will stop liking us.

You cannot build a healthy relationship without feeling vulnerable. Think of vulnerability as the glue that binds the two of you together. Knowing that someone loves you the way you are and for who you are is the ultimate gift you can get from a relationship. On the other hand, loving your partner for who they are is also one of the most fulfilling experiences you can get from life.

Realize that when you choose to fear vulnerability, you are choosing to sabotage yourself. It is this kind of fear that will stand in the way of you giving your all into your marriage.

But maybe you are wondering how you could know if your partner will embrace your vulnerabilities. Well, you can find that for yourself. If you are afraid of vulnerabilities, the chances are that you will feel the need not to expose your personality to your partner. You may feel that keeping a distance from them makes you feel safe and in control. In other instances, you may feel embarrassed to share your true feelings with them.

Whatever it is, note that vulnerability is often thought of as a sign of weakness, but in fact, it is a strength. Trust me, no one is born comfortable in their skin. However, it takes so much strength, self-confidence, and character to show your vulnerability to someone else. If your partner is genuine, then they will respect you for allowing them to see the real you. Putting your vulnerability out in the open is something truly attractive, and only honest people can appreciate others' authenticity and imperfections.

If your partner does not see it, then he or she does not deserve you!

CHAPTER 28:

Learn To Trust in Your Relationship

We humans continually adapt as social, mental, and physical beings. On the one hand, this adaptive ability allows us to manage future situations more effectively. On the other side, it can keep us from taking on new opportunities. Our past experiences determine how we behave rather than see a person or circumstance as something different. Our memory ends with us, rather than the other way around. Maybe the best example is trust?

If a friend betrays us, when a business partner switches us quickly, when a lover becomes unfaithful, our willingness to trust is shattered. The next time a friend makes a vow, a business partner proposes, or a lover asks us where they are, the error is assumed by our unconscious minds.

Even if we believe that everything is ok, our perception is clouded by the reminders of the past. Worse still, bearing this emotional residue will keep us in friendship, company, or relationship from creating healthy new connections.

So how can we once again learn to trust? Can the words of the past be silenced and genuinely open to others? The solutions are more accessible than you could imagine. You can see people and situations through a more straightforward lens through regular practice and adherence to a few basic principles.

You have all the courage and strength to go through any challenges that occur in your life. You have a vast reserve of energy that you may not be sure of. You have the wisdom to know what you have to do in the situation in which you live. You can trust yourself to deal with what needs to be done. Confidence, and moving through every condition, one step at a time, will give you the trust and strength to move forward in your life.

Be mindful that the critical step in learning to trust is to look carefully at your reactions. You don't have to criticize yourself or try to change your behavior. Only listen. What are the things you have had in the past? If you experience mistrust, where does it come from specifically? Once past feelings surface, you will have a better understanding of why trust is hard for you. This perspective is going to inspire change.

Find your natural state. We trust life entirely in our hearts. We know that we're on the right path for us already. Yet our mental and spiritual powers don't always share this feeling. Restore faith is a matter of linking our hearts and opening up in us the root of love. We instinctively want to feel satisfied, secure, and willing to trust others, whether in the bedroom or the boardroom. It may take compassion, validation, and good old-fashioned hard work, but it's invaluable to be able to trust again.

Learn to Trust Your Love

Confidence in love is an important and exciting subject and should not be underestimated. We will see ways to learn to trust your love, your love for someone else, as in your ability to love, and as in the person you love.

What Is Confidence?

Confidence is the firm belief in someone's reliability, reality, capability, or power. Trust does not usually occur immediately, but it evolves as a gradual evolution over time. Some may happen faster than others which depends on your relationship to trust.

You must trust yourself before you can trust anyone or anything else. This includes embracing, controlling the goals, and acknowledging disappointment as a human being. Confidence does not mean that we must be flawless and not make errors; it is instead, a sense of faith and belief in our abilities that integrates with realistic expectations that matter.

Confidence in your relationship is positively related to your past experiences in marriage. If it is unresolved, you will work through it and let go if you do not want to repeat it in your current relationship. Instead of doubting the present situation, we prefer to see current events through the filters of the past, and if the screens have a negative effect, we would have to delete the screen.

Confidence in someone else you love, as described above, and self-confidence is something that develops over time as a gradual development. This creation may be affected, depending on your background. Tell yourself if the controls are in question or if the terms, acts, and behavior of the other person are questionable. You may need medical help from a therapist, psychologist, or coach to answer this question. Be conscious that if you ask friends, they can only send you their views based on their backgrounds and filters.

Creating Your New Esteem State

Since your faith may be outdated and need to be restored, ask yourself: what do you need to trust? What kind of confidence would you like to accept in your trust? Which other states (e.g., clarity of thought, approval, peace, trust, light-heartedness, conviction, etc.) do you want to be in?

How to Create Trust in a Relationship?

Trust is life's glue. It is an essential component of effective communication. It is the fundamental principle that governs all relationships.

Healthy relationships are always founded on an intangible foundation of confidence. Since they are living organisms that operate in an ever-changing environment of constant flux and transition, there is nothing like a stable or static relationship. It is important to remember how easily trust can be lost and how difficult it can be to regain once lost. If we do not intend to build a stable foundation of faith in all of our ties, we will not be able to withstand or cope with the disputes and tension that change brings.

Faith is not only essential in relationships with others, but it is also essential that we have internal faith. After no-one knows for sure what tomorrow brings or what the future holds, self-confidence is the force invisible to welcome hope and to push towards that unknown future with esteem. We are assured that we have the power and ability to face any obstacles for us in the future. The future quickly becomes a dangerous source of fear and anxiety without self-confidence.

Whether we speak about trust in one's relationships or faith in one's partnerships, there are four equally essential components or competencies that need to be adopted.

First of all, we understand that our words and actions always have to be consistent. When we state that we love someone, our works must be "good." When we claim to love someone and then harm them by not caring or doing compassionate acts, they tend to remember our actions, not our words. In other words, we generate stress for other people, and we start to weaken the trust our relationships are founded on when our actions and attitudes are inconsistent.

The second is our willingness to be accurate; to say what we feel frank without blaming other people for our feelings, or to pretend that we do not feel something. Our words will only be truthful and true if we have learned to be honest and genuine.

Honesty means that we must first be confident with our emotions and then be willing to share them freely, or to express the truth as we see it; to ourselves and others. Then we need to know how to let things evolve without trying to force them one way or another.

Instead of saying, "You're a jerk who refuses my emotion," for example, we might simply say, "Your silence feels critical and rejects me." In other words, speak your feelings respectfully and stop using the word "You." Too often, the term "You" is related to guilt.

Understanding to be honest in our relationships with ourselves and others requires practice, but building and retaining trust are good things. Through time, our friends will trust us to be honest and real. The person they see is the person we are.

Thirdly note that you have to respect and consider your actions and behavior. In other words, sometimes it may be better to say nothing, simply to allow things to be as they are. Not every single mistake in any partnership should be focused on. If the actions of the other party remain detrimental, then you will ultimately have to be truthful and genuine with them and share your feelings.

It is often complicated to be compassionate when coping with thoughts and behaviors that we are not confident within ourselves. Our ability to offer kindness to others or ourselves is very minimal without development in self-consciousness, self-honesty, and self-authenticity.

Fourthly, note that our primal ego is highly reactive, and honestly thinks that it is always right, and those emotions reflect reality directly. In other words, if others feel dismissive of our primitive ego, our primitive ego wants to blame them for thinking so. The truth is that nobody can make us feel anything within us already. Others can only note that we are very open to criticism.

The idea that nobody can make you feel anything that is not inside you already is a significant truth when it comes to building trust. The end is simple: learn to have your feelings. The problem is, of course, that this is very complicated for our primitive ego. Also, our ego can be vigilant and self-aware; it is always subjective to understand how our feelings are. They're still our sensations. It is like asking "them" to take an aspirin when we have the pain that causes the other person to change his behavior.

Many relationship failures are due to the inability to our emotions, and the responsibility for our weak egos then projects towards the other individual.

We no longer feel helpless and dominated by others when we learn to hold our feelings. We must not blame others for our feelings anymore. Indoors, we should search for the root of our opinions. At the same time, if we believe that we cannot "make" others feel bad, we start to love ourselves more. They don't have to take ownership of it when others say, "shame on you because it makes me feel depressed or otherwise." It is essential to learn to love ourselves, to trust that we are OK because we can't love others until we learn to love ourselves. Much of the tension that we see today in the world is because we often "respect" others as severely as we love ourselves.

Such four threads, when woven together, contribute to a trust that facilitates every partnership. But, when it's lost, trust is complicated to repair. The rule of thumb in restoring faith is simple; you only have one shot, and typically it takes a long time. When trust is broken twice, it is a rare partnership that can be remedied successfully. Fortunately, trust in our relationship is always available to heal through self-awareness development.

Conclusion

Jealousy can raise its head in any relationship. It's a fatal feeling; it can choke out an upbeat organization and separate the trust that was there. Jealousy can make you experience a scope of emotions, from insecurity and doubt to dismissal, dread, outrage, or tension. Numerous individuals glamourize jealousy by saying it's a sign of affection. It's most certainly not! It's a sign of insecurity and intelligence of considering you to be as an article to be controlled. It's a negative feeling originating from both want and uncertainty, yet not love. On the chance that your partner gets unreasonably envious, it might be a pointer that they are moving their feeling of the blame on to you. This sort of projection is a great way that miscreants attempt to conceal their wrongdoings. A jealous person can't change. Frequently this is because a desirous individual either won't change or will not concede they are off base.

From the early days of mythology to the current century, jealousy still haunts our very being and meaning as a human race. The autonomy of belief in the thread that connects us all is quite strong on religious and spiritual grounds.

Jealousy is a disease, as well as a cure. This can be quite ironic, coming from the source of all good things reputable. People need to work on relationship standards before we can say we are fully developing into a universal oneness.

We have delved deep into the emotion that spells fear, doubt, clouds judgment, and destroys relationships. We have also seen how the wise can use this emotion to get ahead in building their relationships, breed trust, and enhance friendships and familial bonds with their siblings and parents.

Therefore the next time you get the chance with your significant other to play the jealous victim role, always put yourself in their shoes and mull over a few thoughts.

Are these feelings new?

Could it not be the first time they're acting this way?

It is imperative to note that someone with a tendency and nature to be obsessive and controlling even in their previous relationships will not go down easy. Time and a lot of it will be spent in much-needed therapy sessions with a professional. You will be lucky to find a partner willing to change and take the steps necessary to take control of their emotions.

It would be wise to say that using everything at hand, including emotions as a tool to make things better in our daily lives, is a skill learned and should be used at every opportunity when necessary.

Chances to be overwhelmed with jealousy should be overcome by taking heed to the steps outlined in this book, as well as taking the chance to repair the cracks in any relationship. The beginning and end of a relationship is a choice.

Lightning Source UK Ltd.
Milton Keynes UK
UKHW021223040321
379769UK00001B/45